Survival Through Adaptation:
The Chinese Red Army and The Extermination Campaigns,
1927-1936

A thesis presented to the Faculty of the U.S. Army
Command and General Staff College

by

WILBUR W. HSU, MAJOR, U.S. ARMY
M.S., Tsinghua University, Beijing, China, 2011
B.S., United States Military Academy, West Point, N.Y., 1999

Fort Leavenworth, Kansas
2012-01

The cover photo courtesy of the Library of Congress is that of General Dwight Eisenhower giving orders to American paratroopers in England.

Abstract

Survival Through Adaptation:
The Chinese Red Army And The Extermination Campaigns, 1927-1936
by Major Wilbur W. Hsu

This study analyzes the Chinese Red Army from 1927 to 1936 to determine how the Red Army survived attacks from external military forces and also successfully overcame the threats to its existence posed by changing Chinese Communist Party (CCP) policies. During this period, the CCP attempted to develop, expand, and professionalize the Chinese Red Army as a way to defend Communist base areas from a series of Kuomingtang (KMT) Extermination Campaigns. Also during these years, changes in the CCP leadership often placed the Red Army in dangerous situations by underestimating the KMT military threat and overestimating Red Army capabilities. This re-examination of the origin and development of the Chinese People's Liberation Army looks at the Chinese Red Army's strategy, tactics, organization, and training and identifies four themes that helped it adapt and survive: a pragmatic strategy focused on long-term success; creating local populace support through adaptation; strong soldier recruiting, training, and retention; and a comprehensive officer development system.

Objectives of the Art of War Scholars Program

The Art of War Scholars Program is a laboratory for critical thinking. It offers a select group of students a range of accelerated, academically rigorous graduate level courses that promote analysis, stimulate the desire for life-long learning, and reinforce academic research skills. Art of War graduates will not be satisfied with facile arguments; they understand the complexities inherent in almost any endeavor and develop the tools and fortitude to confront such complexities, analyze challenges, and independently seek nuanced solutions in the face of those who would opt for cruder alternatives. Through the pursuit of these outcomes, the Art of War Scholars Program seeks to improve and deepen professional military education.

The Art of War Program places contemporary operations (such as those in Iraq and Afghanistan) in a historical framework by examining earlier military campaigns. Case studies and readings have been selected to show the consistent level of complexity posed by military campaigns throughout the modern era. Coursework emphasizes the importance of understanding previous engagements in order to formulate policy and doctrinal response to current and future campaigns.

One unintended consequence of military history education is the phenomenon of commanders and policy makers "cherry picking" history—that is, pointing to isolated examples from past campaigns to bolster a particular position in a debate, without a comprehensive understanding of the context in which such incidents occurred. This trend of oversimplification leaves many historians wary of introducing these topics into broader, more general discussion. The Art of War program seeks to avoid this pitfall by a thorough examination of context. As one former student stated: "The insights gained have left me with more questions than answers but have increased my ability to understand greater complexities of war rather than the rhetorical narrative that accompanies cursory study of any topic."

Professor Michael Howard, writing "The Use and Abuse of Military History" in 1961, proposed a framework for educating military officers in the art of war that remains unmatched in its clarity, simplicity, and totality. The Art of War program endeavors to model his plan:

Three general rules of study must therefore be borne in mind by the officer who studies military history as a guide to his profession and who wishes to avoid pitfalls. First, he must study in **width**. He must observe the way in which warfare has developed over a long historical period. Only by seeing what does change can one deduce what does not; and as much as can be learnt from the great discontinuities of military history as from the apparent similarities of the techniques employed by the great captains through the ages....Next he must study in **depth**. He should take a single campaign and explore it thoroughly, not simply from official histories, but from memoirs, letters, diaries. . . until the tidy outlines dissolve and he catches a glimpse of the confusion and horror of real experience... and, lastly, he must study in **context**. Campaigns and battles are not like games of chess or football matches, conducted in total detachment from their environment according to strictly defined rules. Wars are not tactical exercises writ large. They are...conflicts of societies, and they can be fully understood only if one understands the nature of the society fighting them. The roots of victory and defeat often have to be sought far from the battlefield, in political, social, and economic factors which explain why armies are constituted as they are, and why their leaders conduct them in the way they do....

It must not be forgotten that the true use of history, military or civil... is not to make men clever for the next time; it is to make them wise forever.

Gordon B. Davis, Jr.
Brigadier General, US Army
Deputy Commanding General
CAC LD&E

Daniel Marston
DPhil (Oxon) FRHistS
Ike Skelton Distinguished Chair in the Art of War
US Army Command & General Staff College

Acknowledgments

This thesis has been a labor of love that could not have been accomplished without the support of key individuals. First, I want to thank Amy for your love and support throughout my career, especially through the Art of War program. You have graciously put up with the long nights, mountains of books, and esoteric discussions on the intricacies of the Chinese Red Army. This study could only have been completed with your unwavering love and support.

To Dr. Bjorge and Mr. Babb. Thank you for your guidance throughout this writing process. Your wisdom properly guided this study from an oversized idea to its current, manageable state. Your contribution to my education and learning cannot be overstated.

To Dr. Marston. Thank you for selecting me to be part of this amazing program, and believing in me. The Art of War program has opened my eyes to what a military officer should know and understand as part of his profession. To Dr. Stephenson, Dr. Hull, and Dr. Murray. Thank you for helping me to learn and grow as an officer. And to Chuck, Chris, Darrell, Kevin, Mark, and Tom. Thank you for your patience, comments, and advice throughout this experience, I have learned so much from our discussions, and appreciate all your candor.

Lastly, I want to express my appreciation and gratitude to the Combined Arms Library, the Fung Library, the Harvard-Yenching Library, and the Hoover Institution Library for their support and patience during my research.

Table of Contents

Abstract iii
Acknowledgments vi
Table of Contents vii
Glossary viii
Chapter 1: Introduction 1
Chapter 2: Late Qing to Early Republican China (1850-1926) 9
Chapter 3: The Chinese Red Army
and the Jingang Mountains (1927-1930) 33
Chapter 4: Li Lisan Line
and First Three Extermination Campaigns (1930-1931) 69
Chapter 5: Twenty-eight Bolsheviks
and Final Extermination Campaigns (1932-1934) 109
Chapter 6: Epilogue 149
Chapter 7: Conclusion 163
Appendix A: Military Organization of Red Army 171
Bibliography 177

Maps

China 2
Jiangxi-Fujian-Hunan Area 37
First Extermination Campaign 77
Second Extermination Campaign 81
Third Extermination Campaign 85
Fourth Extermination Campaign 115
Fifth Extermination Campaign 120

Glossary

CCP	Chinese Communist Party
COMINTERN	Communist Internatinal
CSBA	Central Bureau of Soviet Areas
CWPRA	Chinese Workers and Peasants Red Army
CY	Communist Youth
KMT	Kuomingtang [Chinese Nationalist Party]
NRA	Nationalist Revolutionary Army

Chapter 1
Introduction

China's meteoric rise to superpower status in the past forty years has sparked the interest of academics and policy makers around the world. Much scholarly research has been devoted to understanding the history, development, and modernization of China's military since the Great Reform and Opening in 1979.[1] Documentation and historical materials from these more-recent events remain difficult for foreigners to obtain. On the other hand, historical materials from pre-1949 China have been more accessible and have led to an increase in a reexamination of historical events.[2] With that said, there still remains a dearth of new academic research on the development of the Chinese Red Army in its first ten years of existence.

This time period is often overlooked in Chinese military history, and sometimes seen as an extension of the chaos of the early Republican China period. It is sometimes viewed as a period of guerrilla warfare, most likely influenced by the recent resurgence in the popularity of Mao Zedong's book of the same name. However, under closer examination, 1927 to 1936 was a critical time for the Chinese Red Army and its leaders. The Chinese Workers and Peasants Red Army, the precursor of today's Chinese People's Liberation Army (PLA), was created and many of the PLA's cultural traditions date back to this early period. Many of China's leaders took part in this crucible experience, influencing their perspective and outlook forever. Additionally, while guerrilla tactics were used during this time, the Chinese Red Army also adopted conventional military tactics to fight the Nationalists. It also created institutions to professionalize its forces, even while under severe constraints of war and deprivation. Using primary resource materials, classic studies of the period, and recent Chinese historical research, this study reexamines one of the most influential times in Chinese military history, the Extermination Campaigns.[3]

Research Questions

This study seeks to answer the following research question: How did the Chinese Red Army survive and grow from 1927 to 1936 while under constant attack from external and internal threats? In support of answering the above question, this study will also examine the following questions:

1. How did different perspectives on the same communist political ideology affect tactics and strategy?

2. How did the Chinese Red Army survive the five Extermination Campaigns?

3. How were guerrilla and conventional warfare tactics incorporated and used within the Red Army?

4. How did the Red Army create, organize, and train its own forces?

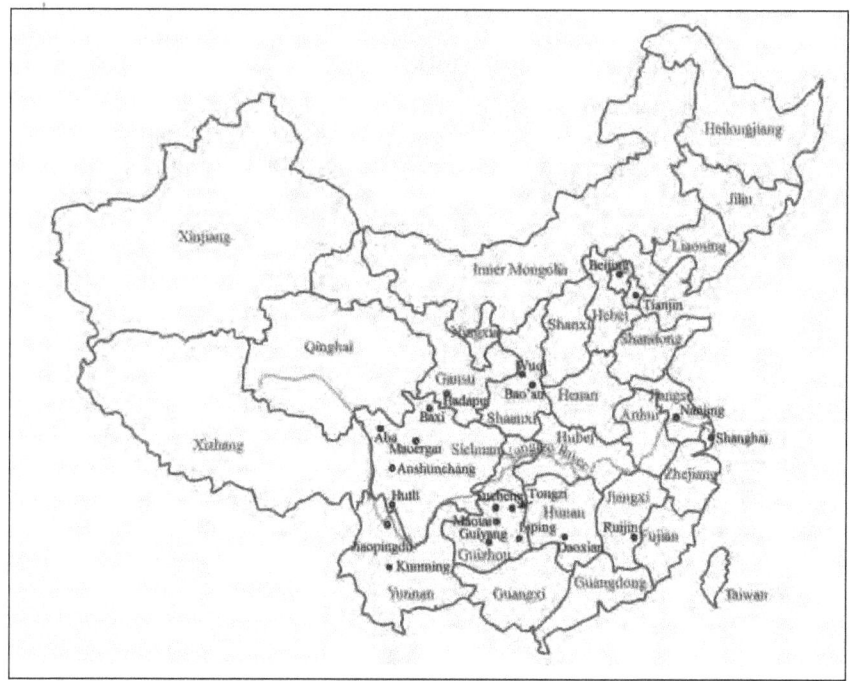

Figure 1: China
Source: Created by author

What measures or policies did they employ to compete with the KMT for recruits?

Methodology

The primary methodology for this research is the historical analysis of key events involving the Chinese Red Army from 1927 to 1936 based on both Chinese and English primary and secondary sources. The study examines changes and adaptation within the Army through the perspective of four different categories: strategy, tactics, organization, and tactics. The definition and criteria of these four categories is expanded further in Chapter 2. These categories are not meant to be prescriptive or inclusive of the changes within the Red Army, and simply provide a framework to analyze the Red Army during different time periods.

The study begins with Chapter 2, which provides a historical background on the development of military forces in China starting in the late Qing dynasty. The review focuses on the challenges the Qing dynasty faced in the late 19th and early 20th centuries and its responses to those challenges. It also examines the developments of military power within early Republican China, specifically looking at the development of the warlord armies, the Chinese Nationalist Party, known as the Kuomintang (KMT), and the Chinese Communist Party (CCP). The chapter ends with a description and brief discussion of the analytical framework and specific categories for analysis.

Beginning with Chapter 3, this study conducts an in-depth analysis of three consecutive time periods of the Chinese Red Army. The time periods selected for each chapter highlight specific periods of development within the Chinese Army and help to highlight specific changes and adaptation within the Chinese Red Army. Each chapter begins with a descriptive analysis of the greater political and economic environment during that time period. It then flows into case studies of specific battles and campaigns. The chapter concludes with analysis of adaptations and changes of the Chinese Red Army within the analytical framework outlined in Chapter 2.

The first time period examined is 1927 to 1930. This time period is a critical time for the Red Army as it struggled to survive in the Jinggang Mountains and the Jiangxi Soviet. The time period shows how the crucible of multiple threats of extermination while in a hostile environment encouraged the Chinese Red Army leaders to adapt and innovate in order to survive. Some of the policies and measures adopted in this early period would later become cornerstones of the modern Chinese People's Liberation Army. This time period also introduces the reader to the political discord within the Communist Party that would remain a constant struggle for the remainder of its time in Jiangxi.

The study moves forward to 1930 to 1931 when the Chinese Red Army expanded its operations within the Jiangxi Soviet. The conflict within the CCP erupted when the Chinese Red Army failed to successfully foment urban insurrections, and laid bare a growing disconnect between factions inside the party. The defeat led to the fall of Li Lisan, the Shanghai-based CCP leader, and Mao Zedong and Zhu De filled the power vacuum which helped them to expand Soviet operations within rural China. This period demonstrates a growing maturity of the Red Army as it takes concrete measures toward professionalization of its military force while it combats the Nationalist Revolutionary Army (NRA) Extermination campaigns.

Chapter 5 examines the two-year period of 1932 to 1934 of the Chinese Red Army. During this time, Soviet influence positively contributed to the Red Army effort to further professionalize its military force. On the other hand, the Soviets also forced the Red Army to adopt a strategy and corresponding tactics that were inconsistent with its capabilities. The successes and challenges during this time period demonstrate that a professional military force is not necessarily the best predictor for success in combat.

The Chinese Red Army's Long March from 1934 to 1936 is the epilogue to this study. It provides a descriptive analysis of the leadership decisions and actions taken to preserve the Red Army during its most weakened state. The survival of the Red Army protected the institutions, policies, and traditions that made it successful during the previous seven years for future generations to use.

This study uses Chinese primary and secondary sources in support of its analysis. The author has attempted to remain balanced and objective when using these sources for analysis. Early Mainland China and Taiwan source material is often fraught with propaganda and polemics. Additionally, much of the primary documents from the period were lost during the Long March. What remains of the surviving materials are mostly located in different archives around China where access is limited. With that said, the study uses the *Shi sou zi liao shi gong fei zi liao mu lu*, (known as the *Shih Sou Collection*),[4] a 21-reel microfilm collection of primary source documents seized during the Jiangxi Soviet period and compiled by former NRA commander, Chen Cheng, as a primary resource during research. Additionally, translated primary source materials were also used in this study, to include Tony Saich's *The Rise to Power of Chinese Communist Party,* Stuart Schram's *Mao's Road to Power,* as well as different autobiographies and memoirs from the time period.[5] The lack of access to Chinese archives has forced the author to also rely on English and Chinese secondary research works to assist in analysis. The use of Western works on China presents its own difficulties. Earlier Western historical analysis on China was plagued with an uneven record which is sometimes filled with Western ethnocentric bias.[6] The same can be said about Chinese secondary sources. On a positive note, more modern historical analysis from these two areas has taken a more balanced approach, though historians are still subject to their own historiographical biases and propaganda.[7] Given these biases, this study deliberately chose to use secondary historical research from mainland China to supplement its primary source research. These modern studies have greater access to primary source materials and documentation only available to a select few Chinese nationals. Their research and examination of the Extermination Campaigns sheds new light on the subject by examining the subject through a different perspective. The author has been cognizant of all potential biases during the research process, and has attempted to objectively analyze all information. This study uses the *pinyin* romanization for all Chinese terms, except for terms that are better known by their Wade-Giles spelling, such as Chiang Kai-shek, Kuomintang (KMT), Sun Yat-sen, and Yangtze River. All translations that are not otherwise noted of Chinese materials within this study have been done by author and he assumes full responsibility for all errors that may have occurred.

Summary of Results

Historical analysis indicates that from 1927 to 1936, the Chinese Red Army was successful in adapting its organization and adopting military innovations to overcome a series of external and internal challenges to its existence. The Chinese Red Army's success against the Nationalist Revolutionary Army (NRA) during four Extermination Campaigns can be attributed to its successful adaptation of strategy, tactics, organization, and training to its unique situation and environment. However, once the NRA adapted its own strategy during the Fifth Extermination Campaign to neutralize the communist threat, the Chinese Red Army was forced to retreat into the Chinese interior. The army's survival through the Long March preserved all the innovation and adaptations, setting the conditions for the Chinese Red Army's revival and eventual victory over the Nationalists.

Notes

1. For recent research on the Chinese People's Liberation Army, see Dennis Blasko, *The Chinese Army Today: Tradition and Transformation for the 21st Century* (New York: Routledge, 2012); Richard Fisher, *China's Military Modernization: Building for Regional and Global Reach* (Stanford: Stanford Security Studies, 2010); David Shambaugh, *Modernizing China's Military: Progress, Problems, and Prospects* (Berkeley: University of California Press, 2004).

2. For more recent research on the development of the Communist party prior to 1927, see Hans J. van De Ven, *From Friend to Comrade: The founding of the Chinese Communist Party* (Berkeley: University of California Press, 1991). For more recent research on the Sino-Japanese War, see Stephen MacKinnon, Diana Lary, and Ezra Vogel, eds., *China at War: Regions of China, 1937-45* (Stanford: Stanford University Press, 2007); Mark Peattie, Edward Drea, and Hans van de Ven, eds, *The Battle for China: Essays on the Military History of the Sino-Japanese War of 1937-1945* (Stanford: Stanford University Press, 2010). For more recent research on the Third Chinese Revolutionary War, see Gary Bjorge, *Moving the Enemy: Operational Art in the Chinese PLA's Huai Hai Campaign* (Fort Leavenworth: Combat Studies Institute, 2004). Christopher Lew, *The Third Chinese Revolutionary Civil War* (New York: Routledge Press, 2011); Michael Lynch, *The Chinese Civil War, 1945-49* (Oxford: Osprey Publishing, 2010); Odd Arne Westad, *Decisive Encounters: The Chinese Civil War, 1946-1950* (Stanford: Stanford University Press, 2010).

3. In this study, the term "Extermination Campaigns" will be used to describe five specific Chinese Nationalist military campaigns that occurred from 1930 to 1934 to encircle and destroy the communist forces. The term Extermination Campaign is synonymous with "Encirclement Campaign." The Extermination Campaign does not included the battles and skirmishes conducted prior to 1930, when the Nationalist Revolutionary Army and provincial forces also conducted military campaigns to encircle and destroy the communist forces.

4. *Shi sou zi liao shi gong fei zi liao mu lu* [Shi Sou Collection] (Stanford: Hoover Institution, 1960), microfilm, 21 reels. Hereafter cited as SSC.

5. Tony Saich, *The Rise to Power of The Chinese Communist Party* (Armonk: M.E. Sharpe, 1996); Stuart Schram, ed., *Mao's Road to Power*, vol. 1-4 (Armonk, M.E. Sharpe, 1992).

6. Paul Cohen, *Discovering History in China: American Historical Writing in the Recent Chinese Past* (New York: Columbia University Press, 1984).

7. For more information on the use of propaganda within modern China, see Ann-Marie Bradey, ed., *China's Thought Management* (London: Routledge, 2011).

Chapter 2
Late Qing to Early Republican China (1850-1926)

This chapter provides a historical background on the development of military forces in China from the late Qing Dynasty to just prior to the outbreak of the First Chinese Civil War. During the late Qing Dynasty, advances in Western military technology, weaponry, and tactics had surpassed the Chinese military. Strapped with a bloated, ineffective military fighting force, the Qing Dynasty suffered a series of military defeats at the hands of more advanced foreign armies. Multiple attempts at reform were largely unsuccessful in addressing the structural and cultural impediments to developing a strong national military force, and contributed to the fall of the Qing Dynasty. The subsequent early Republican era was filled with constant war as former Qing military units battled each other for power and control. With the help of the Soviet Union, the Chinese Nationalist Party was able to raise a professional, loyal military force that would become the foundation for future armies in China.

Late Qing History
Military Developments

The late 19th century saw the decline of the Qing dynasty as conflicts with both foreign and domestic adversaries damaged the imperial court's reputation and its ability to rule its people. Domestic problems caused by population growth, poor governance, and natural disasters fed public discontent. Large population growth in rural China stressed the heavy-tilled farmland.[1] Corruption infiltrated all corners of the Qing imperial court, degrading the overall economy and enraging the peasants.[2] Alternating bouts of floods and droughts brought periods of famine and pestilence to China's interior, killing millions of the population.[3] These internal challenges were exacerbated by foreign intervention. Western imperial intervention in China almost bankrupted the Qing Dynasty. The British introduced opium to Chinese society to help address trade imbalances, which led to decreased Chinese labor productivity and a host of medical issues. British imperialism in China expanded during the First and Second Opium Wars, whereby the British Empire gained favorable terms of trade and further access to Chinese ports in Hong Kong, Guangzhou, and Tianjin.[4] These external and internal disturbances fomented public discontent into a series of rebellions against Manchu rule. Three major rebellions, the Taiping Rebellion, the Nien Rebellion, and the Muslim Revolts, erupted across China creating multiple civil wars.[5]

In the midst of all the unrest and foreign intervention, the Qing leadership entered a period of serious reflection and reform. The combination of civil unrest, imperialist intervention, and unequal treaties pushed many Chinese bureaucrats to question the relevance of the traditional Chinese model. Some members looked to Western models, specifically the importation of Western technology, to help strengthen the economy and military. The death of the Xianfeng Emperor in 1861, the subsequent Xinyou coup, and the rise of the Empress Dowager Cixi and Prince Gong as the Prince-regent was a catalyst for greater reform. Under Prince Gong's leadership, the Self-Strengthening Movement began as the Qing government instituted a series of institutional reforms to restore China to its former greatness.[6] One of the major areas of focus was the Qing military. Prince Gong began a series of reforms to develop a more capable military force that could prevent foreign intervention and maintain stability at home.

By the late 19th century, the Qing military forces, to include the Eight Banners Army and the Army of the Green Standard, were ineffective. The name Eight Banners Army was first established in 1643, when the Manchus first divided its military forces according to banner colors. The army actually consisted of 24 armies, divided by ethnicity into Manchu, Han, and Mongols.[7] Banner garrisons were stationed along frontier areas and population or economic centers, with the primary mission focused on preventing and quelling internal disturbances. The Army of the Green Standard was created as a paramilitary force stationed in the provinces to help maintain domestic order.[8] The command and control of these two military organizations reflected the political constraints of the period, and negatively affected the two armies.

One of the major concerns for the Qing government was ensuring imperial loyalty. To maintain loyalty, both armies received imperial funding for salaries and allotments.[9] Additionally, commanding officers at the company level and above were rotated to different units in different garrisons to prevent the development of personal loyalties that might interfere with imperial loyalties.[10] Qing emperors initially maintained centralized control of the armies to ensure their subordinate princes or governor-generals did not have the "power of the gun." The central imperial court relied on its military forces to enforce many of its edicts at the provincial level. However, lack of oversight of the Eight Banners Army and the Army of the Green Standard contributed to their decline. Over time, the lack of communications with distant garrisons required the Qing imperial court to gradually devolve power to the provincial level.[11] Another factor leading to the armies' decline was poor leadership. The officer accession program did not bring capable officers into the force. Those officers in the force abused the system, and over-reported personnel accountability numbers to pocket nonexistent soldiers' income. Officer maltreatment of soldiers was commonplace. Army commanders also allowed a decadent and sedentary lifestyle to overcome the military garrisons around China. Many soldiers were addicted to opium, and often had terrible gambling habits.[12] The illiteracy rate was extremely high in most of the units. The Banners Army or Green Standard units did not train for combat operations; instead, they stayed in the garrison for weeks on end.¹³ All these weaknesses manifested over years deteriorated the combat effectiveness of the armies, and contributed to their inability to protect the empire from foreign intervention or internal disturbance.¹⁴

While the Eight Banners Army and the Army of the Green Standard were unable to put down the different rebellions, other military units were instrumental in suppressing internal revolts and orders. Some of the more successful Chinese military units, such as the Ever-Victorious Army during the Taiping Rebellion, were led by foreign officers trained in foreign tactics and equipped with foreign weapons.¹⁵ The success of these foreign-led units set a precedence for future Qing and Republican China units to take a positive view toward Western tactics, training, and weapons.¹⁶ Other regional armies established by the Qing, such as the Hunan-based Xiang Army led by Zeng Guofan and the Anhui-based Huai Army led by Li Hongzhang, were critical in the suppression of the Taiping, Nien, and Muslim rebellions. These units' successes were due in part to their unique command and control structure. Unlike the Qing banners armies that were beholden to the imperial court, the regional armies leveraged soldiers' traditional Confucian hierarchal loyalties to their own leaders. These strong bonds maintained accountability among soldiers and officers and increased their combat effectiveness.¹⁷ The regional forces also recruited locally, changing the ethnic make-up of the army from a predominately Manchu force to a Han Chinese force and planting the seeds for ethnic nationalism.¹⁸ This new type of command and control structure became the archetype for the personal armies of warlords in Republican China.¹⁹

Qing Military Reform

The Qing imperial leadership, with the help of regional military forces, was finally able to suppress the rebellions; however, the incidents demonstrated a clear requirement for military reform. Under the auspices of the Tongzhi Restoration, Prince Gong, with the help of Li Hongzhang, pushed a broad platform of change to the military. The first aspect was the modernization of military equipment. The Chinese leadership attempted to shore up its weaknesses by replacing outdated equipment with more modern Western, especially German, weapons.²⁰ The Qing imperial court also authorized the creation of multiple arsenals, with the largest domestic arsenal established in Jiangnan in 1865, which used modern machinery to manufacture the latest rifles and guns. The development of equipment extended to maritime forces as the Qing court attempted to expand its fleet with steamships. Other areas of focus were tactics and training. The Qing hired German, French, and British advisors to train its officers on Western military equipment and employment tactics. Some of these officers were dispatched to Germany to attend advanced military training, and later they became the training core for their units.²¹ The training program expanded and formalized with the creation of a two military academies; the first one in Tianjin in 1885, and later one school near Guangzhou.²² While these reforms helped to equip and train a more professional force, the impact of the changes was limited.

The Qing court's attempts at reform were always hampered by political calculations, inefficiencies, and nepotism, which hastened the empire's demise. The Qing court was riddled with internal strife as Confucian traditionalists and xenophobic bureaucrats stonewalled reforms.[23] Corruption and graft during the procurement process slowed down modernization efforts.[24] Reforms that made it to the Eight Banners Army and Army of the Green Standard were met with lethargy and inertia.[25] Other reforms were directed at the higher quality regional armies, tipping the balance of power away from the imperial court toward provincial governor-generals, causing controversy.[26] While the modernization and expansion of the regional forces was constrained by provincial budgets, these forces did improve and began to assume the primary defensive role from the Army of the Green Standard.[27] Because of corruption and nepotism, the imperial court failed to deactivate the replaced units from the Green Standard, leaving the national force bloated and ineffective.[28] These forces continued to drain precious economic resources and contributed to the lack of consistent funding for key military investments. Li Hongzhang's personal goal of developing a strong maritime defense, especially after the creation of the Beiyang navy in 1882, also diverted key resources from the land forces.[29]

In total, the lack of substantial reforms within the Qing military exposed China to multiple foreign-relations crises. In the 1870s, the Qing court experienced huge setbacks with Great Britain and the Margary Affair, Russia and the Ili Crisis, and Japan and the Mudan Incident near Formosa and the Ryukyu islands.[30] The challenges continued as the Qing military failed to defeat the French in Annam, present-day Vietnam, in 1884 during the Sino-French War and later, the Japanese in Korea during the First Sino-Japanese War in 1895.[31] With continued internal strife in different provinces, Qing bureaucrats finally made a concerted push for military reforms and changes starting in 1895 to establish better security. Changes and reforms that occurred at the provincial levels only served to reinforce provincial loyalties over imperial loyalties.[32] However, the biggest change was the creation of two Western-style military units. These two formations were the first to completely adopt Western military reforms in order to defend China against future Japanese aggression.[33]

The first unit was the Self-Strengthening Army, predominately based in the Yangtze River area in Southern China. The Self-Strengthening Army received its funding through provinces and was led by Zhang Zhidong.[34] He believed that the traditional Chinese military model was ineffective, and aimed to create a professional military modeled after Western military armies. He bucked Chinese tradition and recruited young, healthy, and literate peasants from villages near Nanjing to fill his ranks.[35] The soldiers received generous pay, uniforms, room and board as a way to retain quality talent. These soldiers were organized into standard modern Western brigades, with eight battalions of infantry, two squadrons of cavalry, two battalions of artillery, and one battalion of engineers. Zhang then employed 35 Prussian officers and non-commissioned officers to train the Self Strengthening Army. Prussian officers also initially led the units until Chinese officers were trained and ready.[36] To ensure the Self-Strengthening Army no longer relied on foreign officers, Zhang created a military academy in Nanjing in 1896 modeled after the Prussian military school system. All these reforms helped create a 10,000-man division-plus military force.[37] Zhang Zhidong later spread these reforms across southern China as he instituted similar reforms when he was transferred to Wuchang.

The Rise of Yuan Shikai

The second unit was the Newly Created Army, based in Northern China. Under the lead of Yuan Shikai, the army was expressly created for the defense of Beijing and centrally funded by the imperial government to ensure loyalty. Unlike the Self-Strengthening Army, the Newly Created Army fell in on the foundations of a Chinese military unit undergoing transformation. In 1894, the original unit, the Pacification Army, was created under the recommendation of Herr von Hanneken, a German military adviser to the imperial court.[38] The Pacification Army was designed initially as a large modern imperial army loyal to the Emperor. After the Pacification Army was designated the Newly Created Army in 1895, Yuan Shikai took over command and oversaw the training and development of the 7,000-man force. The Newly Created Army adopted organizational and training policies that were similar to those of the Self-Strengthening Army. Yuan ensured that his soldiers were taken care of, received adequate pay, and were even able to send a portion of their pay back to the soldier's home.[39] The Newly Created Army's organization paralleled the Self Strengthening Army; consisting of an infantry regiment, a cavalry squadron, three artillery battalions, and an engineer company. Prussian officers were used as well to train modern tactics, to include staff operations, communications, and night maneuvers.[40] All in all, these reforms helped improve the Chinese military in terms of training and capabilities.

However, these initial reforms still failed to address the deep institutional and cultural issues within the Qing military system. Political inertia within the imperial court continued to slow down many of the reforms. The Qing imperial court continued to allow the bloated and inefficient Eight Banner Armies and Army of the Green Standard to exist, taking away resources and manpower from the other units. The coup against Emperor Guangxu in 1896 also put a hold on many reforms. The inertia was also felt at the provincial level where military reform was needed. The imperial court had difficulties enforcing any reforms at the provincial level, demonstrating a shift in the balance of power towards provincial leadership.[41] The reforms also did not address the cultural issues within greater Chinese society that affected the military. The education level of the standard soldier was still low, even with the higher recruiting standards. The lack of prestige for military service within Chinese culture contributed to lackluster recruits.[42] The officers who did attend military academies were still small in number and they were unable to make a marked difference in the overall army effectiveness.[43] Some officers could not grasp simple military concepts and were unable to properly employ soldiers in battle.[44] Other officers still maintained the traditional military virtue that solely focused on brute strength and courage, and ignored tactical acumen. Lastly, the Qing government simply did not have the funds to finance the full modernization of its forces. Unfair foreign treaties exacerbated a weak Qing economy, which in turn constrained the budget necessary to create a modern army. A large proportion of the military budget was spent on foreign arms to meet the immediate demand of equipping a stronger army, as well as to satisfy the rapacious demands of corrupt Qing officials. This pragmatic choice left less money to be invested in domestic arms manufacturing capacity, which further fed the dependence on foreign arms.[45]

In 1901, the Qing military forces had improved greatly, but still were an insufficient defensive force. They suffered a humiliating defeat at the hands of foreign militaries and local insurgent forces in the Boxer Rebellion.[46] Finally realizing the critical need for a strong, centrally controlled, professional army, Empress Dowager Cixi supported full-scale military reforms. The Empress Dowager abolished the antiquated military examination system and charged each province to create its own military academy.[47] An imperial general staff was created to oversee the standardization of military training, equipment, and pay.[48] The Army of the Green Standard was finally cut by 30 percent to help trim down costs and increase efficiencies.[49] Among the most dramatic changes was the promotion of Yuan Shikai to become the Zhili governor-general and Superintendent of the Beiyang Administration, which oversaw the foreign and military affairs of North China.[50] His promotion further entrenched himself and his loyal subordinates into the Qing military structure, and allowed him to consolidate greater control while overseeing military reforms. Yuan Shikai received authorization in 1902 to use his New Army units to form the nucleus around an expanded and modern central military force, called the Beiyang Army. He created a military campus at Baoding in 1902 to train his forces, which included a staff college, military academy, and non-commissioned officer school. Yuan even started sending his officers abroad, especially to Japan's Shikan Gakko to study Western military theory.

The other dramatic shift in reforms was the creation of the Central

Commission for Army Reorganization in 1904. Japan's victory during the Russo-Japanese War heavily influenced the Qing dynasty by demonstrating that a properly trained and organized Asian army could defeat a Western power.[51] The commission's main responsibility was to help recruit and train the Qing military forces and help consolidate the myriad different military forces that were across the country. The commission set a goal for creating a 450,000-man military force made up of 36 divisions by 1912.[52] The Beiyang Army built on Yuan's and Zhang's more stringent recruiting standards by focusing on finding young, healthy volunteers to join the military.[53] The forces would be supported by two sets of reserve forces, which actually incorporated many of the recently demobilized Green Standards soldiers. The Commission also established a four-tier officer education system. At the lowest tier was a three-year provincial elementary military school designed to impart the basic skills needed for an officer. The second tier schools were two-year regional middle schools, located in Beijing, Xi'an, Wuchang, and Nanjing. The next two tiers were built around the Baoding Military Academy complex, with the military academy and staff colleges rounding out the military education system.[54]

By 1908, the military reforms made the Beiyang Army the most capable military force in China. The reorganization created a modern combined arms unit with a trained staff that facilitated planning and operations. This force was more mobile due to advances in the domestic rail networks, allowing the Beiyang Army to mobilize and respond quickly.[55] Training was improved as well, with the introduction of forced marches, field problems and night maneuvers into the Chinese military lexicon. Foreign advisers from France, Germany, Great Britain, and Japan oversaw the training, helping to coach, develop, and mentor the Beiyang Army's military capabilities. The educated gentry began filling the Beiyang officer corps, which coupled with the comprehensive military education program, increased the professionalism of the Beiyang army.[56] These improvements were not just limited to the Beiyang Army. Most of the Self-Strengthening Army troops were absorbed into the Beiyang Army; however, Zhang Zhidong continued to be a strong proponent for military reforms. He established an officer and non-commissioned officer school that employed Prussian instructors to help teach modern Western tactics and techniques.[57] With that said, there were still some issues. The regionalization of military forces hampered the army standardization of weapons, equipment and training.[58] Imperial-provincial funding conflicts also undercut modernization and training, decreasing levels of readiness of military units and driving some governments to engage in illicit fundraising activities.[59]

Some of these reforms also actually intensified ethnic and nationalistic tensions within society. Military officers studying abroad became exposed to nationalist or other radical ideologies.[60] Upon their return, these officers joined local organizations, such as the Sun Yat-sen's Nationalist organization, the Tongmenghui.[61] Changes in perception to military service and a growing nationalistic sentiment pushed more intellectuals and educated elite into military service, which increased the revolutionary sentiment in the army.[62] The military profession was now seen as an honorable vocation and a source for national pride for greater Chinese society.[63] As the Qing military forces improved, a sense of pride and patriotism increased in the unit. In response, foreign instructors were slowly phased out and replaced by Chinese officers, and by 1908, they were predominately absent from major training exercises.[64]

The strength of the Qing Army began to become a greater threat than an advantage for the Qing court. Starting in 1906, the Empress Dowager began attempting to consolidate control over the forces. In 1906, four divisions from the Newly Created Army were transferred away, decreasing Yuan Shikai's influence and power.[65] In 1907, Yuan Shikai and Zhang Zhidong were both appointed to ceremonial positions as members of the Imperial Grand Council, removing them from direct command of their forces.[66] Even with his removal, Yuan's influence over his subordinates remained strong. His subordinates were governor-generals of Zhili and Manchuria, along with almost all the division commanders of the New Army.[67] Additionally, the years of Western influence and influx of overseas-trained military officers increased nationalistic sentiment in the local populace and the military.[68] Even worse, the Manchu government received most of the blame. Many Han Chinese began seeing themselves as being very different from the Manchus and blamed the weakness of the Manchu imperial leadership for the poor state of affairs, especially for the defeats against foreign intervention. By 1907, many military soldiers cut off the Manchu-mandated queue, severing this symbol of Manchu rule.[69] On top of it all, the Qing economy was hampered by unfair foreign treaties, natural disasters, and poor crop yields, resulting in inflation and food shortages, which set the conditions for a revolution.[70]

Transition from Qing Dynasty to Republican China
Yuan Shikai Presidency

The Wuchang Uprising by the Hubei New Army in 1911 started a nationalist revolution across China, and ended the Qing Dynasty.[71] The Qing imperial court never gained full control of its new military forces, and its Eight Banners Army and Army of the Green Standard were long since ineffective. In an act of desperation, the imperial leaders asked Yuan Shikai to come back to national service and restore order. Instead, he betrayed the court, supported the revolutionaries, and forced a Manchu abdication.[72] On February 12, 1912, Yuan was named president of the newly established Republic of China. With this new position, Yuan effectively brought order to Chinese society and avoided the outbreak of civil war, but he still faced immense obstacles. The fractured central/provincial government relationship that had benefited Yuan in his rise to power now was an obstacle to his presidency, as provincial governors and their armies were unwilling to submit themselves to central civil authority.[73] Provincial governor-generals and their regional military units had become stronger during the late Qing period, and now wanted concessions and shares in the power. Yuan's attempts in 1912 and 1913 to disband military units or reorganize the military under central government control had little success.[74] By 1913, multiple military organizations of different sizes, abilities, and agendas existed at the city, county, provincial, and national level, thereby making any consensus impossible.[75] The chaos from the revolution took its toll on former Qing military forces, as the professional officers and soldiers were replaced by opportunists looking to profit from the revolution. Yuan Shikai's feud with provincial leaders continued until he suddenly died in 1916, leaving Republican China in a fractured state, with multiple military formations scattered around the country vying for power and control.

Warlords

The warlord period in early Republican China was the culmination of decades of militarism within Chinese society.[76] The Qing imperial court and Yuan Shikai failed to limit the growth of military power at the local and provincial level and contributed to the spread of militarism across society. The 1911 Revolution only increased provincial demand for more local military forces to reestablish order within Chinese society. By 1928, warlords had created hundreds of armies, totaling almost two million soldiers.[77] With that said, a majority of the power was held by former officers who commanded old Beiyang Army, Self-Strengthening Army, and other military units. In the absence of a central government apparatus, these forces competed with each other for power, wealth and control.

While the warlord armies varied in size and quality, they all shared two basic characteristics. First, a strong relationship existed between the army leaders and their subordinates that helped establish a loyal military force. The relationships were built on the traditional Confucian hierarchical structure, with subordinate officers developing strong loyalties for their leaders. Relationships through blood, marriage, and school ties were also used to create strong bonds that could weather the turbulent times.[78] The second characteristic was the occupation and control of land. Territorial control was a critical resource for the armies, providing revenue through taxation and trade, materials for weapons and subsistence, and peasants to fill the soldier ranks. With the control of land came simple government responsibilities and powers. Once tied to a government structure, the warlord armies had legitimacy to conduct war and collect taxes in support of the operations.[79]

While more territory provided greater revenue, materials, and peasants for the warlords, those same requirements were first needed to expand territory, which created a cycle that prevented any warlord army from gaining a distinct advantage. Instead, the warlord armies had to rely on alliances and coalitions to defeat any military challenge. The coalitions were marked by extreme pragmatism, as allegiances shifted over time according to circumstances.[80] The alliances were often territorial or relationship based. Two major cliques, the Zhilli and Anhui, were based on ties to Yuan Shikai that existed in the old Beiyang Army.[81] The Fengtian clique was created through local personal relationship as Zhang Zuolin rose through the ranks in Manchuria. These cliques and alliances of minor military units were constantly formed and dissolved based on short-term interests in increasing wealth and power, often using war to settle disputes.[82] Many armies also exacted taxes from their local areas. Other groups were able to finance operations by issuing bonds or receiving foreign loans. Illicit activities, such as pillaging and opium sales, also accounted for portions of the armies' revenues.[83]

To conduct these wars, the warlords needed weapons and equipment, and there was no shortage of willing sellers. The United States, European countries, the Soviet Union, and Japan were all involved in a brisk arms trade during the warlord period, in spite of an arms embargo established in 1919. The arms trade ballooned over time. In 1927, more than $100 million dollars' worth of foreign weapons entered China.[84] The chaos of the warlord period hampered domestic weapons production, forcing more warlords to rely on outside assistance.[85] Often, the arms trade supported a certain clique or warlord group that protected key foreign economic and trade interests within China, and also helped foreign entities avoid taxation and exploitation from the rapacious warlords. The Russians provided arms and financial support to both Wu Peifu and Feng Yuxiang's armies, whereas the Japanese backed Zhang Zuolin's armies in Manchuria.[86]

Warlords also desperately needed soldiers to fill the expanding ranks of their military forces. They used both coercion and financial incentives to recruit new soldiers. Many peasants saw military service simply as a means to receiving a steady paycheck. Others saw the expansion of military forces as a better opportunity for upward mobility within the army.[87] Some just saw military service as an opportunity to get rich through looting and other illegal activities. Some military warlords even used the promise of looting in lieu of an actual salary. Once in the army, soldiers' performances were varied greatly. Incidents of atrocities, poor treatment of civilians, and shirking of duties were common during this period, and were sometimes a result of poor treatment and neglect by superior officers.[88]

Training during this period was varied. After the 1911 Revolution, the formal military education system declined. The Baoding military campus remained open until 1923, though its ability to train officers suffered after 1911.[89] Some warlords supplemented the education system with their own schools. Feng Yuxiang conducted lectures and discussions on military and political indoctrination topics. Yan Xishan created small study groups in Shanxi to increase unit discipline and espirit de corps. Wu Peifu established his own specialty schools to train his units.[90] Even with these measures, the military officer remained plagued with issues. Schools did not have enough funds, trained teachers, or even a proper curriculum. An anti-intellectual culture was also prevalent at the time, as soldiers and officers tried to emulate the courage and charisma of the self-made warlord general. Issues of gambling and opium use began to resurface in some military units.[91]

All these factors prevented any single warlord from gaining majority power within China. Instead, the early history of Republican China was marred by a series of warlord conflicts as different cliques shifted alliances to gain power and control. A series of different republican governments attempted to gain majority control but failed to gain a consensus. The chaos and disorder prevented any full-scale economy to develop, negatively affecting the quality of life of the average citizen in China. Over time, the Chinese people saw the pluralistic model as simply a deadly competition for power and unsuitable for Chinese society.[92] More and more citizens longed for one strong central authority to gain control and rule over the country.[93] In the early 1920s, the Nationalist and Communist parties believed they could fill that role within the country. Both parties began searching for a way to create their own military force necessary to establish political control within China.

Nationalists and Communists
Creation of the KMT

Since his brief tenure as President of the Republic of China in early 1912, Sun Yat-sen struggled to establish a constitutional republic in China.[94] He and his Nationalist Party, the Kuomingtang (KMT), did not have the allies or the military force to back his vision. He was betrayed multiple times by warlords who took advantage of his lack of a loyal military force. While in exile after the betrayals, Sun gained political and financial support from overseas Chinese and secret societies to help finance his operations. Even with their support, the KMT still needed more financial and technical assistance and fortuitous circumstances to create its own modern military force.

The Soviet Union's involvement with the Chinese Communist Party is well documented. In 1922, Lenin saw the potential for revolutionary movements in China that could support the Soviet Union's greater communist plans. At the same time, the Soviet Union also supported other political and military organizations within China. Pragmatic assessments of its national interests contributed to the Soviet shift towards the KMT. Since before the Russo-Japanese war, Manchuria and Mongolia had been areas of economic and security interests for Russia. To ensure that these areas remained free from interference, the Soviets initially backed Wu Peifu's warlord armies in order to check the anti-Soviet warlord, Zhang Zuolin, and his Manchurian armies. However, Wu's loyalties towards the Soviet Union and communism shifted after his suppression of a communist labor strike in 1922, leading the Soviet Union to find a more reliable partner.[95] While the Soviet Union backed Feng Yuxiang's clique to balance Wu Peifu, it also saw value in the KMT brand and the charismatic abilities of Sun Yat-sen.

In January 1923, Adolf Joffe, the Communist International (COMINTERN) representative for the Soviet Union, arrived in Shanghai and negotiated a new partnership with the KMT that was outlined in the Joint Declaration. In exchange for helping the KMT unify the nation by training and equipping a KMT military force, Sun Yat-sen agreed to protect Soviet interests on the China Eastern Railroad and allow the stationing of Soviet forces in Mongolia.[96] The introduction of Soviet support for the Nationalists was one of key factors that helped raise the KMT and Nationalist movement from a symbolic icon to a powerful agent for change in China. With the help of pro-KMT Guangxi warlord armies, Sun Yat-sen established a base in Guangdong to begin Nationalist operations.

In October 1923, the Soviet Union dispatched Michael Borodin as the head of the Soviet mission and political adviser to Sun Yat-sen. Upon his arrival, he began a comprehensive reorganization of the KMT to increase its productivity and appeal to the masses. Borodin's initial assessment of the KMT was bleak. With his help, the KMT established a provisional Central Executive Committee in Guangdong to draft party rules and plan a KMT congress in 1924. He also helped to establish a propaganda branch to distribute materials to help recruit new members.[97] Additionally, the KMT instituted some financial reforms that helped to ease some of the pressure. Corruption, graft, mismanagement, and bloated bureaucratic systems placed enormous strain on the Guangdong economy, and left little revenue to support the KMT's plan to create a military force. The actual cost to fund the various Guangdong military forces was half the military expenditures budget.[98] Tax reforms, issuance of new debts, and consolidation of power in the area, helped to fortify revenue streams. While the Nationalist government still ran a deficit in its budget, it had established a revenue source to supplement Soviet assistance. The revenue streams also directly supported the military, taking away any incentive to loot or exploit the local populace for financial gain.[99] With all these reforms, the KMT looked to expand operations outside of Guangdong. A KMT office was established in Shanghai, which became a conduit for cooperation and coordination with a nascent political group known as the Chinese Communist Party.

Creation of the Communist Party

The creation of the Communist party was the result of a confluence of international and political events that stimulated a group of intellectuals to choose a different political path to address the pressing issues of the time.[100] One of the biggest influences was the strong student reaction to the Versailles Treaty's apportionment of Shandong provincial territory to the Japanese. The subsequent May Fourth Movement forced many Chinese to begin questioning traditional Chinese thinking and increased the appeal of Marxist thought.[101] Many Chinese students could identify with Marxist theory, relating concepts of class struggle, the oppressed, and exploitation to the corrupt and inefficient early Republican Chinese government.[102] Different cultural study societies at universities across China began discussing these and other communist theories, coming to the conclusion of rejecting Sun Yat-sen's republican ideal for China.[103] Communist cells began growing in Beijing, Hunan, Chongqing, Chengdu, and even among overseas Chinese in Europe. The main hub of communist activity was in Shanghai where Chen Duxiu was publishing *New Youth*.[104]

The Soviet Union also looked to China as a possible place to spread communism. The Chinese had history of supporting the Bolsheviks, with close to 50,000 Chinese serving in the Red Armies during the Russian civil war.[105] In 1919, the Soviet Union established the Communist International (COMINTERN) to help spread communism outside its borders, and a year later established its Far Eastern Section. In April 1920, the COMINTERN dispatched Voitinsky as its representative in China, where he was introduced to Chen Duxiu. With Voitinsky's help, Chen Duxiu expanded his propaganda and organizational operations. In May 1920, they established a Provisional Central Committee to help coordinate operations and help move the movement towards the actual creation of a communist party.[106] By the middle of 1921, the communist cells expanded across China. The First Party Congress was conducted in Shanghai in July, officially founding the Chinese Communist Party (CCP).[107] The first few years were a struggle for the nascent CCP as it attempted to consolidate and organize different branches, and gain consensus on a platform for issues. One of the major issues was partnership with the KMT.

The First United Front

The proposal for having the communists work within the KMT was initially made in July 1922 by Soviet adviser Maring.[108] He believed that the weak communists groups could only expand their operations through partnership with the KMT. He proposed that the Chinese communists construct a "bloc within" the KMT, where the communists could maintain their independence within the KMT.[109] CCP opposition to joining the KMT was strong, until a compromise was struck at Third Party Congress. In 1923, the CCP Central committee finally agreed to the "bloc within" policy, but established certain preconditions. Communists could enter the KMT as individuals and accept KMT leadership. Over the next few years, the CCP made inroads within the KMT, especially within the Whampoa Military Academy. A majority of the political instructors at the military school were CCP members, including the head of military instruction, Zhou Enlai.[110] Overall, the United Front helped to expand the Communist party by tapping into the KMT propaganda network and military operations. However, the communist party still did not have its own military force. The success of the KMT military forces during joint KMT-CCP operations in Guangzhou in 1925 reinforced the need for a separate communist party army.[111] Second, for all its efforts, the CCP had difficulties remaining fully independent within the KMT structure. Support from COMINTERN and Russian advisers helped the communist cause, especially in creating a left-leaning group within the KMT.[112] Overall though, both communist and nationalist leaders expressed doubts of the long term viability of the United Front.

Creation of the NRA Army

By 1924, the KMT recognized that within China's political arena, a military force controlled by the party was a necessity. The constant shifting of alliances and wars between factions made it necessary for the KMT to establish a military force. While the creation of a KMT military helped to defend against warlords, the explicit goal of the KMT military force was to help bring about nationalist revolution, expel Western imperialism from Chinese territory, and defeat Japanese aggression.[113] Sun Yat-sen also saw that a military and national conscription was a means of changing the social dynamics within society through discipline and moral correction.[114] The creation of a national military force would establish the cohesiveness and discipline needed in a modern society to prevent any relapse back to the old warlord ways.[115] Ultimately, a modern Chinese army would reinvigorate pride within the Chinese society, and demonstrate that China was not a pariah on the international stage.

Creating a modern Chinese military force was not that simple, though. The warlord culture still permeated across the ranks of the different units. When the Russian advisers arrived in China to survey Sun Yat-sen's forces, they were shocked at the abysmal state of affairs. The units were untrained with outdated equipment and poor leadership. The Guangdong economy and industries were also weak, and did not have the capacity to fully support all the necessary reforms.[116] The KMT had to rely heavily on Soviet technical and financial assistance. Whereas Borodin focused on the reorganization of the KMT political structure, the Soviet Union sent its best officers to help reorganize the KMT military force along Soviet doctrine. Soviet military legends such as A.I. Yegorov, Vasily Bluecher, and Georgi K. Zhukov were all assigned to China in the early 1920s to help develop the KMT military forces.[117] The Nationalists also established political commissars within each unit to help politically indoctrinate soldiers. The political commissar was meant to be a bulwark against any negative influences in the unit. They also provided a key role in training and educating the soldiers, which would help increase morale and courage.[118] In conjunction with these reforms, the KMT First National Congress authorized the creation of a new military school to develop junior officers, which would serve as the foundation for a new KMT military force.

This school, Whampoa Military Academy, was established on a small island off the coast of Guangdong in May 1924. Chiang Kai-shek, a loyal subordinate of Sun Yat-sen and graduate of the Shikan Gakko Military Academy in Japan, was designated the superintendent. The faculty consisted of Chinese officers who had attended the Shikan Gakko, Baoding, or Yunnan military schools.[119] There was a handful of Frunze Military Academy-trained Russian instructors on the faculty as well. The curriculum was a six-month course that covered both political and military topics, which was a revolutionary concept at the time. The political training was meant to establish discipline, loyalty, courage, and espirit de corps within the cadet population.[120] Political classes covered classes on Sun Yat-sen's three principles, KMT history, and American and European politics and economics. Whampoa instructors incorporated Western pedagogical methods by adopting the group conference method to encourage all students to participate and discuss political topics.[121] The military curriculum was primarily infantry-based courses, though it also included classes in artillery, engineers, logistics, and heavy weapons. Classes on gymnastics, fencing, and Russian were also given. To facilitate rapid learning, the instructors often used practical exercises and hands-on demonstration to improve comprehension.[122] By November 1924, the first class of 490 students graduated from the course and joined the KMT military force. Just prior to graduation, the Soviet Union shipped 8,000 weapons to Whampoa to outfit the KMT's new army.

Upon graduation, the new officers joined cadets and faculty to create the first model regiment in October 1924. The force was put into action very soon after and demonstrated strong leadership, tactical acumen, and professionalism. In late October, the Model Regiment suppressed an uprising of angry merchants and their private militia forces, collecting 10,000 Belgian Mauser rifles as part of the spoils. In partnership with Yunnan and Guangxi warlord forces friendly to the KMT, the Whampoa military defeated Chen Jiongming's old Guangxi clique military force, collecting 12,000 rifles, 110 machine guns, 30 artillery pieces, and eight million ammunition rounds. In June 1925, the KMT military force further burnished its record by defeating the invading Yunnan and Guangxi warlord forces, collecting 16,000 rifles, 120 machine guns, and six gunboats.[123] These victories, coupled with continued Soviet financial and technical assistance, helped create a reliable, dedicated, disciplined, and loyal military force. The Whampoa force later was the initial part of what later became the National Revolutionary Army (NRA), and would become the foundation for the expansion of KMT military power. Some of the officers trained at Whampoa would also become key leaders within the CCP's military force when it was created in late 1927.

Analytical Framework Categories

This study will use four factors to analyze the adaption and innovation of the Chinese Red Army: strategy, tactics, organization, and training. These factors are not meant to hold any predictive value for successful adaptation. On the contrary, the factors are only meant to be an objective marker to analyze change due to external and internal stimuli. Second, the factors are not mutually exclusive; rather they are interrelated and interdependent within a complex system. Changes in the external environment often directly stimulate change of one specific factor; however, the resulting change causes a chain reaction, creating second and third-order effects on the other factors. The resultant change may be greater or less than the proposed change given the complex relationship of the factors. These factors are not an exhaustive list of the possible factors in the adaptation cycle of a military unit. Lastly, the observed adaption within this analysis construct is not meant to prescribe any normative value to the changes within the military unit.

Strategy

This study employs B.H. Liddell Hart's definition for strategy as the art of distributing and applying military means to fulfill the ends of policy.[124] The examination of strategy will include analysis of the overall vision and endstate for a nation, party, or military unit, the supported political objectives and goals, and the plan for the application of military power in pursuit of accomplishing the goals. It will also look at the challenges within the process of translating political goals into military action.

Without a concrete strategy, any military organization will aimlessly wander in its operations and eventually fail. A strategy provides the overall vision that guides actions and operations to effect positive change. It also connects political ideas and goals to military operations. In other words, strategy helps make war "a continuation of policy by other means."[125]

Change in the political environment is the primary stimuli for change and adaptation of strategy. New political leadership with a different ideological or philosophical view can change the ends, ways, and means of a strategy. A change in political goals will affect the sequencing and coordination of supporting military operations and engagements. Simply a different view on the application of military power can change the way a strategy is executed. A strategy is also based on the current conditions of the nation, party, or military force, which may limit or delay the accomplishment of certain goals. Lastly, external economic, social, and cultural factors can also constrain the development and accomplishment of any strategy.

Tactics

Carl Von Clausewitz defined tactics as the use of armed forces in the engagement.[126] He elaborates further, saying that tactics focus on the form of the engagements.[127] The form is determined by the specific techniques and procedures employed by individuals and units used in the engagement. For this study, military tactics used in combat operations and political mobilization will be examined to identify change and adaptation.

Tactics are the concrete actions taken by individuals and units in support of a strategy. A majority of military training is focused on the practice of certain tactics, techniques, and procedures in combat. Tactical proficiency for soldiers and military units is a critical skill and an important factor in determining a unit's combat effectiveness. Tactics are also specific to a given task in a given environment, and are directly affected by the terrain, equipment, personnel, and their training level.

Change and adaptation of tactics often occurs with the introduction of new technology and equipment to the formation. New weapon systems may change how individuals or units move in formation or individually on the battlefield. The training and education of soldiers can also determine their employment in combat. Highly trained soldiers may be more trustworthy, and allow for the application of decentralized tactics on the battlefield. Changes in military organizations and formations can also affect tactics, changing the sequence of actions and operations or employment of certain weapon systems.

Military Organization

Military organization is defined as the formation and arrangement of individuals and units into larger, functioning, integrated combat units within a hierarchal structure. The scope of this analysis will include analysis of the recruitment and retention of soldiers, the arrangement of tables of organization and equipment for the army, and the development of the command and control structure within its hierarchal organization.

A properly organized military organization transforms individual actions into a unified, synergistic effort. It combines strategy and tactics into concrete action on the battlefield. The hierarchal structure within the military organization serves as a conduit for reports and orders and is the link between units of action and their headquarters. It also allows facilitates the delegation of tasks and operations which increases the range and scope of operations within the battlefield.

The primary determining factor in shaping the structure of an organization is the number of available soldiers. As the size of the military unit increases or decreases, corresponding changes are made to ensure the proper span of control. Technological advances in communication equipment can also determine the size of the military organization. To leverage new weapon systems' strengths, a military organization may change its formation, sequence, or organization of units. Increased training and confidence in unit abilities can also expand or contract the delegation of responsibility within an organizational structure. Political imperatives and economic conditions can also become an external factor on the recruitment and retention of soldiers, changing the organization structure.

Training

For this study, military training is defined as using practice and instruction to bring an individual or unit to a predetermined standard of proficiency in order to be successful in combat. It includes formal military school instruction, informal class instruction, military training exercises, hands-on training with combat equipment, and informal discussions and debates on military topics. Most times, military training is conducted prior to any combat operations; however, it is not uncommon for on-the-job training to occur during combat.[128]

Proper training is a key component to the success and survival of any military unit. Proper training ensures that soldiers and officers have the necessary skills to react under the enormous stress and pressure of combat. Training also facilitates synchronization and coordination of complicated operations between individuals and military units. As the scale and size of the battle increases, the more important proper synchronization and coordination becomes, which also increases the importance of proper training.

Changes to the environment can precipitate adaption within a military unit. Employing new military equipment or modern military tactics will require instruction and practice. The education and literacy level of soldiers and officers can constrain the difficulty and depth of military training. Funding for training equipment can also constrain military training. Additionally, the amount of key leadership focus on training can determine the frequency and quality of military training. Lastly, external political and economic factors can also influence the amount of time and funding allocated to military training.

Notes

1. For more information on the impact of population growth on food supply, see James Lee, "Food Supply and Population Growth in Southwest China, 1250–1850," *The Journal of Asian Studies* 41, No. 7 (1982): 711-746; R. Bin Wong, "Food Riots in the Qing Dynasty," *The Journal of Asian Studies* 41, No. 7 (1982): 767-788.

2. For in-depth analysis of the depth of corruption within Qing dynasty society, see Bradley Reed, *Talons and Teeth: County Clerks and Runners in the Qing Dynasty* (Stanford: Stanford University Press: 2002).

3. For more information on famine during this period, see Walter H. Mallory, *China: Land of Famine* (New York: American Geographical Society, 1926).

4. For more information on the Opium wars, see Peter Ward Fay, *The Opium War, 1840-1842* (Chapel Hill, NC: University of North Carolina Press, 1975); John King Fairbank, *Trade and Diplomacy on the China Coast; the Opening of the Treaty Ports, 1842-1854* (Stanford: Stanford University Press, 1964); James M. Polachek, *The Inner Opium War* (Cambridge: Harvard University Press, 1992); Arthur Waley, *The Opium War Through Chinese Eyes* (Stanford: Stanford University Press, 1968).

5. For more information on the Taiping Rebellion, see Youwen Jian, *The Taiping Revolutionary Movement* (New Haven: Yale University Press, 1973); Philip A. Kuhn, *Rebellion and Its Enemies in Late Imperial China; Militarization and Social Structure*, 1796-1864 (Cambridge: Harvard University Press, 1970); Ssu-yu Teng, *Taiping Rebellion and the Western Powers: A Comprehensive Survey* (London: Oxford University Press, 1971). For more information on the Nien Rebellion, see Elizabeth Perry, *Rebels and Revolutionaries in Northern China, 1845-1945* (Stanford: Stanford University Press, 1980); Ssu-yu Teng, *The Nien Army and Their Guerrilla Warfare, 1851-1868* (Paris: Mouton Press, 1961). For more information on the Dungan/Muslim Rebellion, see Hodong Kim, *Holy War in China: The Muslim Rebellion and State in Chinese Central Asia, 1864-1877* (Stanford: Stanford University Press, 2004); Jonathan N. Lipman, *Familiar Strangers: A History of Muslims in Northwest China* (Seattle: University of Washington Press, 1998).

6. The Self-strengthening movement soon became synonymous with the Tongzhi Restoration Period, named after the Tongzhi Emperor who nominally ruled during this period. The movement encompassed not only reforms, but also a fundamental shift from traditional Chinese culture and norms. For more information on the Self-Strengthening Movement, see Ssu-Yu Teng and John Fairbank, *China's Response to the West: A Documentary Survey, 1839-1923* (Cambridge: Harvard University Press, 1979); Mary C. Wright, *The Last Stand of Chinese Conservatism: The T'ung-chih restoration, 1862-1874* (Stanford: Stanford University Press, 1964).

7. Ralph Powell, *The Rise of Chinese Military Power: 1895-1912* (Princeton: Princeton University Press, 1955), 8.

8. Powell, *The Rise of Chinese Military Power*, 9.

9. Kwang-Ching Liu and Richard J. Smith, "The Military Challenge: the

north-west and the coast," in *The Cambridge History of China, Vol. 11, Late Ch'ing, 1800-1911, Part 2*, eds. John K. Fairbank and Kwang-ching Liu (New York: Cambridge University Press, 1980), 202.

10. Liu and Smith, "The Military Challenge: the north-west and the coast," 203.

11. Powell, *The Rise of Chinese Military Power*, 14.

12. Powell, *The Rise of Chinese Military Power*, 31.

13. Powell, *The Rise of Chinese Military Power*, 17-18.

14. Hsi-sheng Ch'i, *Warlord Politics in China, 1916-1928* (Stanford: Stanford University Press, 1976), 11.

15. For more information on the American and British officers who worked with the Chinese during the Taiping Rebellion, see Caleb Carr, *The Devil Soldier: The American Soldier of Fortune Who Became a God in China* (New York: Random House, 1995); Andrew Wilson, *The "Ever-Victorious Army": A History of the Chinese Campaign under Lt. Col. C. G. Gordon and of the Suppression of the Tai-Ping Rebellion* (Cambridge: Cambridge University Press, 2010).

16. Powell, *The Rise of Chinese Military Power*, 28.

17. Liu and Smith, "The Military Challenge: the north-west and the coast," 202; Powell, *The Rise of Chinese Military Power*, 32.

18. Ch'i, *Warlord Politics in China*, 12; Powell, *The Rise of Chinese Military Power*, 33.

19. Powell, *The Rise of Chinese Military Power*, 23.

20. Liu and Smith, "The Military Challenge: the north-west and the coast," 244.

21. Powell, *The Rise of Chinese Military Power*, 40-42.

22. Liu and Smith, "The Military Challenge: the north-west and the coast," 266-269; Powell, *The Rise of Chinese Military Power*, 41.

23. Liu and Smith, "The Military Challenge: the north-west and the coast," 153-156, 172-179, 209-211.

24. Powell, *The Rise of Chinese Military Power*, 39.

25. Liu and Smith, "The Military Challenge: the north-west and the coast," 208.

26. Liu and Smith, "The Military Challenge: the north-west and the coast," 26.

27. Liu and Smith, "The Military Challenge: the north-west and the coast," 37.

28. Liu and Smith, "The Military Challenge: the north-west and the coast," 30.

29. Edmund S.K. Fung, *The Military Dimension of the Chinese Revolution: The New Army and its Role in the Revolution in 1911* (Vancouver: University of British Columbia Press, 1980), 12.

30. For more information on the Margary affair, see Shen-tsu Wang, *The Margary affair and the Chefoo agreement* (London: Oxford University Press, 1940). For more information on the Ili Crisis, see Immanuel C.Y. Hsu, *The Ili Crisis: A Study of Sino-Russian Diplomacy 1871-1881* (Oxford: Clarendon Press, 1965). For more information on the Mudan Incident, see Edwin Pak-Wah Leung, "The Quasi-War in East Asia: Japan's Expedition to Taiwan and the Ryūkyū Controversy," *Modern Asian Studies* 17, No. 2 (1983): 257-281; Leonard Gordon, "Japan's Abortive Colonial Venture in Taiwan, 1874," *The Journal of Modern History* 37, No. 2 (1965): 171-185.

31. For more information on the Sino-French War, see Lloyd Eastman, *Throne and Mandarins: China's Search for a Policy during the Sino-French Controversy, 1880-1885* (Cambridge: Harvard University Press, 1967). For more information on the Sino-Japanese War, see Edward J. Drea, *Japan's Imperial Army: Its Rise and Fall, 1853-1945* (Lawrence: University of Kansas Press: 2009); S.C.M. Paine, *The Sino-Japanese War of 1894-1895: Perceptions, Power, and Primacy* (Cambridge: Cambridge University Press: 2003).

32. Hatano Yoshihiro, "The New Armies" in *China in Revolution: The First Phase 1900-1913,* ed. Mary C. Wright (New Haven: Yale University Press, 1968), 367.

33. Yoshihiro, "The New Armies," 371.

34. Roger Thompson, "Military Dimension of the 'Boxer Uprising' in Shanxi," in *Warfare in Chinese History,* ed. Hans J. van de Ven (Leiden: Brill, 2000), 290.

35. Yoshihiro, "The New Armies," 371.

36. Powell, *The Rise of Chinese Military Power*, 62.

37. Powell, *The Rise of Chinese Military Power*, 63.

38. Fung, *The Military Dimension of the Chinese Revolution*, 13.

39. Yoshihiro, "The New Armies," 371.

40. Powell, *The Rise of Chinese Military Power*, 76-77.

41. Powell, *The Rise of Chinese Military Power*, 84.

42. Powell, *The Rise of Chinese Military Power*, 56.

43. Edward A. McCord, *The Power of the Gun: The Emergence of Modern Chinese Warlordism* (Berkeley: University of California Press, 1993), 32.

44. Powell, *The Rise of Chinese Military Power*, 50.

45. Powell, *The Rise of Chinese Military Power*, 100.

46. For more information on the Boxer Rebellion, see Paul A. Cohen, *A History in Three Keys: the Boxers as Event, Experience, and Myth* (New York: Columbia University Press, 1997); Joseph Esherick, *The Origins of the Boxer Uprising* (Berkeley: University of California Press, 1987).

47. Chuzo Ichiko, "Political and Institutional Reforms 1901-11," *The Cambridge History of China, Vol. 11, Late Ch'ing, 1800-1911, Part 2*, John K. Fairbank and Kwang-ching Liu, eds., (New York: Cambridge University Press, 1980), 384.

48. Powell, *The Rise of Chinese Military Power*, 133.

49. Ichiko, "Political and Institutional Reforms 1901-11," 384.

50. Powell, *The Rise of Chinese Military Power*, 138.

51. Fung, *The Military Dimension of the Chinese Revolution*, 16.

52. Fung, *The Military Dimension of the Chinese Revolution*, 20.

53. Ichiko, "Political and Institutional Reforms 1901-11," 385.

54. Yoshihiro, "The New Armies," 373.

55. Jonathan Spence, *The Search for Modern China* (New York: W.W. Norton and Company, 1999), 249-251.

56. Fung, *The Military Dimension of the Chinese Revolution*, 75.

57. Powell, *The Rise of Chinese Military Power*, 19.

58. Powell, *The Rise of Chinese Military Power*, 240.

59. Fung, *The Military Dimension of the Chinese Revolution*, 55.

60. Yoshihiro, "The New Armies," 366.

61. Fung, *The Military Dimension of the Chinese Revolution*, 77

62. Yoshihiro, "The New Armies," 375.

63. Fung, *The Military Dimension of the Chinese Revolution*, 97.

64. Fung, *The Military Dimension of the Chinese Revolution*, 84.

65. Ichiko, "Political and Institutional Reforms 1901-11," 385.

66. Powell, *The Rise of Chinese Military Power*, 254.

67. Stephen R. MacKinnon, "The Peiyang Army, Yüan Shih-k'ai and the Origins of Modern Chinese Warlordism," *The Journal of Asian* Studies 32, No. 3 (1973): 413.

68. Michael Gasster, "The Republican Revolutionary Movement," in *The Cambridge History of China, Vol. 11, Late Ch'ing, 1800-1911, Part 2*, eds. John K. Fairbank and Kwang-ching Liu (New York: Cambridge University Press, 1980), 509.

69. Fung, *The Military Dimension of the Chinese Revolution,* 79.

70. Fung, *The Military Dimension of the Chinese Revolution,* 195.

71. For more information on the Wuchang Uprising, see Vidya Prakash Dutt, "The Wuchang Uprsings" in Mary Clabaugh Wright, *China in Revolution: The First Phase 1900-1913,* Mary C. Wright ed, (New Haven: Yale University Press, 1968). For more information on the revolution, see Edwin John Dingle, *China's Revolution: 1911-1912: A historical and political record of the civil war* (New York: Haskell House Publishers, 1972); Joseph Esherick, *Reform and Revolution in China: the 1911 revolution in Hunan and Hubei* (Berkeley: University of California Press, 1976).

72. Powell, *The Rise of Chinese Military Power*, 334.

73. Fung, *The Military Dimension of the Chinese Revolution*, 241.

74. Fung, *The Military Dimension of the Chinese Revolution*, 236-247.

75. Gasster, "The Republican Revolutionary Movement," 528.

76. The term warlords is considered a pejorative term for the leaders of military units, militias, and armed groups during early Republican China. Edward McCord uses the term militarist, instead of warlord, to highlight some of the professional aspects of these leaders. See McCord, *The Power of the Gun*, 24-45. This study follows Hans van de Ven's explanation for the use of warlord as the best, albeit imperfect, description for the leaders during this time. See Hans J. van de Ven, *War and Nationalism in China, 1925-1945* (New York: RoutledgeCurzon, 2004), 72.

77. James E. Sheridan, "The Warlord Era: politics and militarism under the Peking government 1916-28," in *The Cambridge History of China, Vol. 12, Republican China 1912-1949, Part 1*, John K. Fairbank, ed. (New York: Cambridge University Press, 1983), 288.

78. Sheridan, "The Warlord Era: politics and militarism under the Peking government 1916-28," 288.

79. Sheridan, "The Warlord Era: politics and militarism under the Peking government 1916-28," 289.

80. Lucian W. Pye, *Warlord Politics: Conflict and Coalition in the Modernization of Republican China* (New York: Praeger Publishers, 1971), 10.

81. Sheridan, "The Warlord Era: politics and militarism under the Peking government 1916-28," 294.

82. Pye, *Warlord Politics*, 38, 78.

83. Ch'i, *Warlord Politics in China, 1916-1928*, 153-156.

84. Ch'i, *Warlord Politics in China, 1916-1928*, 122.

85. Chi'i, *Warlord Politics in China, 1916-1928.*, 120.

86. Sheridan, "The Warlord Era: politics and militarism under the Peking government 1916-28," 304-306.

87. Ch'i, *Warlord Politics in China, 1916-1928*, 84-87.

88. Diana Lary, *Warlord Soldiers: Chinese Common Soldiers, 1911-1937* (Cambridge: Cambridge University, 1985), 74-80.

89. Ch'i, *Warlord Politics in China, 1916-1928*, 102.

90. Chi'i, *Warlord Politics in China, 1916-1928*, 95-96.

91. Lary, *Warlord Soldiers*, 40-41.

92. Sheridan, "The Warlord Era: politics and militarism under the Peking government 1916-28," 319.

93. Pye, *Warlord Politics*, 169.

94. For more information on the challenges Sun Yat-sen faced in the early Republican China period, see Marie Claire Bergere, *Sun Yat-Sen*, trans. Janet Lloyd (Stanford: Stanford University Press, 2000); Harold Schiffrin, *Sun Yat-Sen and the Origins of the Chinese Revolution* (Berkeley: University of California Press, 2010).

95. van de Ven, *War and Nationalism in China*, 79.

96. van de Ven, *War and Nationalism in China*, 79.

97. van de Ven, *War and Nationalism in China*, 81.

98. van de Ven, *War and Nationalism in China*, 89.

99.. van de Ven, *War and Nationalism in China*, 88.

100. Hans J van de Ven, *From Friend to Comrade: The Founding of the Chinese Communist Party, 1920-1927* (Berkeley: University of California Press, 1991), 10. For more in-depth discussion on the creation of the Communist Party, see Arif Dirlik, *The Origins of Chinese Communism* (Oxford: Oxford University Press, 1989); Hans J. van de Ven, *From Friend to Comrade: the founding of the Chinese Communist Party, 1920-1927* (Berkeley: University of California Press, 1991).

101. For more information on the May Fourth Movement, see Chow Tse-tsung, *The May Fourth Movement: Intellectual Revolution in Modern China* (Stanford: Stanford University Press, 1967); Vera Schwarcz, *The Chinese Enlightenment: Intellectuals and the Legacy of the May Fourth Movement of 1919* (Berkeley: University of California Press: 1990).

102. Jerome Ch'en, "The Chinese Communist Movement, 1927-1937," in *The Cambridge History of China, Vol. 12, Republican China 1912-1949, Part 1*, John K. Fairbank, ed. (Cambridge: Cambridge University Press, 1986), 509.

103. van de Ven, *From Friend to Comrade*, 54.

104. van de Ven, *From Friend to Comrade*, 54.

105. James Pinckney Harrison, *The Long March to Power: A History of the Chinese Communist Party, 1927-72* (New York: Praeger Publishers, 1972), 24.

106. Harrison, *The Long March to Power*, 28-29.

107. Ch'en, "The Chinese Communist Movement, 1927-1937," 515.

108. For more information on the United Front, See Tony Saich, *Origin of the United Front: The Role of Sneevliet (Alias Maring)* (New York: E.J. Brill, 1991); Lyman Van Slyke, *Enemies and Friends the United Front in Chinese Communist History* (Stanford: Stanford University Press, 1967).

109. Saich, *The Rise to Power*, 32.

110. Harrison, *The Long March to Power*, 56.

111. van de Ven, *From Friend to Comrade*, 169.

112. Saich, *The Rise to Power,* 103-104.

113. van de Ven, *War and Nationalism in China*, 13.

114. van de Ven, *War and Nationalism in China,,* 68.

115. van de Ven, *War and Nationalism in China,,* 69.

116. C. Martin Wilbur, "The Nationalist revolution, 1923-8," in *The Cambridge History of China, Vol. 12, Republican China 1912-1949, Part 1*, ed. John K. Fairbank (Cambridge: Cambridge University Press, 1986), 539.

117. F.F. Liu, *Military History of Modern China* (Princeton: Princeton

University Press, 1956), 5-6.

118. Liu, *Military History of Modern China*, 19.

119. Liu, *Military History of Modern China*, 9.

120. Liu, *Military History of Modern China*, 10.

121. Jane L. Price, *Cadres, Commanders, and Commissars* (Boulder: Westview Press, 1976), 56-58.

122. Price, *Cadres, Commanders, and Commissars*, 57.

123. van de Ven, *War and Nationalism in China*, 84-85

124. B. H. Liddell Hart, *Strategy* (London: Faber, 1967), 321.

125. Carl von Clausewitz, *On War* (Princeton: Princeton University Press, 1976), 87.

126. Clausewitz, *On War*, 128.

127. Clausewitz, *On War*, 132.

128. The Chinese Communist Party maintained a tradition of "learning-by-doing" in both civilian and military occupations. For more information on the application of "learning-by-doing" concept in rural industrialization of post-1949 China, see Christopher Bramall, *The Industrialization of Rural China* (London: Oxford University Press, 2006).

Chapter 3
The Chinese Red Army and the Jinggang Mountains
(1927-1930)

From its arrival in Jinggang Mountains in late 1927 until its migration to and expansion of the Jiangxi Soviet in early 1930, the Red Army was in perilous state: weak, scattered across the country, poorly equipped, and riddled with discipline and morale issues. To push forward the communist movement in China, The Fourth Red Army, led by Mao Zedong and Zhu De, maintained its core conviction on the critical mass of the peasant movement within the Chinese communist movement and at adapting the urban-oriented, communist political and military strategies to the realities of the rural areas of inner China. The Red Army used guerrilla tactics to defend itself against a superior enemy and leveraged its victories to make itself stronger with gains in equipment, local support, and new recruits. The guerrilla tactics also incorporated political mobilization of the local masses as a means to recruit, equip, and sustain itself. Within the army, key leaders conducted a series of organizational changes to create unity of command and party control over the army. It also adopted different methods, to include creating training units and conducting after action reviews, to train and develop the peasant force into a legitimate military threat. By 1930, the Red Army had survived its most difficult test to date, and was ready to expand its operations within China.

Creation of the Red Army

The birthday of the People's Liberation Army (PLA) is celebrated on Aug. 1, 1927, the day of the Nanchang Uprisings. The actual creation of the Red Army spanned a longer period of time, and was a result of military revolts and urban rebellions within Republican China. During this period, the dissolution of the United Front coupled with Soviet support for communist revolution were key factors in the genesis of a new military force and created the foundations for the Chinese army today, the People's Liberation Army (PLA).

Dissolution of the United Front

Since the start of the United Front, ideological conflicts and power struggles between the right wing of the KMT, led by Chiang Kai-shek, and the CCP, led by Chen Duxiu, increased tensions and led to the eventual dissolution of the alliance. Initially, Sun Yat-sen's charisma while head of the KMT allowed the United Front to work relatively well. His untimely death in 1925, however, exposed many of the schisms within the alliance. The first schism was between Chiang Kai-shek and Soviet influence, embodied by COMINTERN adviser Michael Borodin. Chiang viewed Borodin's and the Soviet advisory team's growing influence within the Whampoa Academy as overreach, and became increasingly concerned about the politicization of the students, especially their growing sympathy within the army for communist thought.¹ The number of future Red Army leaders that filled the ranks of the Whampoa Academy's cadets and faculty, to include Zhou Enlai, the head of Whampoa's Political Department, only substantiated Chiang's fear. The controversy surrounding the *Zhongshan* Incident in March 1926 further fueled his suspicions, and Chiang adopted a series of measures immediately to limit the Soviet and CCP influence within the National Revolutionary Army (NRA).² In 1926, Chiang began a campaign to consolidate control by launching the Northern Expedition.³ In April 1927, the Northern Expedition was successful and extended its operations into Shanghai. While in Shanghai, NRA troops turned on their Communist allies, arresting or killing many communist union members who actively helped the NRA to seize Shanghai, effectively purging the Communists out of the KMT ranks.⁴

Surprisingly, the Shanghai massacre did not end the United Front. Stalin, through the COMINTERN, remained steadfast about the importance of the alliance, and pushed the CCP to continue cooperating with the leftist "revolutionary" faction of the KMT. The Wuhan-based leftist KMT⁵ faction sympathized and even agreed with many of the communist policies. The partnership was also opportunistic in nature, as key leaders, such as Wang Jingwei, in the Wuhan KMT believed they would receive Soviet financial aid in return for partnership with the CCP.⁶ Cooperation between the left-leaning KMT and the CCP would only last a couple months. The CCP, under COMINTERN direction, continued to foment peasant and urban uprisings against the industrialists, local elite, and gentry classes in Hunan and Hubei provinces, inciting violent responses from the right-leaning KMT faction. In June 1927, the KMT dispatched the Thirty-fifth Army to suppress the insurrection and seized control of Wuhan. Once Wuhan was under rightist control, He Qian, commander of the Thirty-fifth Army, demanded the Wuhan KMT break ties with the CCP.

During this same time, Stalin grew increasingly frustrated with the unreliability of the military effort within the United Front to spread the communist movement.⁷ To rectify the situation, he outlined four specific tasks for the COMINTERN and CCP in his telegram:

1. Confiscate land by the masses from below.

2. Revolutionize the present structure of the KMT by drawing the peasant and working-class leaders into its Central Committee.

3. Organize your own reliable army.

4. Establish a revolutionary military tribunal headed by a prominent non-Communist Guomindangist to punish counterrevolutionary officers.⁸

The Stalin telegram provided new Soviet guidance to the CCP and gave explicit approval for the creation of the Red Army, directing the COMINTERN to create its military force from the "revolutionary workers and peasants" and "utilize the students of the school for commanders."⁹

Wang Jingwei, the left-leaning KMT leader, struggled to maintain peace within the United Front until he became aware of a secret telegram from Stalin. The telegram outlined the COMINTERN's plan for subversion, and Wang Jingwei dissolved the alliance in July. As a result, COMINTERN representatives Borodin and Roy returned to the Soviet Union, and the KMT-Soviet partnership ended as well. The United Front did not last long; however, it was a portent example of a growing trend of KMT factions and groups with sympathies towards the CCP that would turn "Red."

Urban Uprisings as the Solution

Stalin blamed the failures in Wuhan on the CCP, and directed them to take active measures to correct the current situation. Chen Duxiu's leadership as the Chief of the CCP was labeled "opportunist" and he was replaced by Qu Qiubai. Stalin still insisted that the KMT was a legitimate partner with the CCP and all efforts of the revolution should remain under the KMT flag. CCP members continued to work to infiltrate the KMT and the NRA. The break pushed the CCP activities and members underground. Proactive measures were taken to promote both agrarian peasant revolutions and urban insurrections to set the conditions for the communist revolution. Besso Lominadze, a confidante of Stalin, replaced Borodin and Roy in China to help lead the movement. The new plan was to shift the communist movement to the offensive, and combine military rebellion, urban insurrections, and peasant movements.[10] The first opportunity to attempt this new strategy was in August 1927 with military units within the KMT Second Front Army.

The Nanchang Uprisings occurred on August 1, 1927.[11] The CCP did not have its own army and viewed the subversion of KMT army units as a quick way to increase its military force. The Second Front Army, led by Zhang Fakui, had recently arrived in Nanchang and had many Communist members and supporters within its ranks. Among the key members of the unit were the Twenty-fourth Division commander, General Ye Ting, Twentieth Army commander General He Long, and Chief of Public Security in Nanchang, Zhu De. Other officers inside the unit include Liu Bocheng, Lin Biao and Li Lisan. The intent of the subversion was to (1) gain control of the Second Front Army; (2) convince Zhang Fakui to support the communists; and (3) use the military forces to expand communist control. Two members from the Central Committee, Zhang Guotao and Zhou Enlai, joined Lominadze in Nanchang to help plan and oversee the operation. On the day of the uprising, Zhang Fakui was in Guangdong, and communist loyal forces disarmed their compatriots and took control of Nanchang. The communist forces established a revolutionary committee under the KMT banner to oversee the city. The uprising lasted only three days. When Zhang returned to Nanchang, he sided with the KMT and sent loyal units to suppress the rebellion. The communist forces retreated, breaking into two groups. He Long and Ye Ting's forces moved south to

Shantou. Zhu De's forces broke from the main body and took a circuitous route through Guangdong before arriving in Hunan.

Following the failed Nanchang Uprising, the CCP called an Emergency Conference on August 7, 1927, and pushed for continued uprisings within the cities, though a new strategy emerged. Stalin and the COMINTERN promoted the idea that peasant revolutions would complement the urban worker-proletariat movement. Reports of the success of peasant revolts, albeit on a smaller scale, had been sent back to the CCP headquarters in Shanghai as early as 1926.[12] The Central Committee tasked a local CCP organizer, Mao Zedong, to create an army from the peasants and incite a series of rebellions around Changsha that would spark a nationwide movement. He created the First Division, First Army of the Workers and Peasants Revolutionary Army, made up of miners from Anyuan county and peasants from three counties in Hunan province.[13] Mao had reservations with the plan,[14] but was overruled. On September 8, 1927, Mao and the First Division, First Army of the Workers and Peasants Revolutionary Army attempted to seize Changsha as part of the Autumn Harvest uprisings.[15] The uprising failed because a small number of urban workers and proletariats appeared to support the insurrection. Within five days, the rebels were kicked out of Changsha and the surrounding areas, and were forced on the run. During the uprising, Mao was briefly captured but managed to escape.[16]

By late 1927, Moscow and the CCP leadership all realized the urban insurrection plan had failed. The failure of the Guangdong Commune Uprising[17] in December 1927 further demonstrated that point. In response to the series of insurrections, Chiang Kai-shek instituted a series of Communist repression campaigns in the city, killing or arresting many other communist members, with the remainder going underground in the cities or fleeing to the rural areas. Most of the armed communist forces retreated to the rural areas to evade NRA pursuit. KMT repression of communist activities in the city severely hampered communications between the Central Committee and its forces, ceding the leadership and direction of the party to the military leadership in charge of the guns. Qu Qiubai's short tenure as the CCP Chairman ended as a result of the failed uprising and created a power vacuum within the CCP. The entire episode demonstrated to key leaders of the CCP the need for a professional military force. The masses of workers and peasants could initiate strikes and rebellions to take city centers, but a dedicated, professional military force was needed to maintain those gains in the face of the NRA.[18] That much-needed force would emerge from the Jinggang Mountains.

Push for Survival in the Mountains

Retreating communist leaders were forced to adopt pragmatic measures to survive in the highlands. Their experiences in the uprising reinforced the idea that a strong military force was the necessary push

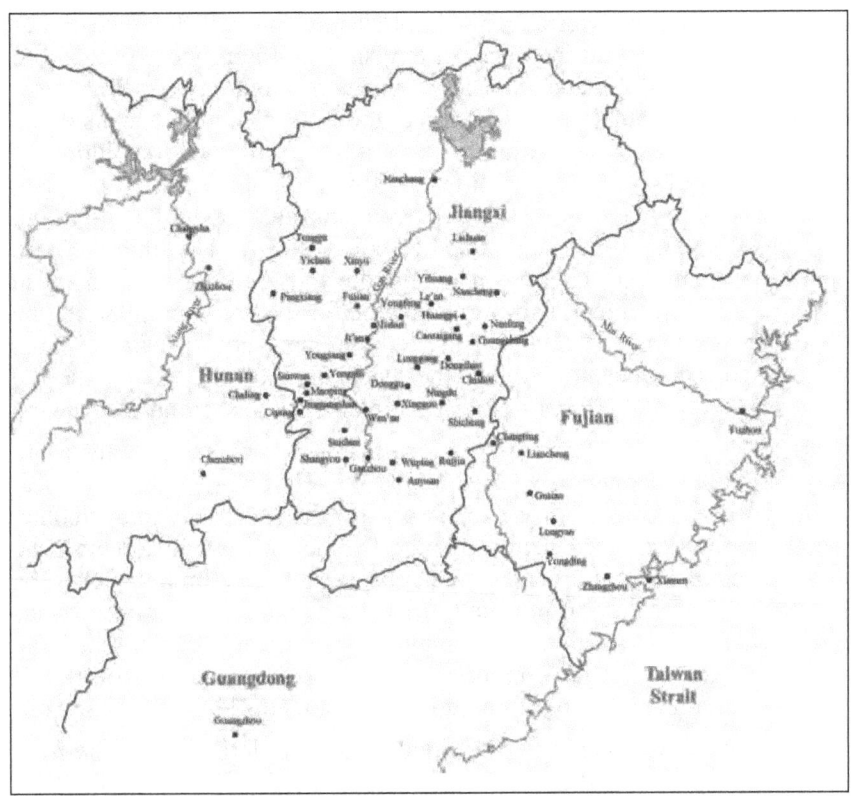

Figure 2: The Jiangxi-Fujian-Hunan Area
Source: Created by the author

to create the agrarian-based communist revolution. To develop the conditions for revolution, Mao Zedong and Zhu De adapted the Red Army and communist policies to the local conditions in order to recruit, sustain, and retain loyal soldiers, and began to improve the symbiotic relationship between the army, the local populace, and party.

The Journey to Jinggang Mountains

After the collapse of the Autumn Harvest Uprisings, the Workers and Peasant Red Army scattered to the rural areas. Mao narrowly escaped capture by the Nationalists and linked up with the remnant forces of the Workers and Peasant Red Army in Sanwan, Jiangxi province. Many of the soldiers were killed, arrested, or had deserted. Less than one thousand soldiers remained from of the original force.[19] Many of them were simply exhausted and homesick. Low morale, lack of a unified mission, and conflicting loyalties pervaded the unit, and even worse, some troops began to blame Mao for the losses and separation from family. In order to counteract these claims and strengthen the remaining forces into a cohesive force, Mao held a conference in Sanwan on September 29, 1927, and implemented a series of radical policies to stave off the implosion.[20] He reorganized the unit from the 1st Division, Peasants and Workers Red Army to the First Regiment, First Division, Peasant and Workers Red Army, streamlining the command and control of the unit.[21] Second, Mao instituted political representatives within each unit to instill the "revolutionary spirit" within the soldiers. A political cell was established in each squad, a branch at company level, and a party committee at the battalion and regimental level.[22] Next, he established soldiers' Soviets within the unit, providing "democratic centralism" within the unit. Additionally, Mao spun the narrative to his favor, shifting the blame for the uprising failure to the collective poor understanding of the revolutionary course within China, rather than incompetency among the leadership. Lastly, to appease the homesick soldiers, the First Regiment moved back to their native Hunan.

The Worker and Peasant Red Army initially planned to return to Anyuan, the hometown of a large number of soldiers; however, the local military forces in the area were too strong for the Red Army to overcome. Another option was needed, and quickly. The sick and wounded within the unit created a sense of urgency to establish a base area immediately. The lack of stable location to medically treat the wounded had a deleterious effect on morale.[23] The nearby Jinggang Mountain area presented an opportune site to laager temporarily,[24] especially since one of Mao's former Peasant Movement Training Institute students knew the area well.

Jinggangshan, meaning Well Ridge mountain, derived its name from the five villages around the main city of Ciping: Big Well, Middle Well, Little Well, Upper Well, and Lower Well. The mountain is situated within the Luoxian range that straddles the border between Jiangxi and Hunan province. The mountainous area is also the point where four different counties converge: Lingxian, Suichuan, Ninggang, and Yongxin. Its location along the county and provincial borders made it a good area for defense. Factional and political differences prevented most provincial forces from coordinating operations or massing effects in these border regions.[25] Jinggang's mountainous terrain also provided natural obstacles favoring the defense. The area was remote, away from any major urban concentration, county headquarters, and major road networks. The mountain's inhospitable terrain did not invite much industry and shielded it from any undue attention. For its remoteness, the area also had some strategic advantages. It stood midpoint between Changsha, Nanchang, and Guangdong, which allowed the Red Army flexibility to return to the sites of the failed insurrections.[26] Additionally, the revolutionary movement was more mature and developed in the Hunan area, and the Red Army could find greater local support for their operations.[27] All in all, the Jinggangshan mountain area provided a sensible alternative for the Red Army to consolidate its forces and start over its operations.

In their weakened state, the Peasant and Worker Red Army could not simply occupy Jinggangshan by force. The lack of military presence in these border regions often made its occupants subject to exploitation of roving bandits. The Jinggang mountain region was controlled by two bandits, Yuan Weicai and Wang Zuo, and Mao had to employ adroit negotiation skills to gain access into the area. Both sides had concerns about a new arrangement in the Jinggang mountains. The Peasant and Worker Red Army's biggest concern was the trustworthiness of Yuan and Wang. At a meeting in Gucheng, some members of the Front committee and representatives of soldier Soviets doubted the revolutionary character of Yuan and Wang and believed they were simply bandits.[28] Mao, on the other hand, argued that the two and their loyal followers were important part of the communist movement. For Yuan and Wang, they primarily worried about the impact of a new military force effect on the local balance of power. The mountain areas outside the cities had a complex power arrangement. Bandits and local elites maintained a status quo, and any change in power often led to an attack to return an area to a balanced state. Additionally, the mountain region had a distinct ethnographic population. A significant Hakka ethnic minority population considered the Jinggangshan their ancestral land, and the Han settlers were simply guests in the area. Ethnic tension between the minorities and the Han remained a flashpoint, and any addition of new guests had to be vetted.

Mao first convinced Yuan Wencai how the partnership would be mutually beneficial. In exchange for housing, food, and local support, the Red Army would provide weapons, training, and support Yuan and Wang's operations. Mao presented Yuan with a gift of 100 rifles as a symbol of the new relationship. Mao later made a similar gesture to Wang Zuo, sending him seventy rifles. The issue of a base was settled with the Red Army entering Jinggangshan; however, the prickly issue of differentiating between a bandit and a revolutionary soldier would remain a thorn in the Red Army's side.

Upon arrival at Jinggangshan, the Worker and Peasant Red Army began conducting guerrilla operations and peasant mobilization. On October 7, 1927, the Red Army started operations in Maoping, and moved across Jinggangshan area to Ciping. While on this march, the Red Army passed through Lingixan and Shuikou villages, attacking the local elite and their militia, opening up the local jails, and holding mass rallies as a way to promote the communist message. On October 22, Mao's forces moved to Dafen, where they were attacked by a local militia. The local militia used its knowledge of the local terrain to its advantage and inflicted heavy losses to the Red Army. The retreating forces of about 300 rallied at Dajing, linking up with Wang Zuo. Wang had yet to meet Mao and remained suspicious of his intentions. Fortunately, Mao won him over with similar promises of weapons and training for his force. Additionally, Mao promised to help Wang against some of his local rivals, which included

Xiao Jiabi. Wang's forces and the Red Army joined forces in Dajing, and seized Shimen. The final stop of the operation was Ciping, and on October 15, 1927, the Red Army seized the city center. In the span of one month, the Red Army established a stretch, albeit tenuous, of territory for a base to expand operations.

With a foothold established, the Red Army expanded its influence in the surrounding areas. The Red Army often preyed on local areas where government control was weak or in flux. On November 16, the Red Army sent a battalion to the west and took Chaling. The success in Chaling allowed the Red Army to expand its operations into Suichang in January 1928. On February 18, 1928, the Red Army got its largest catch with the occupation of Xincheng, Ningang County. Within two months of action, the Red Army almost doubled its territory and now occupied portions of three counties.

The concrete effects of the Red Army attacks were often temporary. It often could not hold the territory it seized during the raids. Traditional hierarchies of power remained entrenched in the region. The material gains from the attacks were consumed almost immediately.[29] Yet the military action itself served an important purpose by subverting the legitimacy of the traditional governing apparatus. Prior to the Red Army arrival, many villages maintained traditional governing system for decades. The attacks of the Red Army cracked the illusion of invincibility, and demonstrated to the people there was an alternative. Such a breakthrough within the psyche of the peasants helped to create greater support for the communist movement.[30] Additionally, the opportunity presented through revolution was an attractive alternative to many peasants. Life for a peasant since the fall of the Qing was difficult, to say the least. Natural disasters in 1918, 1924, and 1926 destroyed the lands peasants needed for subsistence.[31] At the local level, exploitation by the powerful or wealthy was common. Nationalist attempts at reconstruction were ineffective and had little positive impact on the peasantry, leaving them ultimately open to communist influence.[32]

The Arrival of Zhu De to the Mountain

For the most part, Mao was left alone because of the political shake-up within both the Central Committee and COMINTERN in response to the multiple failures to sustain the uprising in metropolitan areas.[33] Contact with the provincial and regional CCP community still existed. Zhou Lu, a member of the South Hunan Special Committee, heard about the communist expansion in the mountain areas and came to inspect the conditions. While at Jinggangshan, he gave Mao orders to dispatch his unit to support Zhu De's forces in an uprising in Southern Hunan.[34]

After the failed Nanchang Uprisings, Zhu De and the remnants of his forces evaded Nationalist forces and wandered around southern Jiangxi and Fujian until he linked up with a fellow Yunnan graduate and Nationalist army leader, Fan Shisheng. His stay with Fan was temporary once word had travelled a NRA unit was harboring fugitive communist forces.[35] The Communist forces left in January 1928 for southern Hunan to support some urban uprisings. Upon their arrival, Zhu De's capable military force became the critical addition to the Hunan communists' plan. Zhu De was augmented by peasants and levies from the surrounding Hunan areas. Zhou Lu was also supposed to provide additional forces from Jingggang Mountains to support the insurrection. The insurrection started on in late January, but it never got off the ground. The urban workers and local populace did not rise as originally planned. Instead, local support turned against the communists as revolutionary policies were seen as too harsh.[36] Additionally, Mao's forces never made it to Southern Hunan; instead, he dragged his feet and stayed in Central Hunan holding rallies and mobilizing the local peasant population.[37] Recognizing the growing threat within their spheres of influence, warlord armies in Guangdong and Hunan banded together and pursued Zhu De's forces. The Red Army and warlord armies had a series of engagements along the Jinggang Mountains as Zhu De and the Hunan regiments slowly retreated to the Jinggang Mountain base.[38]

Once Zhu De and Mao's forces arrived safely in the Jinggangshan area, the leadership from the two units retreated to Maoping to hold a conference. On May 20, 1928, Zhu De and Mao agreed to establish the Jinggangshan Special Committee, with Mao as the general secretary.[39] Additionally, the army reorganized the military forces, and established the Fourth Red Army, named after the original famed Fourth "Ironsides" Army.[40] The initial number of forces varied but the consensus estimates the force to be between 10,000 and 12,000. The forces consisted of Zhu De's Nanchang Uprising force (later designated Twenty-eighth Regiment), Mao's Autumn Uprising force (later designated Thirty-first Regiment), Yuan Wencai and Wang Zuo's former bandit force (later designated Thirty-second Regiment), and the Hunan Uprising force[41] (the Yizhang unit remained and was later designated Twenty-ninth Regiment).[42] Zhu De's arrival in Jinggangshan also brought in a traditional military mindset that assisted in the professionalization of the Red Army. The famous guerrilla tactics quote, "When the enemy advances, we retreat; when the enemy halts and encamps, we harass them; when the enemy seeks to avoid battle, we attack; and when the enemy retreats, we pursue," is attributed to Zhu at the first conference of Maoping, and would remain a guiding principles for Red Army action.[43]

Attacks against the Mountain

The increased strength and size of the Fourth Red Army attracted the attention of neighboring Jiangxi and Hunan military leaders. The first set of military campaigns against the Red Army was from May to June 1928 and was led by the Zhu Peide and the Jiangxi provincial military forces.

The first campaign was based out of Yongxin. The Jiangxi government dispatched the Twenty-seventh Division to attack the Red Army. With one regiment garrisoned at Yongxin as the reserve, the division sent one regiment to attack the Red Army stronghold in Nanchang with another regiment flanking to the east. The Red Army countered the action by stationing one regiment in the mountains to protect the base, one regiment to defend the mountain passes, and two regiments to conduct a spoiling attack on the flanking Jiangxi regiment. The Red Army regiments destroyed the flanking unit, which retreated back to Yongxin. The Red Army pursued into Yongxin, destroying the garrison regiment as well. The Red Army then effectively maneuvered to the rear of the Jiangxi division, causing the remainder of the division to withdraw to Ji'an to avoid complete defeat. The Red Army secured Yongxin, established a Worker-Peasant-Soldiers government, and expanded the Soviet across the county.[44]

The second encirclement campaign occurred relatively immediately afterward in late May, with the same Jiangxi Twenty-seventh Division in the lead. With new reinforcements, the Jiangxi Division took back Yongxin, and began a slower, more deliberate approach to attack the mountains. Red Guard units conducted guerrilla attacks to expose weaknesses for the Red Army to exploit, with little success. When the Twenty-eighth Regiment left to reinforce a distressed Red Army force in neighboring Chaling county, Zhu Peide saw an opening to attack the mountain passes. However, the Jiangxi Division did not account for the Red Army's mobility, as the Thirty-first Regiment quickly assumed the Twenty-eighth Regiment's former defensive positions and gave the Jiangxi forces a stiff fight. The Twenty-eighth Regiment quickly returned and reinforced the Thirty-first Regiment for the advance on Yongxin, seizing the enemy's rear once again. Choosing to survive rather engage in a losing battle, the Jiangxi forces retreated back to Ji'an.[45]

The last encirclement campaign occurred in June 1928 and was a combined operation with a Hunanese division attacking from the east. The Jiangxi Ninth Division was deployed in combination with the remaining two regiments of the Twenty-seventh Division from the previous campaigns. The Jiangxi forces conducted a frontal attack up through the mountain passes with three regiments. The Red Army first established a feint to the east to occupy the Hunanese forces, and then deployed one battalion augmented by local guerrilla groups to the western flank of the mountain passes. The threat of guerrilla attacks on the eastern flank of the Jiangxi forces caused the commander to maintain two regiments garrisoned the reoccupied Yongxin as a reserve. Using the mountainous terrain to its advantage, the Red Army destroyed one regiment as they funneled up to through the passes. The victory brought numerous weapons and new soldiers, and the Red Army retook Yongxin.[46]

At the end of June 1928, the Jinggangshan base area hit its apex in terms of size. It controlled the entire area of Ninggang, Yongxin, and Lianhua counties. It also had control of portions of Ji'an, northern Suichuan county, and Anfu city.[47] Chiang Kai-shek took notice of the Communists' gain and directed a new campaign against the Communist bandits.

Another series of combined campaigns incorporated the Hunan and Jiangxi armies against the Fourth Red Army, and started in July 1928. The Hunan Eighth Army forces began its attack from the west through Ninggang, whereas the Jiangxi Army deployed eleven regiments from the Third and Sixth Army through Yongxin along the eastern border of Jinggang Mountains. The Red Army kept two regiments to defend the bases, while the Twenty-eighth and Twenty-ninth Red Army Regiments moved west and slipped behind the Hunanese Eight Army rear and conducted raids. At the same time, local Red Army militia forces implemented a "scorched earth" strategy, removing all food, contaminating water sources, and vacating villages in order to deny the enemy forces any supplies. The combination of these tactics forced the Eighth Army forces to retreat. With its flank secured, the Red Army turned around its forces and moved towards Yongxin to attack the Jiangxi regiments. The success of this campaign would be overshadowed, though, by the "August Defeat" incident.[48]

The Red Army had an initial string of victories, especially with its recent victory against the Hunanese forces in Ninggang. However, the "August Defeat" incident demonstrated how tenuous the situation really was. As the Twenty-eighth and Twenty-ninth regiments moved west to support the attack against the Jiangxi forces, the regiments abruptly changed courses, and headed south towards Southern Hunan, citing orders to assist the Southern Hunan Special Committee.[49] The two regiments attacked the city of Chenzhou, about 200 kilometers from Jinggang Mountains, and defeated the local enemy force. However, the Red Army did not pursue the retreating forces; instead, soldiers and officers uncharacteristically strolled through the streets as if they were civilians once again. Some soldiers left to visit families in nearby villages and incidents of looting were also reported during that time.[50] The enemy reorganized and engaged in a fierce counterattack. The Twenty-eighth Regiment withdrew quickly with minimal casualties. The Twenty-ninth Regiment did not fare so well. The surprise attack exploited the excitement of being home, and the unit did not respond quickly enough to retreat before the enemy cut off the only bridge leading out of town. The stragglers who survived were incorporated into the Twenty-eighth Regiment. The Twenty-eighth Regiment slowly made its way back up to the base area, where the remaining Red Army forces were in a nasty fight with the Jiangxi military.[51]

With the two regiments gone from the mountain, a reinvigorated KMT force attacked once again. Three regiments of reorganized Hunanese troops joined the same eleven Jiangxi regiments. The remaining Red Army forces defended the Jinggang mountains by employing every tactic possible to survive. The Red Army gave up terrain as the enemy military forces moved forward to take the mountain base, relying heavily on the recently constituted village militias to disrupt and delay the advance. Given the shortage of personnel, the Thirty-first and Thirty-second regiments became the main defensive force, and retreated to the protection of the high ground, and established hasty defensive positions along key routes in order to mass fires. The force was actually smaller than reported, since Mao Zedong went with one battalion from the Thirty-first Regiment south to escort back the Twenty-eighth Regiment.[52] Small guerrilla and raid units attacked the flanks and rear of advancing forces as the KMT forces attempted to attack up the rugged mountain side in the dead heat of summer. After repeated failed attempts to scale the mountain, the Hunan and Jiangxi forces finally withdrew and the mountain was safe. On September 9, the Twenty-eighth Regiment returned safely back to the Jinggangshan. The Red Army continued to fight and retake land lost during the campaign. By October 1928, they had retaken the Ninggang county, and parts of the surrounding Suichuan, Lixing, and Yongxin county, but were never able to recover all the territory.[53]

The last campaign coincided with an economic blockade and the arrival of Peng Dehuai's Fifth Army forces. The Jiangxi and Hunan forces adopted an economic blockade tactic, normally used against bandits, to deprive the Red Army and its local support network access to the local markets in the lowlands. Starting in the fall of 1928, military forces and local militia established checkpoints along all routes and trails leading to and from the Jinggang mountains. Private militia, manned with soldiers intimately familiar with the local area, conducted interdiction patrols to capture any blockade runners. The blockade effectively halted local trade of goods, such as timber, tea, and tea oil from the mountains. It also stopped the importation of medicine, clothing, food, and most importantly, salt.[54] The blockade exacerbated local tensions, as the supplies and patience were running short. Conditions in the areas began to worsen, with people simply subsisting on sweet potatoes and pumpkins. Peng Dehuai's Fifth Army[55] arrived in December 1928 and worsened the burden on the area. At the same time, NRA forces from Fujian, Jiangxi, and Hunan provinces began to surround the mountains and prepare for attack.[56]

In the face of all these tensions, the Fourth Red Army leadership convened a conference at Bailu to discuss their options. The discussion focused on how to neutralize the threats looming down the mountain as well as how to integrate the new forces. The options were limited. One recommendation was to repeat the same tactics used before to isolate and attack enemy forces as they moved up the mountain; however, the invading forces had adapted as well and had better coordination and larger units. The next option was to withdraw to a safer area momentarily, and then conduct a counterattack. The economic hardships from the blockade exacerbated civil-military relations in the mountain areas, and any sign of disloyalty to the local populace might end their support for the Red Army. The last option was to mount a defense of the mountain range against the enemy, which did not allow for any withdrawal route for the 6,000 soldiers. The council decided to adopt a hybrid solution for the operation. The Fourth Red Army would break through the blockade in an effort to draw forces away from the mountain area, and at the same time ease the logistical demands on the local populace. The Fifth Red Army, which was understandably worn thin from its recent march, would remain in the mountains and defend the base.[57] On January 14, 1929, the Fourth Red Army led by Zhu De and Mao, broke through the blockade and headed south to Jiangxi.

The Fourth Red Army's initial foray into southern Jiangxi was filled with challenges. They were initially met with success as the units moved south, facing scant resistance as they seized Suichuan and Shangyu, on the way to Dayu, Jiangxi province. At Dayu, however, three regiments from the Jiangxi Army were waiting, and attacked the unprepared Red Army forces, forcing them to retreat north back to the Xingguo-Ji'an area. While moving along the snow-covered winter roads, the Red Army found little local support in the area. The revolution had yet to reach these areas, making logistical and intelligence support difficult at best. The Red Army marched for about 30 days, sometimes covering up to 30 miles a day to avoid pursuit, all the while taking casualties and losing equipment. The Red Army arrived in Dabaidi village, in the Ningdu-Ruijin area, Jiangxi province, on February 10, 1929 and had a fierce battle with two regiments from the Fifteenth NRA Division. The Red Army routed the force, temporarily capturing the two regimental commanders, and gaining about 800 soldiers and weapons in the process. The victory gave the Fourth Red Army well-needed rest after its harrowing escape from the mountains.[58]

After the Red Army secured its place in Jiangxi, the KMT became engulfed in internal strife as Chiang Kai-shek continued his quest to consolidate power from regional warlords. These efforts consumed the NRA's attention and resources and left the Red Army to its own devices. During this period, Mao and Zhu expanded the Jiangxi Soviet through a series of campaigns into West Fujian province. In February 1929, the Fourth Red Army incorporated two independent guerrilla regiments into its force, and leveraged its new combat strength to expand the Soviet area to include Ji'an, Ningdu and Ruijin. In March 1929, the Red Army entered Western Fujian and seized Tingzhou. In the wake of the victory, the Red Army secured a small arsenal, with more than 2,000 weapons and machines guns, plus a clothing factory, providing the army with new uniforms. The Red Army also had 3,000 former KMT soldiers transfer over to the Red Army.[59] Once the Red Army established the Jiangxi Soviet, it rapidly accumulated more success in its battles and operations. Red Army forces continued to conduct guerrilla operations and political mobilization in the areas. By April 1929, the Red Army had expanded the Jiangxi Soviet to encompass more than 20 counties in Jiangxi and Fujian.[60] In light of their successes, Mao sent a letter in April 1929 to the Central Committee,[61] highlighting the achievements in Jiangxi and Fujian, as well as describing the tactics and strategies that led to the Red Army's success.[62] In May 1929, the Red Army conducted its second campaign into Western Fujian, and seized Longyan and Yongding, further expanding the footprint. With each campaign, the Red Army gained more soldiers, more equipment, more territory, and more money.

During the early days of the Jiangxi Soviet, one of the major concerns was control over the direction of the Red Army. Through the expansion, different factions with contrary opinions and directions festered in the Red Army. Issues with militarism, warlordism, "adventurism," and "opportunism" continued to pervade the army.[63] Additionally, the question of the leading role of politics in the Army remained contentious. On June 22, 1929, the Fourth Red Army held its Seventh Representative Congress in Longyan to discuss many of these issues but failed to reach a consensus. During the meeting, many of Mao's ideas of party control of the military faced stiff resistance, and his ideas' unpopularity contributed to his failed bid to be the Front Committee secretary-general.[64] In the wake of the loss, Mao left for Fujian to assist in mass mobilization and became very ill. During that time, Chen Yi, representing the Fourth Red Army in Shanghai, briefed the Central Committee on the unit's status and progress. Based on the reports, the CCP sent a letter of instruction to the Fourth Red Army in September 1929, indicating its full support of political communist control of the Red Army and the application of military force to push political mobilization as the means to continue the spread of the revolution across China.[65] Vindicated by the Central Committee support for his ideas, a healthy Mao attended the Ninth Representative Congress in Gutian county, Fujian province, and issued his famous statement, "On the Rectification of Incorrect Ideas in the Party,"[66] which outlined his view on the current status of the Red Army and his plan to correct those ideas.

The conference also gave Zhu De and Mao a platform to push for centralization of power within the Red Army. With casualties, desertions, and new recruits changing the composition of the Red Army, Mao saw a need to adjust the organization structure.[67] Factional differences within the army became more apparent with new recruits. Additionally, the conference also addressed the role of the Communist party in the army. More education and centralized control was needed to ensure the Red Army maintained a unity of effort.[68] A more through discussion on the specific measures adopted at the Gutian Conference is discussed later in this chapter, but in summary, the resolutions from the Gutian conference effectively established party control over the Red Army. It also clarified the critical importance of the Red Army's dual political and military role in supporting political mobilization in the Communist revolution. Lastly, the Gutian conference symbolized Mao's consolidation of power within the Fourth Red Army against other factions and set the conditions for future actions.

Analysis

Situational Assessment

The myriad of threats of Red Army faced in the Jinggang Mountain remained constant throughout the 10-year civil war. The first set of threats was external to the Army. Besides the obvious threat of the KMT military force, the Red Army also had to contend with the different warlord armies, bandits, and militias. The local militias were among the most threatening. The communist revolution and land reforms directly threatened the interests of the local gentry class, and many of them raised private militia to protect themselves. Some militia forces not only defended lands, but also attacked Red Army forces, especially in the base areas. Equipped with more modern equipment, these forces leverage their intimate knowledge of the local area to strike the base areas and disrupt Red Army activities.[69] The Red Army also had to be prepared for dangers when working with the local populace. Jinggang Mountain areas were occupied by the Hakka minority, and the communist forces worked to ensure their "guest" status in the area remained secure. Prior to leaving Jinggangshan, the ethnic strife flared up due to the economic blockade, and was one of the contributing factors for the Red Army's departure.[70] Even Han support was not guaranteed in the areas. Miscalculations on the extent of revolutionary fervor in the cities contributed to the failure of the uprisings in 1927. The locals surrounding the route to Ruijin were unsympathetic to the communist cause, and gave little support to the fleeing Fourth Red Army.

The other set of threats came from within the Red Army. The biggest internal threat during these first two years was desertions.[71] The horrendous conditions and homesickness pushed many soldiers to voluntarily leave the army and return home. Conditions at the time were extremely tough. At the Jinggang Mountain base areas, food became so scarce the soldier's meals simply consisted of pumpkins.[72] The Red Army units were also constantly short of the necessary logistical and financial resources. The Red Army required a minimum of 50,000 yuan a month to survive,[73] which was difficult to raise, especially when engaged in almost constant conflict. The stark differences in background and culture within the disparate Red Army units also led to many internal conflicts. The Red Army was an amalgamation of different groups coming together less out of common goal, but more out of survival. Many of the soldiers were former peasants. Other Red Army soldiers were former KMT or warlord soldiers. The bad traditions of the warlord and KMT armies coupled with the lack of educational background in the rural areas created a boiling pot of inappropriate behaviors that decreased morale.[74] Under these difficult conditions, the Red Army leadership adopted a more flexible strategy in order to survive.

Strategy

Initially, the main goal of the Red Army was survival. From the above description, the Red Army faced overwhelming circumstances that could easily end the unit's existence. Mao and Zhu De recognized that in its current state, the Red Army would lose in a conventional battle against a superior army.[75] With this understanding, the Fourth Red Army created a new political-military strategy in the Chinese rural areas to protect and grow the communist peasant revolution.

The first strategy adopted by Mao was making alliances. Through these alliances, the Red Army could increase its forces, gain legitimacy, learn about the local area, and expand its territory with little extra work. Mao understood that alliances were important, even if they were frowned upon by the Central Committee of the CCP. In 1928, a resolution from the CCP Sixth Party Congress viewed bandits as a major threat to the Red Army and communist organizations, and they should be immediately expelled.[76] Such an extreme stance ran counter to the reality in Jinggang Mountains, and the contributions made by Yuan Wencai, Wang Zuo, and the members of the Thirty-second Regiment could not be overlooked. To remedy the situation, Mao made no mention of the point in discussions, and actually vetoed any plan to attack Yuan and Wang.[77]

The second strategy was adapting communist policies to the local conditions, specifically, altering the targets of the revolution depending on the circumstances. The Red Army was more pragmatic than dogmatic when it came to fomenting revolution. Contrary to CCP guidance, attacks on landlords and rich peasants were limited to those who were disliked within the local community.[78] The Red Army purposely avoided attacking popular landlords or rich peasants since the actions undermined the political mobilization and did not engender local support. Instead, the Red Army would target its propaganda efforts and negotiations at the popular members of the local gentry class to gain their backing. The pragmatic viewpoint on strategy became a constant theme throughout the war.

Over time, the strategy changed from survival to slow expansion. Mao described the expansion as a series of waves. He saw the systematic development of rural Soviets as the way to encircle the cities and create the conditions for revolution.[79] His grand strategy to expand Soviets in China was time and labor intensive. With that said, it also took into account the external and internal conditions of the Red Army, and provided a road map that could reach their goal. It also required more than the simple application of violence and force from the Red Army. Mao realized early that the Red Army had to have multiple roles in the communist struggle.

Tactics

To survive and expand, the Red Army had to create a new way to fight and defeat superior enemies. The famous quote "The enemy advances, we retreat" encapsulated the Red Army practical application of the best tactics given the Red Army's limitations at the time.[80] During this period, The Red Army combined mobile warfare, guerrilla tactics, and political mobilization in its operations as a way to beat the KMT.

During the Jingangshan and Jiangxi Soviet period, the Red Army is most associated with guerrilla warfare. While Mao is known for his writings on guerrilla warfare, he admitted that he did not invent this style of warfare; rather, it was a product of the collective experiences of the Red Army during these formidable times. At a strategic level, Mao adopted guerrilla warfare because he understood the weakness of the Red Army vis-à-vis his enemies. The purpose of the guerrilla warfare was not to gain decisive victory, but rather gain time, supplies, and equipment while preserving strength. The guerrilla tactics employed in Jinggangshan and Jiangxi remained focused on small-unit tactics, with emphasis on scouting, patrolling, cover and concealment, marksmanship, mobility, and troop leading. The guerrilla units were normally local militia units, trained and sometimes led by Red Army officers, most often political leaders. These forces primarily engaged in ambushes, raid, and feints at the rear and flanks of the enemy to distract and disrupt enemy operations. The Red Army faced immense challenges even before making contact with the enemy, and adopting guerrilla tactics was effective in preserving its combat power for those specific opportunities for the decisive attack.

While guerrilla warfare is often synonymous with the Red Army, its main forces engaged in conventional warfare as the main weapon to defeat the KMT and warlord armies. Red Army units did incorporate some guerrilla tactics in their operations, but for the most part engaged in conventional warfare. The methods of attack were seen as different because the Red Army used small-unit tactics that relied on speed, surprise, and mobility.[81] These functions were not based on a strict following of a guerrilla tradition, but rather an acute awareness of their limitations and shortcomings. During its battles with the Jiangxi Army, the Fourth Red Army used interior lines within the mountains to reinforce weak positions and attack the enemy on the flanks and rear. The Red Army also used the terrain, weather, and light to its advantage to find, expose and mass fires against an enemy's weakness. The Red Army's victory in the second combined Jiangxi-Hunan campaign against an overwhelming force was a direct result of leveraging the restrictive mountain passes to canalize and mass fires on the enemy.

Logistical concerns also limited the Red army's ability to sustain protracted battles, thus making quick attacks a more sustainable choice. As "guests" in a minority area, Red Army leaders were sensitive to the logistical burden it placed on local society, and did not want to consume all the resources in the area. The Red Army's cache was also limited to what they could seize after battle. Therefore, the Red Army had to be economic and efficient in its use of combat power, and leveraged its size and mobility in its attack, and looked for ways to make the most gains from battle. The capture of Tingzhou in early 1929 is a good example of good economic choices. The Red Army picked up two arsenals and a clothing factory, which helped to both increase morale and combat effectiveness of the units. Lastly, conventional battles were often conducted at a larger scale. Mao discussed how, given the quality of soldiers and training, dispersion of forces was a difficult concept.[82] Thus, conventional operations with stronger command and control through key leaders were the primary mode of operations for the Red Army at this time.

Within the Red Army, guerrilla tactics also encompassed political mobilization. These tactics represented a new, distinct direction for the Red Army. Instead of engaging in strictly conventional military activity of fighting, true success of the Red Army during this period was not gained on the battlefield, but rather through local society. The new communist military model transcended traditional offensive or defensive operations and expanded into political mobilization of the masses. These political operations leveraged guerrilla warfare tactics as well as political tactics not necessarily utilized in conventional warfare.[83] The blurring of lines between the military and political realm would eventually create a wedge within the party in the future. However, during this period the Red Army leveraged political mobilization for all its benefits.

The biggest tangible benefit from political mobilization was the creation of an administrative and logistical backbone to support Red Army operations. Local support in a village translated into recruitment, supply and intelligence networks, and revenue streams. To develop the local base, the Red Army refined its peasant mobilization process to increase efficiency and meet any shortfalls. It also used guerrilla tactics to disperse soldiers to mobilize the masses.[84] Political mobilization during this period had four major stages in its operation.[85]

The first stage of the peasant mobilization process was the reconnaissance and assessment. Prior to entry into a new town or village, the Red Army leadership conducted a hasty assessment of the local conditions to determine the mobilization process time.[86] Once in the village, the Red Army conducted a more in-depth assessment, focusing on the following areas: peasant situation, opposition parties' situation, economic conditions, land distribution, geographic conditions, and road networks.[87] The assessment gave the Red Army commander and political commissar a deeper understanding of the local conditions in order to tailor tactics to the local realities. Based on the assessment, the leaders created local elite targeting lists, developed themes for propaganda, and established criteria for negotiations.

The second stage for the Red Army was propaganda dissemination. Red Army units created specific propaganda teams, each assigned with five soldiers. Each team had two sections, one oratory section and one product section, made up of three soldiers and two soldiers, respectively. The oratory section was responsible spreading key communist propaganda themes by speaking at village marketplaces, center areas, and halls to all willing listeners. The products section was responsible for creating propaganda products. They went around town and pasted signs and banners with communist slogans to increase awareness. Usually within a month, the propaganda team held a large mass rally in the central area of the town or village to agitate local support for the movement.[88] Propaganda themes were based on the local assessment. The team tailored specific messages to leverage pre-existing social and political wedges in the community. Propaganda served three main purposes. First, it helped to recruit new members to the Red Guard and Red Army. Mao argued that the primary purpose of the guerrilla operations was to help "expand[ing] the Red Army and the local armed forces."[89] Second, it helped to elicit support from the local populace, especially for Red Army operations. Third, it helped the local populace differentiate the Red Army from local bandit groups. In the past, some Red Army units did a poor job spreading propaganda, and simply posted some banners while passing through villages. Unaware of who the armed group actually was or what the slogans actually meant, many villagers just assumed the Red Army was just another group of roving bandits pillaging the rich in the area.[90] The lack of awareness contributed to low local support for the Red Army, which made its mission of survival and expansion temporarily unfeasible.

The third stage for the Red Army was organizing the people. Once the local populace was sufficiently agitated by the social inequalities neatly identified by the propaganda team, Red Army leaders made a call for action to topple the local government, and pushed the people to organize themselves and create a new government. During the overthrow, not every bureaucrat was targeted. The Red Army did not always have the personnel or experience to replace the local leadership and associated bureaucrats, nor were those skills and experiences always present in the local populace. Instead of a wholesale execution or imprisonment of the opposition, the Red Army used a selective coercion technique of attacking and publicly executing key leaders who were often the communists' most ardent opponents.[91] The remaining elites whose experience and knowledge of a specific field was irreplaceable were kept in place and continued their service to the local government. The party cadre would just fill in the key member positions in the government that were recently vacated. The new arrangement allowed the communist party to enact its policies while maintaining the technical expertise to institute the new vision.

The new local apparatus also included the establishment of multiple organizations in the towns. Every citizen became a member of at least one organization, from the communist party to labor unions. Some locals volunteered directly for the Red Army. Many of the volunteers were sent on practice missions to collect information to ensure their loyalty and reliability.[92] Once verified, they would fall in on one of the multiple organizations within the Red Army. The Communist Youth organization was a feeder unit to the Red Army by training and integrating local teenagers and young adults into the Red Army. The Red Guard was a local militia group that protected the community, and supplemented the Red Army in combat if needed. Guerrilla units or independent regiments were paramilitary forces that operated outside their locals areas in support of the Red Army. The goal of these organizations was to grow the security teams organically at the lowest levels. The local militia, out of self-interest, would guard its own village from attack. Those who demonstrated zeal for the job would be incorporated into independent guerrilla units and support the Red Army. Personnel from these units also entered the Red Army and became soldiers. The entire system ensured that the Red Army had multiple layers of defense tied into the local community, and supported a viable and sustainable military force within the Red Army.

The last stage in the political mobilization was revenue generation. The Red Army did not have any organic industries or trade to rely on for revenue, so a large portion of its money came from attacking wealthy landowners.[93] The main revenue stream came from extorting the wealthy locals in the villages. The toppling of landlords and rich peasants was both consistent with communist doctrine and also benefited the Red Army's bottom line. It was not surprising that the direct targeting of wealthy elites led many locals to believe the Red Army were a group of bandits. A second source of revenue for the Red Army came from taxing businesses in the cities. This stream was smaller because the Red Army targeted middle to large businesses, which were often based in urban areas outside Red Army territories. The last and smallest source of income for the Red Army came from taxes paid by the local populace.[94] Since previous warlords and local leaders extorted high taxes from their constituents, the Red Army tried to avoid levying taxes on the populace in order to maintain its support in the area.

The proper application of mobile warfare, guerrilla tactics, and political mobilization was the key to the success to the Red Army in its early phases. Stephen Averill analyzed Mao's initial tactics in Jingangshan and summarized the Red Army's tactics in five basic steps:

1. Initial lightning attacks on key enemy military forces and county

seats, accompanied by the destruction of official buildings, opening of jails and other similar anti-government acts.

2. Appropriation of cash, grain, and other useful property from yamens[95] and local elites, some of which was kept by the Red Army and some distributed to the local populace.

3. Selection of a few local elites as exemplary targets for punishment (often execution) at public rallies.

4. Dispersion of Red Army units and CCP cadres into towns and villages to proselytize, investigate, and otherwise interact with the local population.

5. Re-concentration of forces, accompanied by further rallies announcing the formation of Communist-run local governments.[96]

The Red Army successfully applied these tactics, and variations to the core themes, in Jiangxi, Hunan, and Fujian to expand the communist revolution and become a serious threat to the KMT legitimacy.

Organization

The Red Army instituted a series of organizational changes to meet two needs, establish loyalty and commitment to the Chinese Communist Party, and establish a flexible organizational structure that allowed for both dispersion of its forces for guerrilla operations and the concentration of firepower. Initially, the Red Army applied the Russian and NRA model, but changes were needed to adapt to local conditions.[97]

To increase the political control of the party, Mao instituted a series of measures, beginning in Sanwan. The Sanwan reorganization helped to establish party rule over the army by establishing party representatives and soldier Soviets. The purpose of the political party representatives was two-fold. It established equal footing between the army leaders and communist party as well equal control of the army units.[98] It also gave party representatives greater oversight into the issues and concerns of the soldiers, especially if it could affect positive change and lower the number of desertions and bad behavior. Mao also established soldiers' committee to improve the quality of life and treatment of soldiers in the Red Army. Yelling and beating soldiers was commonplace within NRA and old warlord army units.[99] The democratization was a method to reverse decades of poor treatment of soldiers and make the soldiers and officer equal.[100] Mao believed that the success of the Red Army could be attributed to democratization, as the benefits of soldiers committees gave Red Army soldiers more courage to be fearless on the battlefield.[101] While the democratic process could have instilled more courage into soldiers, its greater impact within the unit was integrating soldiers into the decision-making process. Soldier's committees empowered them and made them part of a team. In turn, they felt more vested in the decisions and operations of the unit, and led to greater committment on the battlefield. The soldier's committee lasted for only about two years until it began to overshadow the control of the party. Mao alluded to some of the growing concerns with the committees, using terms such as absolute egalitarianism and extreme democratization to describe the errant ways pervading some Red Army units.[102]

The Gutian Conference in December 1929 adopted more initiatives to help consolidate military power under party control. Under the resolutions adopted at the conference, the Red Army adopted the political commissariat system from the Soviet Red Army to place greater control of the army into the hands of the political commissar. Beside their special role in political training and mobilizing the masses, the political commissars also held veto power over military operations, whereas military commanders did not have the same power over political operations.[103] With this resolution, the party seized effective control of the military. Political training was still needed to ensure enforcement of this rule. The introduction of former KMT forces into the Red Army increased the need for political indoctrination. For example, only ten percent of Zhu De's original force were party members.[104] Additionally, the Gutian Conference reiterated the equality among the soldiers and officers as well as between the military and civilians.[105] This statement re-emphasized the importance of soldier retention, as improvement in quality of life could help decrease desertions, especially preventing Red soldiers from joining the NRA.

Concerns about unity of command and control pushed the Red Army to conduct a series of reorganizations of its units. One of the major issues the Red Army continued to run into was the uneven distribution of manpower across Red Army units. Local area recruitment and casualties all affected the personnel numbers in Red Army units, and made assessing, organizing, and directing units very difficult. Some companies had less than sixty soldiers, others had more than 160.[106] In its "Outline of Military Work" issued in May 1928, designated the force from the "Chinese Workers and Peasant Red Army" to simply the "Red Army."[107] Additionally, it outlined a temporary force structure of a 3-5 model. Each squad was made of 12 soldiers. Three squads made up one platoon, and five platoons were assigned to one company. Each battalion had five companies, each regiment had five battalions, and finally five regiments were in one division.[108] By 1930, the Red Army had reformatted the organization, and established a 3-3 reorganization plan.[109] Based on a KMT military table of organization, the Red Army established the 3-3 model at the company and platoon level. Each company had three platoons, with three squads each. Each squad had ten soldiers in each unit. At the battalion level and above, there were more variations. Battalions varied from three to six companies, and a regiment had two to three battalions, with an artillery battery and/or a specialty unit, such as engineers, communications, or cavalry.[110]

Training

Mao and Zhu understood the important role of military training for the Red Army. The most important purpose of the training was to dismantle previous habits and biases and align individual interests with the greater good of the party. As discussed previously, the disparate origins of Red Army soldiers added personal, institutional, and cultural baggage which inhibited the Red Army from becoming an effective fighting force.[111] Second, the military training made up for the Red Army's collective lack of experience and knowledge to conduct sustained combat operations. While two major groups of soldiers, former NRA soldiers and officers and graduates of the Peasant Movement Training Institute, did receive some level of formal training, they also received the bulk of casualties in the initial fighting. The majority of the Red Army ranks were now filled with peasants with little to any combat experience.[112] Furthermore, the lack of experience at the local Red Guard and guerrilla unit level pushed experienced officers away from the front line to lead these units.

The strategic aim of political and military training was to reduce the commitment of Red Army leaders and soldiers to specific Soviet areas. By developing a competent and trained local force, the Red Army could move outside its borders to expand the regions.[113] Additionally, Mao's experience at the Hunan-based Peasant Movement Institute highlighted the importance of large-scale military training. The Peasant Movement Training Institute's curriculum was heavily military focused, given that the use of force was necessary to overcome local landlords. However, the low success rate of the graduates pointed to issues with scale. The number of graduates paled in comparison to the number of peasants they had to lead, and there were not enough graduates to sustain the efforts of the communist movement pre-1927.[114]

Communist strategy and tactics depended on smalls units and disciplined soldiers to properly interact with their leaders and the local populace. Given the disparate origins, old military traditions, and impoverished upbringing of many soldiers, incidents of theft, assault, and property damage were common. Mao and Zhu De took proactive steps to increase the discipline of its units by instituting the famous "three disciplines and eight points of attention." Mao initially instituted the three disciplines in 1927:[115] (1) obey orders in all your actions; (2) don't take anything from the workers and peasants; and (3) when attacking the local bullies, turn over [whatever you take from them].[116] The eight points of attention were initially six when first issued in 1930.[117] The points included: (1) Put back the doors [you have taken down for bed boards]; (2) put back the straw [you have used for bedding]; (3) pay fairly for what you buy; (4) return everything you borrow; and (5) pay for anything you damage.[118] Mao and Zhu later added two more points of attention: (7) defecate only in latrines, and (8) do not steal from captives.[119]

The purpose for these rules was two-fold. The Red Army leadership used these disciplines to curb reckless soldier behavior that negatively impacted the local populace because the Red Army needed the local population to be supportive, not neutral. The Red Army units were guests in many villages, often inhabited by both ethnic minority tribes and Han settlers. Some soldiers married local women, and became part of the community.[120] Any offensive behavior jeopardized the army's security, food, recruiting base, and home. Second, the disciplined behavior differentiated the Red Army from NRA units, warlord armies, or bandit gangs. To prevent local villagers from mistaking the Red Army for another gang, Red Army soldiers had to distinguish themselves in both word and action. These actions had a strong propaganda effect on both the local populace and the NRA.

Discipline alone did not guarantee success for the Fourth Red Army. Military and political training were desperately needed to improve effectiveness. The Red Army initially used the NRA and Huangpu Military Academy training structure to develop its training methodology. The Red Army continued an old NRA training method, known as the "Three drills, two talks, and one roll call."[121] The Red Army established training units to help develop junior leaders and local cadres. Many of the Red Army's senior leaders were trained at Baoding, Whampoa, and Yuannan military schools. Yet at lower levels, the level of military experience was uneven, and these training units were one method to cross-level the experience across the units to ensure a minimum standard. Mao established the first training unit, the Thirty-first Regimental Training Unit, in December 1927 at Longjiang Academy in Jinggang Mountains.[122] Zhu De and Chen Yi established a similar unit in January 1928, before their arrival at the Jinggang Mountains.[123] Initially, military training was quite basic given the unit's lack of experience in conducting military training.[124]

In June 1928, these units combined to form the Fourth Red Army Training Group, and oversaw the training of the Fourth Front Red Army. These classes incorporated pedagogical training styles from Huangpu Military Academy Shiko Gan Military Academy, and Yunnan Military Academy as the basis for its training.[125] The arrival of Zhu De's unit did bring more experienced cadre to help in the training efforts of peasants and new soldiers.[126] During training, Zhu De and Mao Zedong periodically gave lectures on specific topics. Commanders from field units were also invited to the school to teach courses and lead exercises to ensure the curriculum remained relevant.[127] The overwhelming majority of students were leaders at the company level and below, as well as key cadre members of Red Guards at the villages and counties around the Jinggang Mountain border areas.[128] The first class of 100 students graduated from the Fourth Red Army Training Group training in December 1928.[129] All these measures helped to establish a minimum base of military education across the Red Army.

Once in Jiangxi, the Red Army established mobile schools that accompanied units to the front lines to continually train its forces. While the Jiangxi Soviet remained under continuous threat of attack, the increased stability of the new location allowed for the expansion of training for the Red Army. The expansion of Red Army forces and increased casualty rate created a larger demand a more robust training regimen.[130] The pressures from the KMT extermination campaigns also made it almost impossible to create a normal education system. The Red Army responded to the requirement by establishing accompanying military schools.[131] On the foundation of the training units, the accompaniment schools were created to teach a curriculum and program designed for specific military units. In June 1929, the Fourth Red Army established its first accompanying military school in Changning.[132] These schools were unique in two regards. First, the schools were not in a fixed location. As the name suggests, the schools moved with the unit as they travelled across the area. Second, the teachers' unit maintained a combat role as well and fought as a unit. The Red Army still required all its personnel to fight when needed, and the school was no exception. The accompaniment school's curriculum length ranged from three months to a year.[133] The focus of training remained at the lowest levels, with training tasks focused on basic guerrilla tasks.

While schools were important, for many soldiers the only way to learn was from doing. Sometimes conditions did not allow for the training, and the students were thrust into combat immediately. Mao stated "to learn warfare through warfare—this is our chief method."[134] While Mao touted the efficacy of learning by doing, in reality, Red Army soldiers did not have a choice.[135]

The biggest contributor to the practice of learning by doing was the adoption of specific measures to complement the process. To simply assume that the success of learning by doing through a Darwinian method of improvement would be folly. The practice was actually complemented by a strong after-action review program. Zhu De is cited for specifically importing the practice of after-action reviews.[136] After battles, the leadership conducted meetings and led discussions on areas of improvement for the battle.[137] If meetings couldn't be conducted, the leadership wrote reports analyzing the battles and identifying key areas for improvement. This self-critical examination helped to modify behavior and improve the model of learning by doing. The learning by doing also was directed at ensuring the peasant soldier remained engaged in the process. Many of these new recruits and junior leaders never received formal education, and much of the classes and training were boring. To make sure that classes remained interesting, practical exercises were used to maintain interest.[138] Lastly, learning by doing melded theory with practice. Instead of simple lecture programs, the instructors would incorporate practical exercises to apply the theory in areas. This tradition had its roots in the Hunan Peasant Movement Institute, where practical exercises were conducted as well. Practical exercises were in actuality real missions supervised by instructors. Students went into villages and organized the local populace during exercises to gain a better understanding of how operations were conducted.[139]

Political indoctrination was also a critical part of the training program as it helped to increase the education, loyalty, and effectiveness of new soldiers. At Sanwan, one of the key initiatives was the establishment of political training as part of party control of the army.[140] Political training's main function was indoctrination. It allowed members of the Red Army to coalesce around a common mission, language, doctrine, and tradition. The training also attempted to separate the soldiers from the cultures and traditions the army deemed harmful, such as "warlordism, extreme democratization, egalitarianism, militarism, individualism, etc."[141] These pejorative labels were part of the Red Army's narrative to limit activities associated with divergent traditions. The initial political training curriculum covered a range of topics, to include the nature of revolution, principles of Marxist-Leninist ideology, roles and responsibilities of a people's army, and social and economic surveys of local areas.[142]

In terms of political training, the Red Army began to adapt its pedagogical methods for political training in order to mass its effects on the peasants. Expansion of the military, Soviet territory, coupled with casualties from combat, made political training a constant activity to indoctrinate and train members of the Red Army. By 1929, the Red Army had established seven pedagogical methods to conduct political training: (1) large lectures; (2) formal class instruction; (3) informal instruction during formations; (4) after-action reviews; (5) literacy classes; (6) mass rallies; (7) soldier committees; (8) publication of propaganda periodicals.[143] Similar to military training, one key pedagogical method was the use of positive and negative feedback to correct behavior. Whether in lectures, class instruction, or in formation, Red Army leaders used praise to demonstrate to their soldiers "correct" behavior. They criticized mistakes made by soldiers to identify prohibited activities.[144] More subliminal propaganda was also used to change political behavior. Initial literacy workbooks for soldiers were heavily laced with communist propaganda, emphasizing the exploitation of workers and class struggles.[145] Slogans, cadences, songs, and poems during this period were also filled with propaganda to help indoctrinate new recruits and locals into loyalty with the party.

Conclusion

By the beginning of 1930, the Fourth Red Army had expanded its territory from Jinggangshan to Jiangxi, Fujian, and Hunan. An additional seven other Soviets scattered across the Chinese interior and demonstrated the viability of the CCP. The success of the Red Army was attributed to the leadership's ability to adapt communist policies to local conditions. Mao and Zhu also created new policies and training programs to develop a military force capable of defeating the enemy. Interwoven in all these factors was the instinct to survive.[146] While the Red Army had established a strong base in Jiangxi Soviet, there still were many problems within the unit. Mao addressed many of these different ailments, such as militarism, extreme democratization, adventurism, and subjectivism in his comments at the Gutian Conference. These labels carried both a pejorative meaning as well as links to certain political factions and members. While the labels were definitely used to gain public support against a certain movement or faction, stripping away the political propaganda did not change the core issues affecting the Red Army. Issues with desertion, toxic leadership, insubordination, failure to follow orders, incompetence, lax enforcement of standards, lack of motivation to conduct political operations, abuse of power, and uneducated soldiers still remained in the army. The Red Army initiated greater political training programs to weed out these problems, but they would persist for a long time. Continued conflicts within the party would test the Red Army's ability to adapt while in contact.

Notes

1. For more information on Borodin and his role as a COMINTERN Representative, see Daniel N. Jacobs, *Borodin: Stalin's Man in China* (Cambridge: Harvard University Press, 1981).

2. On March 18, 1926, an NRA naval gunboat, *Zhongshan*, was anchored off the coast of the Whampoa. Nationalist historiography contended that the boat captain, a communist party member, was part of a larger conspiracy to kidnap Chiang Kai-shek. Communist historiography argued that Chiang and the KMT manufactured the claim to attack the Communists and declare martial law. As a result of the incident, Chiang instituted punitive measures against the CCP. The KMT demanded a list of all CCP members in the KMT and all CCP members in top ministry positions were removed. For a balanced account on the incident, see Hans J. van de Ven, *War and Nationalism in China, 1925-1945* (New York: RoutledgeCurzon, 2004), 101-104.

3. For more information on the Northern Expedition, see Donald Jordan, *The Northern Expedition: China's Revolution of 1926-1928* (Honolulu: University Press of Hawaii, 1976).

4. The NRA was also supported by the Green Gang, a secret society with connections to local businessmen who saw the labor strikes as detrimental to their business interests. The Shanghai massacre began a general purge of the KMT enemies, with between 3,000 to 4,000 CCP members killed; 25,000 people were also imprisoned during this time. See Hans J. van De Ven, *From Friend to Comrade: The founding of the Chinese Communist Party* (Berkeley: University of California Press, 1991), 193.

5. Within the KMT party, there were marked differences between the factions. It was a disparate polity of union leaders, communists, former warlords, secret society members, foreign sympathizers, and wealthy entrepreneurs, all who created a cacophony of conflicting, separate interests. Unity of effort was elusive for the KMT, and many of its decisions were reached through realpolitik negotiations among its interest groups. John Schrecker, *The Chinese Revolution in Historical Perspective* (Westport: Praeger Press, 1991), 159.

6. Pengfeng Chi, "The Chinese Army and the Kiangsi Soviet" (Ph.D dissertation, George Washington University, 1977), 22.

7. Joseph Stalin, *Marxism and the National and Colonial Question* (Honolulu: University Press of the Pacific, 2003), 249.

8. Stalin, *Marxism and the National and Colonial Question*, 249.

9. Stalin, *Marxism and the National and Colonial Question*, 249.

10. John P. Harrison, *The Long March to Power: A History of the Chinese Communist Party, 1927-72* (New York: Praeger Publishing, 1972), 121.

11. For more information on the Nanchang Uprising, refer to C. Martin Wilbur, "The Ashes of Defeat," *The China Quarterly* 18 (1964): 3-54; Jacques Guillermaz, "The Nanchang Uprising," *The China Quarterly* 11 (1964): 161-168. Bruce Elleman, *Moscow and the Emergence of the Communist Power in China: 1925-30* (New York: Routledge, 2009), also provides a different perspective on

the Nanchang Uprisings by examining the intraparty struggles in Moscow and its effect on the Nanchang Uprising.

12. Mao spent a year observing the revolts, and sent back an extensive report that was received with little fanfare. In the "Report of an investigation into the Peasant Movement in Hunan," he argued that the conditions of the peasant movement were of such magnitude that they could change the face of the communist revolution. Furthermore, the character of the Chinese revolution was, contrary to Soviet ideology, instinctively peasant-based. Mao Tse-Tung. *Selected Works, Vol. 1* (New York: International Publishers, 1954), 21-62.

13. William Whitson, *The Chinese High Command: a History of Communist Military Politics, 1927-71* (Westport: Praeger Press, 1973), 28.

14. Mao's main contentions were two-fold. First, he believed the loyalty and quality of his peasant recruiting base was insufficient, and his force should be augmented by two military regiments. Second, he disagreed with the continued partnership with the KMT, which was in name only, and pushed for the rebellion to be led under an independent communist banner. John Rue, *Mao Tse-tung in Opposition: 1927-1935* (Stanford: Stanford University Press, 1966), 75.

15. For more information on the Autumn Harvest Uprising, see Roy Hofhejnz, "The Autumn Harvest Insurrection," *The China Quarterly* 32 (1967): 37-87.

16. Supposedly, Mao bribed his Nationalist captors, who were unaware of his identity, to release him. He successfully escaped and evaded capture by hiding in small villages until he made it back to Sanwan.

17. For more information on the Guangzhou Commune Uprising, see Arif Dirlik, "Narrativizing Revolution," *Modern China* 23, No. 4 (1997): 363-397; Hsiao Tso-Liang, "Chinese Communism and the Canton Soviet of 1927," *The China Quarterly* 30 (1967): 49-78.

18. John Fairbank, *The Great Chinese Revolution, 1800-1985* (New York: Harper and Row Publishers, 1987), 232.

19. Chong Kun Yoon, "Mao, The Red Army, and the Chinese Soviet Republic" (Ph.D dissertation, The American University, 1968), 44.

20. Jun shi li shi yan jiu bu. *Zhongguo ren min jie fang jun de qi shi nian* [Seventy Years of the PLA] (Beijing: Jun shi ke xue chu ban she, 1987), 49. Hereafter cited as *Seventy Years of the PLA*.

21. The regiment was made of two battalions, three companies, and one Specialty Company. The regiment also maintained one training unit and one medical unit. Zhongguo ren min ge ming jun shi bo wu guan, *Zhongguo zhan zheng fa zhan shi* [History of the Development of War in China] (Beijing: Ren min chu ban she, 2003), 831. Hereafter cited as *History of the Development of War in China*.

22. Harrison, *The Long March to Power*, 133.

23. Stephen Averill, *Revolution in the Highlands: China's Jinggangshan Base Area* (Lanham: Rowman and Littlefield Publishers, 2006), 158.

24. The choice of Jinggang mountain as a communist base area was under

some debate. Most Chinese official histories argue that Jinggangshan was a predestined spot for the communists. See *Seventy Years of the PLA*, 30. Averill argued that the Red Army's occupation of Jinggangshan was never guaranteed; rather, it started as a temporary position that developed over time, Averill, *Revolution in the Highlands*, 156.

25. Mao, *Selected Works, Vol. 1*.

26. Averill, *Revolution in the Highlands*, 156.

27. Mao, *Selected Works, Vol. 1*, 73.

28. Yuan Wencai actually entered the Communist Party in 1926. He was considered the more educated and wiser of the two, given his better understanding of the communist movement. His group of poor peasants considered themselves a local defense force for the area. Wang Cuo on the other hand, was a tailor by trade. Considered illiterate and self-indulgent, he often followed Yang's lead on decision. Peter Short, *Mao: A Life* (New York: Henry Holt and Co., 1999), 212-213. Averill, *Revolution in the Highlands*, 163.

29. Averill, *Revolution in the Highlands*, 170.

30. Averill, *Revolution in the Highlands*, 171.

31. Andrew J. Nathan, "A Constitutional Republic: the Peking Government," in *The Cambridge History of China, Vol. 12, Republican China 1912-1949, Part 1*, John K. Fairbank, ed. (Cambridge: Cambridge University Press, 1983), 262.

32. John K. Fairbank and Merle Goldman, *China: A New History* (Cambridge: Harvard University Press, 1998), 301.

33. Averrill, *Revolution in the Highlands*, 190.

34. Zhou Lu's visit added much conflict to the area. He believed the Red Army was in violation of CCP policies by instituting a tolerant and humane treatment of landlords and rich peasants in the area, at the time considered a "rightist" stance. He also informed Mao and his partners that his membership in the party had been revoked due to the failures of the Autumn Harvest Uprising. Averill, *Revolution in the Highlands*, 191.

35. The KMT government found out that Zhu De's forces were hiding with Fan, and they ordered Fan to arrest him. Fan wrote a letter to Zhu De and told him to rebel against his forces so they could escape. Rue, *Mao Tse-tung in Opposition*, 87.

36. Averill also believed the strength of the enemy force would have overwhelmed the Communist forces, even with the addition of Mao's units. Averill, *Revolution in the Highlands*, 192-195.

37. Averill, *Revolution in the Highlands*, 192-194.

38. The movement of the Red Army up the mountainside was slowed by both the difficult terrain and the low morale of many of the Hunan peasants units raised for the uprising. Averill, *Revolution in the Highlands*, 194.

39. Rue, *Mao Tse-tung in Opposition*, 93.

40. Agnes Smedley, *The Great Road: The Life and Times of Chu Teh* (New

York: Monthly Review Press, 1956), 229.

41. Many of the Hunanese peasants experienced homesickness while at Jinggangshan. Their fighting abilities were also suspect, given their inexperience in combat and recent introduction to communist ideology. The lack of logistical support for the enlarged group of the combined Zhu-Mao forces in Jingangshan did not improve the situation either. In late May into early June 1928, the majority of the peasants migrated back home. Those remained were part of a levied forces led by Hu Shaohai, and were a cohesive, well-trained unit. Averill, *Revolution in the Highlands*, 196-199.

42. Averill, *Revolution in the Highlands,*, 197.

43. Smedley, *The Great Road*, 229.

44. Averill, *Revolution in the Highlands,* 199-200; *History of the Development of War in China*, 840.

45. Averill, *Revolution in the Highlands,* 200-201; *History of the Development of War in China*, 840.

46. Averill, *Revolution in the Highlands,* 201-202; *History of the Development of War in China*, 840.

47. *History of the Development of War in China*, 841.

48. Averill, *Revolutions in Highlands*, 273-274; *History of Development of War in China*, 841.

49. The Twenty-ninth Regiment was made up of members of the Hunan Uprising. The soldiers had recently become more dissatisfied with the revolution, especially given their combat fatigue and poor living conditions. Many soldiers missed home, and the operation to Hunan was a welcomed respite. Averill cited some sources that argued some leaders in the Twenty-ninth Regiment the deliberately conducted the Chenzhou operation to get back home. Averill, *Revolutions in Highlands*, 276-278.

50. Averill, *Revolutions in Highlands*, 277.

51. Averill, *Revolutions in Highlands*, 276-278; *History of Development of War in China*, 841.

52. *History of Development of War in China*, 841.

53. Averill, *Revolutions in Highlands*, 280-288.

54. Averill, *Revolutions in Highlands*, 308.

55. For more information about Peng Dehuai's journey to Jinggang Mountains, see Peng Dehuai, *Memoirs of a Chinese Marshal: The Autobiographical Notes of Peng Dehuai (1898-1974)* (Beijing: Foreign Languages Press, 1984).

56. Averill, *Revolutions in Highlands*, 320-324; *History of Development of War in China*, 842.

57. Averill discusses some of the issues with the plan, including the frustrations within both armies. The Fourth Red Army leadership was not happy about abandoning their base, especially Thirty-second Regiment soldiers, who were from the area. The Fifth Red Army soldiers felt as if they were being left

to slaughter in a new and unfamiliar territory. The Fourth Red Army transferred some key personnel to the Fifth Army, effectively ending the dissension. Averill, *Revolutions in Highlands*, 323-324.

58. *History of Development of War in China*, 842-843; Yoon, 74-75.

59. There is some differences in the number of soldiers identified as being transferred to the unit. Yoon stated 3,000 troops were transferred. See Yoon, "Mao, The Red Army, and the Chinese Soviet Republic," 76. Another study quoted 2,000 soldiers. See *History of Development of War in China*, 342. Chi identified a total of 3,000 soldiers: 1,000 from the defeated unit, and 2,000 peasants organized into Red Guard units. Pingfeng Chi, "The Chinese Red Army and the Kiangsi Soviet" (Ph.D dissertation, George Washington University, 1977), 48.

60. *History of Development of War in China*, 843.

61. Stuart Schram, ed. *Mao's Road to Power,* (4 volumes, Armonk, NY: M.E. Sharpe, 1992), Vol. 3, 153-161.

62. The Red Army's tactics and strategies will be discussed more in depth later in the chapter.

63. "Adventurism" was a pejorative term used by the Chinese Communists to describe operations and/or activities deemed to be impulsive, risky, or outside the scope of the operation. See Snow, *Inside Red China*, 168. Kwok-sing Li defined the Chinese Communist use of "opportunism" in two forms, "right opportunism" and "left opportunism." Right opportunism did not acknowledge changes in society that went counter to their position, and instead attempted to return or maintain society in its original state. Left opportunism also did not acknowledge the objective situation, and instead pursued "fantasy and rash actions." See Kwok-sing Li, comp., *Glossary of Political Terms of the People's Republic of China*, trans. Mary Lok (Hong Kong: The Chinese University Press, 2005), 181.

64. *History of Development of War in China*, 833.

65. *History of Development of War in China*, 833.

66. Mao, *Selected Works*, Vol. 1, 105-115.

67. Rue, *Mao Tse-tung in Opposition*, 179-180.

68. Harrison, *The Long March to Power*, 145.

69. Averill, *Revolution in the Highlands*, 217.

70. Averill, *Revolution in the Highlands*, 307-311.

71. *Seventy years of the PLA*, 49.

72. *Seventy years of the PLA*, 45.

73. Most of the funds went to pay the soldiers' small stipends, and to purchase items and equipment unavailable in the local area. *Zhong yang jun shi tong xun*, [Central Military Report], Vol. 1, (Chinese Communist Party Central Military Committee, January 15, 1930), 39. Hereafter cited as *ZYJSTX*.

74. *Seventy years of the PLA*, 45.

75. *Seventy years of the PLA*, 38.

76. Saich, *The Rise to Power*, 362.

77. Averill, *Revolution in the Highlands*, 317.

78. *ZYJSTX*, 38.

79. Mao, *Selected Works*, Vol. 1, 124.

80. Mao, *Selected Works*, Vol. 1, 124.

81. *Seventy Years of the PLA*, 41-42.

82. Schram, *Mao's Road to Power*, Vol. 3, 154.

83. Whitson, *The Chinese High Command*, 29.

84. Mao, *Selected Works*, Vol. 1, 124.

85. *ZYJSTX*, 38.

86. *ZYJSTX*. Normally, the Red Army chose between a short mobilization timeline, between five to seven days, and a more protracted mobilization timeline, ten days to one month period.

87. *ZYJSTX*. These assessment areas can be traced back to similar assessments taught at the Peasant Movement Training Institute, in which Mao Zedong was principal in 1926. See Jane L. Price, *Cadres, Commanders, and Commissars* (Boulder: Westview Press, 1976), 80. Mao's "Report on an investigation into the peasant movement in Hunan," is a good example of assessments at that time. See Mao, *Selected Works*, Vol. 1, 21-62.

88. *ZYJSTX*, 38.

89. Mao, *Selected Works*, Vol. 1, 125.

90. *ZYJSTX*, 38.

91. Averill, *Revolution in the Highlands*, 158

92. *ZYJSTX*, 38.

93. *ZYJSTX*, 39.

94. *ZYJSTX*, 39.

95. *Yamen* is Chinese for a local bureaucrat.

96. Averill, *The Revolution in the Highlands*, 170.

97. *ZYJSTX*, 26.

98. *Seventy Years of the PLA*, 49-50.

99. For more information on the poor treatment of soldiers in warlord units, see Diana Lary, *Warlord Soldiers,* 49-58.

100. *Seventy Years of the PLA*, 50.

101. Mao, *Selected Works*, Vol. 1, 82.

102. Mao, *Selected Works*, Vol. 1, 108-111. A resolution from the Gutian conference ended soldier's committees. They were replaced by Lenin clubs, which focused more on entertainment and soldier welfare issues, than any political indoctrination or training.

103. Rue, *Mao Tse-tung in Opposition*, 185.

104. Averill, *The Revolution in the Highlands*, 205.

105. Xue, Lianbi, and Zhenhua Zhang, eds. *Zhongguo jun shi jiao yu shi* [History of Military Education in China] (Beijing: Guo fang da xue chu ban she, 1991), 273. Hereafter cited as *Chinese Military Education History*.

106. *ZYJSTX*, 26-27.

107. The four major tasks included: (1) establish a Political Department at the regimental level, and a Political branch at the company level; (2) the local Soviet government should establish a Political commissar within the military units, (3) focus especially on political work; and (4) base military organizational structure on military tasks and weapons available. *Seventy Years of the PLA*, 40.

108. The companies were further designated as musket companies, rifle companies, and pike companies. The regiment also had scouts, transportation, medical, and special units in the formation. Other special units were specific to each regiment. *History of the Development of War in China*, 829.

109. Given the difficulty in communications between the Central Committee and Front committees, the author cannot confirm if the May 1928 reorganization order actually was executed. The information for the 3-3 model comes from a Central Military Committee publication in 1930, which does not specifically address the 3-5 model. It simply stated that the Red Army based its organization off the old NRA model of 3-3. *ZYJSTX*, 26-27.

110. *ZYJSTX*, 26-27.

111. Yuan Wei and Zhuo Zhang, eds., *Zhongguo jun xiao fa zhan shi* [History of the Development of Military Schools in China] (Beijing: Guo fang da xue chu ban she, 2001), 322. Hereafter cited as *Chinese Military School History*. *Chinese Military Education History*, 271.

112. Mao, *Selected Works*, Vol. 1, 79-80.

113. Mao, *Selected Works*, Vol. 1, 69.

114. Price, *Cadres, Commanders, and Commissars*, 73-85.

115. There is some conflict on the origin of the three disciplines. *Seventy Years of the PLA* author argued that the disciplines originated after some soldiers ate some sweet potatoes they were supposed to help the local Sanwan village residents pick. *Seventy Years of the PLA*, 53. Stephen Averill argued the disciplines originated when the Red Army retreated after a defeat. Averill, *The Revolution in the Highlands*, 163.

116. Schram, *Mao's Road to Power, Vol 3*, 283.

117. The six points were initially published by Mao in April 1928. *Seventy Years of the PLA*'s author cites the National Red Army Representative Congress in May 1930 as the issue date of the Three Rules of Discipline and Six Points of Attention. *Seventy years of the PLA*, 53. Schram cited the issue order date of March 21, 1930, in Schram, *Mao's Road to Power Vol 3*, 283.

118. Schram, *Mao's Road to Power, Vol 3*. 283.

119. There is some confusion over one of the points of attention. Schram initially cited that the seventh, "Don't bathe within sight of women," or eighth point of attention was replaced by "do not steal from captives" in 1930. See Schram, *Mao's Road to Power, Vol* 3, 283. *Seventy Years of the PLA's* author cited that the original seventh point, "Don't bathe within sight of women," was used in 1931 with local militia training. See *Seventy Years of the PLA*, 53.

120. Mao married a villager from Jinggangshan, which helped to him to improve local relations with the Red Army. Averill, *The Revolution in the Highlands*, 179-181.

121. Every morning, afternoon, and evening, Red Army units would conduct drills, which included running, marching, and turning movements. In the morning and evening, classes would be given by the leadership, often the political representative, on a range of different topics. At night, there would be one final roll call, which the leadership reviewed key events from the day and reiterate some training points. *Chinese Military School History*, 323, ZYJSTX, 32.

122. The unit was also known as the Officer training unit. Instructors had been trained at Huangpu Military Academy or worked at the Central Military Political School, Wuhan Branch. The unit at its height had 150 personnel, manned by the standard accompaniment of military instructors, administrators, mess officers, quartermasters, and orderlies. The unit was broken down into a political team and military team. Each team had two sections, teaching three classes each. *Chinese Military School History*, 322-323.

123. *Chinese Military School History*, 323.

124. Initial training focused on military movement and positions, such as attention, parade rest, and marching in step. *Chinese Military School History*, 324.

125. *Chinese Military School History*, 325.

126. Averill, *The Revolution in the Highlands*, 197.

127. *Chinese Military School History*, 325

128. Averill, *The Revolution in the Highlands*, 215. *Chinese Military School History*, 325.

129. *Chinese Military School History*, 326.

130. *Chinese Military School History*, 326.

131. The name for the military school translates literally to "school that accompanying a base (*suiying xue xiao*)."

132. *Chinese Military School History*, 328

133. Other tasks included deployment of forces, entrance, expansion, reconnaissance, camouflage, ambush, feints, pursuit, positional attack, positional defense, movement to contact, retreat, night operations, avoiding strengths to attack the weak, and sieges. See *Chinese Military Education History*, 274.

134. Mao, *Selected Works*, Vol. 1, 186.

135. *ZYJSTX,* 35.

136. Whitson, *The Chinese High Command*, 52.

137. *ZYJTSTX*, 32; *Chinese Military Education History*, 273-274.

138. *ZYJSTX*, 32; *Chinese Military Education History*, 274.

139. Price, *Cadres, Commanders, and Commissars*, 79.

140. *Chinese Military Education History*, 271.

141. Mao, *Selected Works*, Vol. 1, 105-116; *Chinese Military Education History*, 271-272.

142. *Chinese Military School History*, 323.

143. *Chinese Military Education History*, 273.

144. *Chinese Military Education History*, 273.

145. *Shi bing ren zi ke ben* [Soldier's Character Reader], Mar 1931, SSC, Reel 8:72.

146. Averill, *The Revolution in the Highlands,* 208.

Chapter 4
Li Lisan Line and First Three Extermination Campaigns (1930-1931)

As the Chinese Red Army settled into its new surroundings, its focus switched to expansion. Its success in Jinggang Mountains and Jiangxi Soviet led the Central Committee of the CCP, located in Shanghai, to make an inflated assessment of the Red Army's abilities. In 1930, the Red Army incited a series of urban insurrections in Nanchang and Changsha that resulted in serious casualties for its units, and ultimately failed to expand the communist revolution. Li Lisan, then the CCP party chief and architect of the insurrection plan, took the fall for the disaster. While the Central Committee reorganized the leadership, the Red Army in Jiangxi Soviet took advantage of the independence and lack of supervision to conduct its own operations. During the first three Extermination Campaigns, the Red Army was still unable to directly engage the NRA in conventional warfare due to the NRA's superior numbers and equipment. Instead, the Red Army adopted a mobile defense strategy, aptly named "lure the enemy in deep," to take advantage of its mobility, knowledge of terrain, and local support. Guerrilla operations and political mobilization were combat multipliers during these three campaigns, as militias and local citizens provided intelligence, logistical, and medical support to the main fighting forces. Political propaganda also helped to turn some officers and soldiers within the NRA forces towards the communist side. The Red Army also expanded its training efforts to improve leaders' and units' proficiency in combat by establishing the Red Army Academy and institutionalizing military training within the political indoctrination program.

Li-Lisan Line
Ideological Underpinnings of Li Lisan Plan

In spite of continued attacks by provincial and NRA forces, the communist movement flourished relatively well in the countryside. The same assessment could not be made in the urban areas. After the failed uprisings in 1927, support for the urban insurrection as the center of the revolution was fragmented. In addition, the KMT implemented an anti-communist campaign inside the cities, repressing communist activities and driving the movement underground. Additionally, the urban labor unions were not very receptive to the communist propaganda. For many of the labor unions and urban workers, their focus was on economic initiatives rather than political changes.[1] The lack of excitement for the communist movement is evident in the party demographics. In 1928, peasants made up three-fourths of the Communist Party membership. One statistic stated the Shanghai labor union members had dropped from 3,000 to 700 by 1930.[2]

In the face of the dreary numbers, the CCP continued to look at the urban centers as the key to the communist revolution. One of the major reasons was philosophical. The Central Committee maintained an unwavering belief that the proletariat should carry out urban insurrections as the means to incite the revolution.[3] As the head of the CCP Propaganda Department, Li Lisan was one of the biggest proponents for the urban insurrection model. Since his return from France in 1928, Li Lisan pushed for reestablishment of the proletariat as the center of the communist movement, stating "the peasantry is petty bourgeois and cannot have correct ideas regarding socialism." He went further to say, "Only a proletarian mentality can lead us onto the correct revolutionary road."[4] Li also maintained a different point of view on the education of the proletarian leadership. He took a more traditional approach, believing that the proletarian spirit solely came from the urban areas, whereas Mao believed through political education, the peasants could gain the spirit even though they were separated from the cities.[5]

For Li Lisan, the push for the revolution was also a political power move to reestablish central control over the Red Army. He openly pushed for the attack and occupation of large cities, rather than the expansion and building of rural Soviets.[6] However, his attempts at reinvigorating the labor movement in the urban centers did not seem to catch on. Recruitment and communist activities within the cities were still weak. His faith in the urban movement initially faltered. In a pessimistic letter to Mao in February 1929, Li lamented the absence of any revolutionary fervor in the cities and felt the revolution's future was in doubt.[7]

At the same time, a strong push from the COMINTERN in the middle of 1929 helped to reinvigorate the CCP and Li Lisan. The COMINTERN continued to stress the urban proletariat as the central theme in the communist revolution. In 1929, Stalin believed the communist revolution in China was on the rise, citing the economic depression in the United States after the market crash in 1929 as evidence.[8] The COMINTERN began publishing a series of guidances and measures in February and June 1929 that gradually reemphasized the urban insurrection line.[9] In September 1929, the COMINTERN made a specific push for the communists to leverage labor unions as means to deliver the revolution to the masses. In October, the COMINTERN estimate reached a crescendo, believing the revolutionary upsurge had finally started.[10] Yet, the COMINTERN remained vague on the exact time period for the revolution to begin, and subsequent guidance would be more confusing and unclear. Some argue the vague and inconsistent guidance left the COMINTERN with a convenient escape if the revolution failed.[11] Even with all the ambiguity, the CCP took the COMINTERN guidance at face value and began preparations to start the revolution.

During this time, the Red Army continued to increase in size and strength and became the only force able to lead the urban insurrections. The uninspired showing from the urban labor movements pushed Li Lisan to rely more heavily on the Red Army.[12] Li planned to gain control of the Red Army by establishing central party control over the Army, while dividing the forces away from its leaders. In April 1930, the Central Committee issued two resolutions for the creation of a General Front Committee to lead the urban insurrection effort. The General Front Committee became responsible for arming all the peasants, organizing them into Red Army units, and deploying them to the urban cities.[13] Li also requested Mao and Zhu De to come to Shanghai in an attempt to separate them from their troops and keep them in the city.[14] While Mao and Zhu De never actually made it up to Shanghai, the introduction of the General Front Committee was the first step in establishing central party control over the Red Army.

By the beginning of 1930, the CCP overcame any awkwardness after the raid on Soviet Union consulates[15] and began promoting the COMINTERN's October directive, stating that the rise in the revolutionary tide in China had begun. The party reaffirmed that the conditions were "ripe," though the CCP also acknowledged the weakness of the current labor movement, stating that the laborers' "timidity," party members' "contempt for the masses," and "negligence" toward organizing the masses were the reasons for the poor showing.[16] In February 1930, the Conference of Delegates from the Soviet Areas convened to "secure the leading role of the proletariat" with the urban worker "taking over leadership of the peasant insurrections."[17] The conference also repudiated Mao's strategy of encircling the cities in favor of urban insurrections. The Central Committee directive chastised Mao and Zhu De's forces as still having a "hide-and-disperse view," and pushed for the Red Army to "concentrate and attack."[18]

Urban Insurrection Plan

The Li Lisan plan was a counter to Mao's strategy. Mao promoted a slow expansion, focused on land distribution and establishing Soviets, rather than any quest for "adventurism" by attacking Changsha.[19] Mao also pushed for the slow bottom-up expansion of the Red Army, starting at the local village militias, then moving to county Red Guard, then to local Red Army forces, and finally to main Red Army units.[20] Li disagreed with Mao's notion. In his initial guidance to the Red Army for the attack, Li criticized Mao's plan to create independent Soviets along the borders areas as erroneous and defeatist.[21] He also placed excessive focus on concentrating weapons in Red Army units, rather than dividing them equally with local militias, which led to a decrease in the combat effectiveness of the Red Guard and guerrilla units.[22] Lastly, Li complained that Mao's strategy was too slow, stating that "by such tactics our hair will be white before the revolution is victorious."[23]

Specific planning for the urban insurrection began in early 1930. The CCP understood that the revolutionary tide around China was not equal. Consequently, the focus was on one or two key provinces and areas to ignite the revolution. The Red Army planned to conduct a series of insurrections in Nanchang and Changsha, with the main target the city of Wuhan.[24] The communists believed that if Wuhan fell, the revolution could then spread to Shanghai, and set off a worldwide chain of revolutionary events.[25]

Success in the uprisings was based on two key assumptions. The first assumption was that the revolutionary fervor was at a necessary level. However, looking at the communist demographic data during this period, the validity of this assumption was strongly questionable. From 1926 to 1930, the working class membership in the CCP dropped from 66 percent to 8 percent.[26] Failure to question this assumption would cause many casualties in the future. The second major assumption was that the Red Army was capable and ready to arouse an urban insurrection. The Red Army had survived the past two years and grown in size. Yet, it still lacked the equipment, training, and personnel needed to conduct such an urban operation.

Recent scholarship has shown that the gap between Mao and Li Lisan's thinking was less than Mao later portrayed it to be. From Mao's historiographical perspective, he was against the rule from the start. In 1938, Mao attacked Li Lisan's line as being "unaware of the protracted nature of the Chinese civil war…consequently, in an attempt to achieve a quick nation-wide victory for the revolution, ordered an attack on Wuhan…thus committed the error of 'Left' opportunism."[27] Additionally, the Red Army's leadership reception was tepid. Zhu De was cautious about implementing Li Lisan's plan, because he understood the strength of the KMT and did not want to have his forces destroyed.[28] Yet, there is evidence that Mao and Zhu De were less skeptical and more willing to follow the Li Lisan line. In his letter to Lin Piao, Mao agreed that the "proletarian leadership is the sole key to victory of the revolution."[29] He later stated:

> At the same time, the development of struggles in the countryside, the establishment of the Red political power in small areas, and the creation and expansion of the Red Army, are in particular the main conditions for helping the struggle in the cities at accelerating the revolutionary upsurge. It is therefore a mistake to abandon the struggle in the cities, and in our opinion it is also a mistake for any of party members to fear the development of the peasants lest it become strong than that of the workers and hence detrimental to the revolution. For the revolution in semi-colonial China will fail only if the peasant struggle is deprived of the leadership of the workers, and it will never suffer just because the peasant, through their struggle, become more powerful than the workers.[30]

Additionally, Zhu De still understood that his inexperience may cloud his judgment, adding, "We had been isolated in the interior for years and such information as we had about the national and international situation was incomplete."[31]

Even with their misgivings, Zhu De and Mao's apprehensions were in the minority, and on June 22, they issued the orders to conduct the attack.[32] Before leaving, as a symbol of solidarity to the Party and the mission, the entire Red army took an oath of allegiance, known as the Li Li-san oath.[33]

Execution of the Plan

With full support for the urban insurrection, the Red Army deployed the newly designated First Red Army Corps, formerly the Fourth Red Army, to attack Nanchang, and the Third Red Army Corps, known before as Peng Dehuai's Fifth Red Army, to attack Changsha.[34] Against Li Lisan's wishes, Mao left three army units back at the Jiangxi Soviet to protect the local area.[35]

The Third Red Army Corps was the first to attack, seizing Changsha on July 29, 1930. Upon arrival, Peng Dehuai established a Soviet government, with Li Lisan as chairman, in absentia.[36] The arrival of the Red Army, however, did not illicit an urban uprising. Most of locals came outside out of curiosity, rather than to support any insurrection. The next day, British, American, Italian, and Japanese navy ships sailed up the Xiang River to protect the foreign concession areas and their investment.[37] The naval bombardment coupled with the lack of any urban support forced Peng's forces to retreat from the city on August 3, taking with them money and supplies collected during their operations.[38] The NRA subsequently occupied the city, and began a systematic purging of all the communist sympathizers left behind.

The First Red Army Corps did not fare any better. Zhu De and Mao's forces were to attack Nanchang, but initially sent in only reconnaissance forces only into the city on August 1.[39] The Red Army made little of any progress in the area, determined the mission was untenable, and moved to Liuyang, Hunan Province. At Liuyang, the First and Third Red Armies consolidated forces into the First Front Red Army, and discussed their next move. At this time, support for the urban line was waning. The assessment of the situation in Changsha and Wuhan was also grim. KMT forces had reinforced the cities, with the NRA setting up a defense in depth and obstacles in Changsha. Foreign naval ships were stationed along the Yangtze River to provide indirect fire support for an even larger force in Wuhan. Zhu De did not believe the Red Army was in a position to conduct "positional warfare" against these defenses.[40] Despite Mao and Zhu's opposition, the First Front Red Army proceeded back to Changsha and participated in the second attack on September 1, 1930.

The second attack on Changsha was a failure. Against a better-equipped enemy in strong defensive positions, the Red Army was no match against the NRA. Within ten days of fighting and in the face of mounting losses, Zhu De and Mao Zedong made a bold decision. Mao gave the withdrawal order on September 13, stating that the Li Lisan plan was incorrect, and there needed to be a change of plan. A deep divide broke through the army, with many of the political commissars objecting to the decision. However, the soldiers obeyed orders and the Red Army conducted an orderly withdrawal. There was a huge division within the ranks, with a sizeable minority, labeled as Li Lisanist or left leaning commissars, calling for a another attack on Nanchang. Mao and Zhu De did not believe one was feasible, especially against a stronger, fortified NRA force. Instead, Mao produced a temporary compromise that won the support of the minority. While the reattack of Nanchang was not taken off the table, the force would first attack Ji'an. Ji'an was a strategic city centered on the Jiangxi Soviet. By capturing the city, the southwestern portion Jiangxi Soviet could be joined together and expand the Soviet area.[41]

On the early morning of October 4, 1930, the Red Army with local militia and CY forces moved into Ji'an from three different directions, and by nightfall, seized the city. The capturing of Ji'an produced a large influx peasant support for the Red Army, with supposedly more than a million peasants going to the city in support of the communists.[42] Additionally, a raid of the KMT headquarters in Ji'an produced secret documents about the upcoming NRA extermination campaign. With this new intelligence, the Red Army's focus shifted from the Li Lisan line, effectively ending the operation, and turned its focus toward the impending NRA extermination campaign.

Aftermath

The collapse of the Li Lisan line created a cascade of intraparty struggles over political power, political direction, and military strategies that culminated with the Futian Incident. With the failure of the second attack on Changsha as evidence of Li Lisan's ineptitude, Mao began attacking Li Lisan to consolidate his own power. At the core, the division within the Red Army resulted in two diverging viewpoints, represented by Mao's gradual rural encirclement strategy and Li Lisan's immediate urban insurrection strategy. While retreating from Changsha, Mao and Zhu attacked the Li Lisan line, arguing the erroneous policy caused the attack's failure.[43] The extreme claim was a shot across the bow inside the Red Army and drove a wedge within the army. Political commissars from subordinate units decried the act as treacherous acts against the Central Committee, whereas peasant soldiers remained loyal to Mao.

Mao was also confronted with the problem of a power grab with the Jiangxi Provincial Action Committee. The recently created committee represented an additional layer of left- leaning bureaucracy and control. After the failure of the second attack on Changsha, the Jiangxi Provincial

Action Committee leadership attempted to gain control of the Red Army. During this time, Mao conducted a rural survey of Xingguo, and while there, identified tenuous linkages[44] between the KMT funded Anti-Bolshevik Corps (AB Corps), a unit of undercover agents charged with sabotaging and subverting communist units, and the local Jiangxi Action committee and Twentieth Red Army leaders, such as Li Wenlin. Armed with this evidence, Mao conducted a huge purge of the Red Army. In November 1930, Mao arrested 4,000 members of the Twentieth Red Army, to include all but two members of the Jiangxi Provincial Action Committee, and charged them with treason. The purge effectively neutralized any left-leaning threat to Mao's control, but also created a huge backlash the next month.

In December 1930, a battalion of the Twentieth Red Army, led by Liu Dizao, marched in and seized the city of Futian. Battalion officers released forty recently purged comrades and suspected AB Corps members. The renegade group crossed over west of the Gan River and established a rival Soviet in Yongyang.[45] From this new Soviet, the unit looked to clear their names, appealing to the Central Committee of the CCP as well as Zhu De and Peng Dehuai. The Twentieth Red Army argued that they were wrongfully accused of being AB Corps members. They were actually maintaining the strict line of the CCP, and attacked Mao's policies as being false, accusing him of attempting to become a "party emperor."[46] One large group of Twentieth Army members left the Soviet under the pretense of attending a peace talk in July 1931.[47] Upon arrival, they were all arrested. Summary trials commenced, and three of the key leaders were summarily executed.[48]

The Futian Incident failed to gain traction within the CCP, especially in light of the COMINTERN and Central Committee condemnation of the Li Lisan line and KMT extermination campaigns. The COMINTERN and Central Committee scrambled to distance itself from Li Lisan after Changsha. Zhou Enlai was sent back from Russia to help clean up after the debacle in Changsha as the Central Committee military representative. Upon his arrival, he distanced himself and the party from the Li Lisan line, which effectively brought the CCP view in congruence with Mao's strategy and helped Mao further consolidate his power.[49] In addition, the COMINTERN sent a letter to the CCP in November 1930 stating that the Li Lisan Line was inconsistent with the COMINTERN guidance and its views were "antagonistic" to the greater communist cause.[50] Li Lisan was recalled to Moscow for questioning in December 1930, where he gave a lengthy *mea cupla* for the botched insurrections. Back in China, the CCP leadership would have a difficult time gaining traction until the end of 1931, when the Twenty-eight Bolsheviks asserted their power over the party.

Official CCP history blamed the AB Corps as the main instigator of the Twentieth Red Army Division revolt at Futian. Further examination of the factors leading up to the incident is required to fully understand the context of the actions leading up to Mao's consolidation of power while under fire. While the power struggle between Mao and remnants of Li Lisan supporters was at the core of the Futian incident, there were other factors that were in play.[51] The military strategy represented by both factions in fact drove one of the biggest wedges within the Red Army. Mao and Zhu De's order to retreat at Changsha challenged many of the loyalists within the Red Army, who saw the act as insubordination. With communication between the CCP and the Red Army intermittent at best during this period, few members knew that the COMINTERN and CCP had already denounced the Li Lisan line. Many of the political commissars believed the urban insurrection was the correct strategy, and should not be changed by Mao or Zhu. Nor did they believe the Red Army should utilize the "lure the enemy in deep" strategy. Mao's opponents were unwilling to cede hard-won territory, nor were they willing to leave the local populace unprotected.[52] These concerns represent concrete disagreements on strategy and tactics, and were further polarized by Mao-Li power politics.

With both Li Lisan and the Jiangxi Action Committee out of the equation, Mao remained in sole control of the Red Army. Years later, Mao's purge would be decried by many people as excessive.[53] While some of the enemies purged were Anti-Bolsheiviks, a majority of them were simply obstacles to Mao's consolidation of power. His choice of brutal tactics may also have been influenced the need for expediency. During this period of internal strife, the Red Army was engaged in a brutal fight with the NRA in the First Extermination Campaign.

Extermination Campaigns
First Extermination Campaign

The initial Nationalist Forces array was the Ninth Route Army, led by the Jiangxi governor, Lu Diping, based out of Nanchang. They were augmented by the Sixth Route Army from Hunan, led by Zhu Shaoling, and the Nineteenth Route Army, led by Jiang Guangnai. The initial force package for the first campaign was 44,000 men, made up of five divisions and three air-bombing corps.[54] The plan was to encircle the Jiangxi Soviets, pressing the communist forces into the mountains and preventing them from maneuvering around the NRA force. Once the encirclement was complete, the NRA would attack Donggu, Longgang and Dongshao to destroy the communist forces.

After seizing Ji'an, the Red Army leadership, in conjunction with the Jiangxi Action committee, held a conference at Luofang on October 25, 1930, to discuss the strategy in response to the upcoming extermination campaign. Initial arguments were for reattacking Nanchang and Jiujiang to divert the NRA forces away from the Soviet. Mao disagreed, and proposed

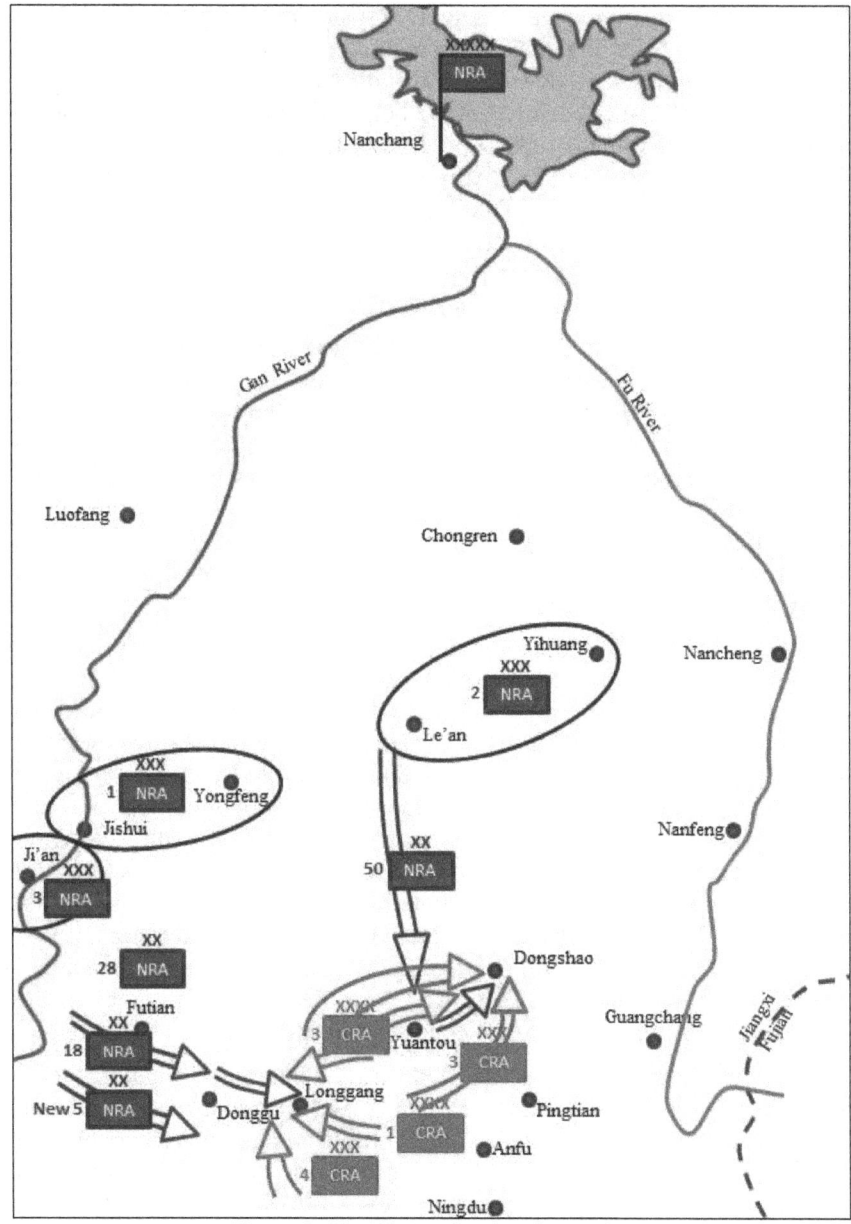
Figure 3: First Extermination Campaign
Source: Created by author

his famous "lure the enemy in deep" strategy. The plan was to give up land for time. Initially, Red Army forces would evacuate the western areas of the Gan River. While moving east, the Red Army would mobilize the local people to raise money, enlist soldiers, and create Red Guard and intelligence units. The eastward movement would also invite the NRA to follow them across the river. As the NRA entered Red Army terrain, it would overstretch its logistical lines and expose itself to attack. The Red Army would attack the NRA on terrain of its choosing, concentrating its firepower on the isolated force. Mao believed that the "lure the enemy in deep" strategy was the only feasible way to defeat the NRA. Once the enemy was destroyed, the Red Army could attack the urban centers. The fortifications in Nanchang and Jiujiang would be unmanned, and the Red Army could move directly in and occupy the city.[55] With some trepidation, the initial strategy of attacking Nanchang and Jiujiang was defeated, and the Red Army adopted the "lure the enemy in deep" strategy.

On November 1, the Red Army began moving forces across the Gan river into Ji'an, Xingan, Jishui, Yongfeng, Le'an, Chongren, Yihuang, and Nanfeng counties. Within six days of operations, the Red Army collected 400,000 yuan and enlisted the support of the local populace.[56] During this time, some members of the Third Red Army Corps, who were originally from southeastern area near Ji'an, rose up against Mao's plan, arguing for the occupation of the western Gan River area. Peng Dehuai was able to suppress the dissension and by the middle of November, the entire Red Army force occupied the eastern bank of the Gan River.[57]

The NRA followed the Red Army across the Gan River, as predicted. On November 18, the NRA moved its forces in three columns: First Column occupied Yongfeng and Jishui; Second Column occupied Le'an and Yihuang; and Third Column occupied Ji'an. The Red Army continued to withdraw as the NRA entered, conducting limited engagements with the NRA, inflicting casualties while conserving its own combat power.[58] On November 26, the second withdrawal was complete, with Red Army forces occupying Donggu, Nanlong, and Longgang.[59] The successful withdrawal was marred by the Futian incident on December 7. The mutiny jeopardized the western flank of the Red Army operation, forcing the Red Army leadership to abandon the Donggu and Futian area on December 15, 1930. The remainder of Third Red Army Corps forces moved to the northern area of Ningdu county, occupying the Pingtian and Anfu areas.[60]

NRA intelligence relayed the Red Army's internal struggles to the KMT leadership, presenting them with a perfect opportunity to attack. On December 16, Lu Diping ordered two divisions to encircle and attack Donggu. The New Fifth NRA Division and Eighteenth NRA Division moved toward the Donggu area. The New Fifth NRA Division was the first to enter Donggu. The Red Army withdrew from the city, engaging units from the New Fifth NRA Division as it left. A ridgeline separated the two NRA divisions as they entered Donggu, with each side unaware of the other. Neither side attempted to deconflict locations through wireless communications. On December 20, 1930 the Eighteenth NRA Division gave the order to attack Donggu, committing fratricide on the New Fifth NRA Division for about half a day before stopping the catastrophe.[61]

By the end of December, the KMT forces had absorbed most of the Jiangxi Soviet. The northern Jiangxi areas were occupied by late November. The Eighteenth NRA Division occupied Donggu, the Twenty-eighth NRA Division occupied Futian, and the Fiftieth NRA Division was en route to Yuantou. However, the NRA forces were overextended, exposing its forces to constant guerrilla attacks. The expanded territory required occupation forces as well. Only one-third of the Third Route NRA Army forces actually were on the front lines, with the rest of the forces stretched across the terrain.[62] These forces occupying the surrounded areas had difficulties with the local residents. The mobilized local populace were uncooperative with the NRA forces and provided little if any information or supplies. Instead, the local populace provided important intelligence to the Red Army, especially about a pending attack on Longgang.[63]

Two brigades of the Eighteenth Division planned an attack Longgang on December 30. Local intelligence quickly alerted the Red Army leadership of the NRA's plan. The Red Army countered with an encirclement of the two brigades, using the mountainous terrain to mass fires and cut off any reinforcements.[64] On the morning of the December 30, the NRA forces entered Longgang, and were effectively encircled by Red Army forces. The First Red Army Corps attacked the two NRA brigades, while the Fourth Red Army and elements of the Third Red Army Corps blocked the Eighteenth NRA Division's rear, preventing any reinforcements from coming to Donggu.[65] By the end of the day, the devastation of the Eighteenth NRA Division was complete. More than 9,000 personnel were captured, to include the division commander, Zhang Huizan, and other key leaders.[66]

With news of the annihilation of the Eighteenth NRA Division, Lu Diping ordered a withdrawal of his forces to consolidate and reorganize. Tan Daoyuan's Fiftieth NRA Division moved south toward Yuantou. Upon receipt of intelligence reports on January 2, 1931, that the Fiftieth NRA Division was moving, the Red Army leadership immediately pursued to establish an ambush. On the morning of January 3, the Red Army attacked the Fiftieth NRA Division near Dongshao from three different directions, causing panic and confusion. The NRA unit disintegrated under the attack, with many soldiers dropping weapons and running away. The Third Red Army was unable to make it in time to complete the encirclement, and many of the Fiftieth NRA Division members escaped. The Red Army captured 3,000 personnel, 4,000 rifles, more than forty machine guns, and a large cache of ammunition. The defeats at Longgang and Dongshao effectively ended the First Extermination Campaign and provided the Red Army with valuable equipment, personnel, and experience.[67]

The destruction of multiple divisions of the NRA yielded weapons and equipment the threadbare communist forces needed to continue their operations. More than 15,000 personnel were captured, and 12,000 weapons confiscated.[68] The victories also validated Mao's strategy and tactics, increasing the confidence of the Red Army. Lastly, these victories helped to spread the word of the communist forces strength in the region, and began to swing the tide of public sentiment for support. The communists sent one strong message with the execution of Zhang Huizan, the commander of Eighteenth NRA Division. His head was sent up to Ji'an, after his public trial, to serve as a warning.[69]

Second Extermination Campaign

The defeat during the Second Extermination Campaign forced Chiang Kai-shek and the KMT to double their efforts against the Red Army. The NRA dispatched four route armies, totaling about 200,000 soldiers, to encircle the Jiangxi Soviet.[70] The NRA forces were arrayed as follows: Fifth Route NRA Army located around Ji'an, Sixth Route NRA Army based in Nanfeng; Nineteenth Route NRA Army based in Xingguo; Twenty-sixth Route NRA Army based in Le'an.[71] This time around, the NRA adopted a different strategy, opting for a slower, more deliberate approach, conducting steady attacks on the enemy.[72]

As the Red Army faced a new threat of encirclement, the leadership and its members discussed strategy. While Mao's "lure the enemy in deep" was successful in the First Extermination Campaign, it still did not engender great support in the subsequent campaign. From March to April, the Red Army held four different meetings to determine the next strategy. On March 18, 1931 the Central Soviet Bureau First Enlarged Conference began debate on an alternative strategy of the Red Army. The alternative was to completely vacate the Soviet areas because of the NRA's overwhelming numerical superiority. The meeting adjourned without a decision. A month later, the CCP Fourth Plenary Session delegation arrived in Jiangxi and sat in on the second meeting of the Central Soviet Bureau First Enlarged Conference. Some members continued to push for vacating the Jiangxi Soviet, this time submitting Sichuan as a new base area. Other members presented a different option, arguing for the Red Army to stay, and divide into smaller units in order to conduct coordinated attacks to break the encirclement and destroy the enemy. This meeting adjourned once again without a decision.[73]

A third meeting occurred a couple days after the second. Acting on the advice of Mao, the Red Army leadership invited the military and political leadership from the different military units to participate. The idea of dividing the Red Army gained traction; however, one caveat was added. Instead of immediately dividing the forces, the Red Army should first conduct a concentrated attack against the Nineteenth Route NRA Army to establish a route out of the encirclement. Mao agreed with the idea, though he submitted the Fifth Route Army as the best target. Attacking the Nineteen Route NRA Army did not make sense since it had been laagered in Xingguo for an extended period of time, had established a strong set of

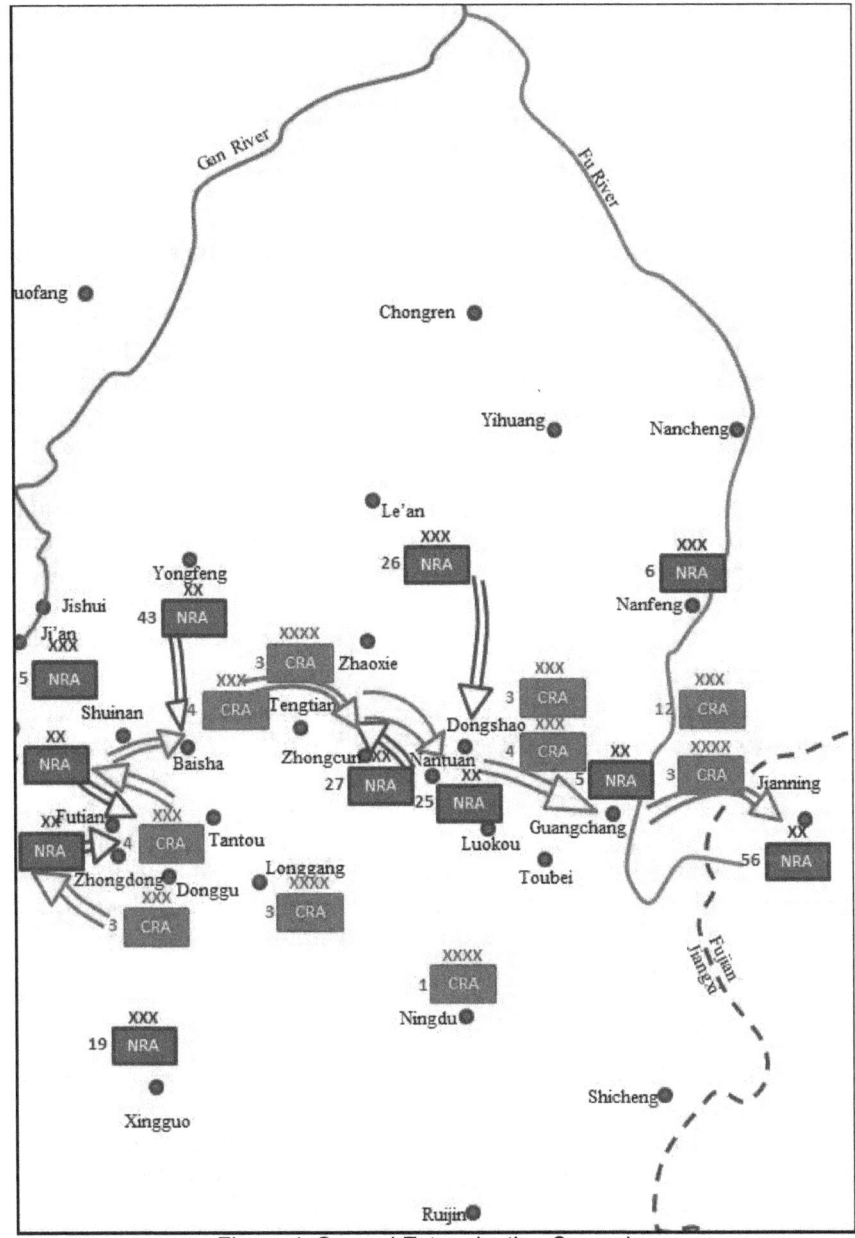

Figure 4: Second Extermination Campaign
Source: Created by author

fortifications, and did not present any weaknesses. Any attack would also take time, which would expose the Red Army to attacks by reinforcements from the north. The Fifth Route NRA Army, though the largest army out of the NRA forces deployed to Jiangxi, had plenty of issues. The Fifth Route

NRA Army was originally from Northern China and unfamiliar with the territory. It also had some issues with morale.[74] The meeting reached a consensus supporting the "attack first, then divide" strategy, but failed to reach an agreement on the target. At a minimum, the decision helped the Red Army leadership give guidance and instructions to its subordinate units.

The final meeting was held at the end of April 1931. All the attendees from the previous meeting joined the final one to discuss the plan. Mao was given the floor to present his view, and he gave an impassioned speech in support of his strategy. He argued that the "lure the enemy in deep" strategy made the most sense because of three factors: the Red Army; the local populace; and the geography. The Red Army and the local populace had the experience and resolve to defeat the enemy. These forces could leverage their intimate knowledge of the terrain in the Jiangxi area to attack the enemy's weaknesses. Mao outlined a strategy of sweeping east across the Soviet, attacking the enemy from Futian to Jianning. The terrain and poor communications between NRA units isolated themselves from mutual support, and allowed the Red Army to use overwhelming firepower to defeat the enemy. Mao's presentation finally worked, his strategy was finally approved, and the Red Army could begin preparations on its attack against the NRA.

During the March-April discussions, the Red Army began withdrawing troops from the fringes of the expanded Jiangxi Soviet in anticipation of the Extermination Campaign. Starting in late March, the Red Army abandoned newly acquired territories in Toubei, Dongshao, Luokou, Zhaoxie, Futian, and Tengtian. Forces also withdrew from Yongfeng, Le'an, Yihuang, and Nanfeng to Guangchang, Shicheng, and Ruijin to increase political mobilization and training in these areas. By April 23, the Red Army forces had relocated, with the Third Red Army Corps based near Longgang, and the rest of the First Front Red Army forces laagering in the vicinity of Ningdu. The Third and Fourth Red Army were stationed in the mountains between Donggu and Futian, awaiting orders.[75]

The NRA forces proceeded slowly according to their new strategy. NRA forces had occupied Futian, and were moving east towards Donggu. The Fourth Red Army, led by Mao and Zhu, was stationed along the Jiucun mountain ridge, overlooking the road leading from Futian to Donggu, and was prepared to conduct an attack. On May 11, the Forty-seventh NRA Division and the Twenty-eighth NRA Division led the NRA movement and walked into an ambush. The attack commenced near Zhongdong five days later. The Red Army forces initially rolled boulders from the mountain tops, causing serious casualties and confusion. The two NRA divisions were taken by surprise and attempted to signal for help, but the Red Army cut off all wired communications. Visibility was poor during the attack, neutralizing any NRA air support to the distressed troops. The Third Red

Army moved quickly from the high ground and attacked the divisions. By the evening of May 17, the NRA forces had been defeated. Five thousand guns, fifty machine guns, thirty artillery pieces, and numerous caches were confiscated.[76]

The second battle occurred in Baisha only two days after the Red Army's victory at Zhongdong. The next target was the Forty-third NRA Division. The division originally was headed toward Tantou, but upon hearing word of the NRA defeat at Zhongdong, it changed direction toward Shuinan. The Forty-third NRA Division planned on crossing the Xiaolong River near Shuinan to consolidate its forces around defensive positions on the northern banks. However, local communist militia groups had already secured the bridge, forcing the NRA to move to Baisha. On May 19, the Red Army attacked and defeated the Forty-third NRA Division at Baisha, collecting more than 4,000 weapons, thirty machine guns, and two mountain cannons. Attempts to send NRA reinforcements were made. However, elements from the Nineteenth Route NRA Army never advanced into Baisha. Instead, they stood on the outskirts, and once the NRA division was destroyed, the unit withdrew back to Xingguo.[77] These two losses effectively destroyed the Fifth Route NRA Army.[78]

The Red Army continued its sweep east, conducting its third battle at Zhongcun. Initial orders for the Twenty-sixth Route NRA Army were to occupy Nantuan in order to gain the southern flank of the Red Army as it advanced east. However, once in the city, its Twenty-seventh NRA Division received orders to reinforce NRA positions in Zhongcun, while the Twenty-fifth NRA Division remained in Nantuan. Before the Twenty-seventh NRA Division could get set, the Third Red Army Corps and Fourth Red Army conducted a combined attack and destroyed the NRA forces in Zhongcun on the morning of May 22, occupying the city by the afternoon. That evening, the Red Army continued to Nantuan and destroyed the Twenty-Fifth NRA Division. The remaining NRA forces retreated to Le'an and Yihuang. The Red Army captured more than 3,000 weapons and ten machine guns, effectively eliminating the Twenty-sixth Route NRA Army.[79]

The fourth battle was a pursuit of the Sixth Route NRA Army near Guangchang. Hearing of the destruction of the Twenty-sixth and Fifth Route NRA Armies, the NRA began withdrawing back to Nancheng. The Fifth NRA Division was the last unit attempting to leave Guangchang, when it was attacked by the Third Red Army and Fourth Red Army on May 27. The Fifth NRA Division put up stiff resistance until nightfall when its commander was injured. The forces withdrew the next day to Nanfeng, ending the fourth battle in the Second Extermination Campaign.[80]

The last battle occurred at Jianning, Fujian province. The Fourth Red Army remained in Guangchang to consolidate gains, with one division moving north toward Nanfeng. The Third Red Army Corps and the

Twelfth Red Army moved east and pursued the NRA forces into Jianning on May 30. The attack caught the NRA commanders of the Fifty-sixth NRA Division completely by surprise. They had yet to make any defensive preparations, believing that the Red Army could not travel at such speed and quickness. By May 31, the Red Army occupied Jianning, destroying an NRA regiment. Along with copious weapons and equipment, the Red Army confiscated caches of sorely needed medicine.[81]

By the end of the two-week campaign, the Red Army had travelled more than 300 kilometers,[82] captured 30,000 POWs, and confiscated 20,000 weapons.[83] The confiscated equipment was enough to outfit the entire First Front Red Army with modern weapons, with the older weapons transferred to local militia and guerrilla forces.[84] Most of the Red Army's success on the battlefield was based on its leadership, morale of soldiers, good intelligence, and its mobility. However, its speed and quickness also placed much strain on its logistical and administrative systems as its forces were stretched across the Soviet, and away from its home base. Expansion of the Soviet grew to almost 5,000 square miles at the end of the campaign.[85] The upcoming Third Extermination Campaign would test the Red Army's ability to regroup and again move quickly back to its base area.

Third Extermination Campaign

In June, First Front Red Army was still in Western Fujian conducting operations. Initially, it did not expect the NRA to initiate the Third Extermination Campaign so quickly. Instead, the Red Army planned a three-phase expansion operation. The first phase was political mobilization in Western Fujian, to include Jianning, Taining, and Lichuan. The second phase involved the Red Army moving back to southern Jiangxi in order to consolidate and strengthen the Soviet rear area. The last phase sent the Red Army back to its original base area, with the focus on the Western Gan River area to connect the Jiangxi Soviet with the Hunan-Jiangxi Soviet.[86] The Red Army conducted political mobilization in Western Fujian throughout June, raising funds for operations and drumming up popular support for the communists. Intelligence reports continued to pour in stating NRA forces were already on the move towards Jiangxi to attack the Soviet.

During preparation to counter the Third Extermination Campaign, the Central Committee issued guidance in June 1931 for the upcoming campaign. The guidance explicitly supported the strategy of the previous two extermination campaigns. Specifically, the Central Committee saw the mobilization of the local populace for guerrilla operations as a critical component to the overall Red Army's success. For the upcoming mission, they stressed the continued political mobilization of the populace. They supported small-unit guerrilla attacks on the NRA forces to prevent them

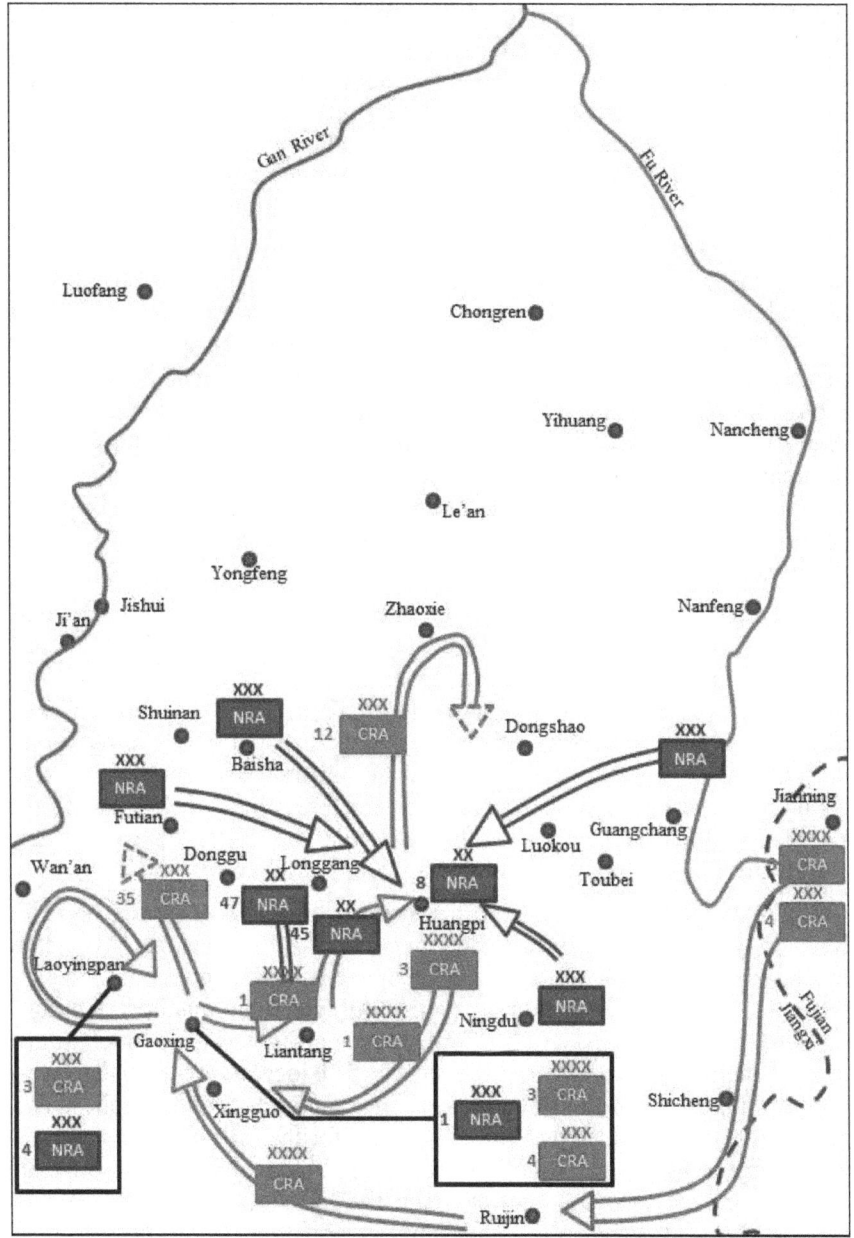

Figure 5: Third Extermination Campaign
Source: Created by author

from gaining a stable footing in the area, setting the conditions for the main Red Army forces to destroy the enemy. The guidance also pushed for the consolidation of the Soviets in the area, to include the Henan-Hubei-Anhui Soviet, Hunan-Hubei Soviet, and the Northeast Jiangxi Soviet. The goal was to connect the noncontiguous Soviets into one contiguous territory in the Hunan-Hubei-Jiangxi area, as well as establish communications with the other Soviets in the north. After issuing the June 1931 guidance, the Central Committee in Shanghai suffered a serious setback from the KMT communist repression campaign, forcing the leadership underground. Not until August 30 did the CCP reestablish communications with the Soviet areas. By that time, the Third Extermination campaign was over.[87]

On June 30, the Red Army leadership finally issued an order to stop the expansion and begin preparation for defense against the extermination campaign. All local militias, Red Guard, and guerrilla units were activated and pressed to conduct mobile defense and guerrilla operations to delay the NRA advance. The Red Army immediately consolidated forces and returned to the central bases areas in Jiangxi.[88] At the time, the Red Army had yet to have a break since the beginning of the Extermination Campaigns, and its number still remained around 30,000 soldiers.[89] This new mission was a difficult task given how spread out the Red Army was across Western Fujian and Southern Jiangxi, especially with the NRA forces scouring the area.

The losses during the first two extermination campaigns grabbed Chiang Kai-shek's attention. The Generalissimo took over the Third Campaign, and brought in his own troops, deploying the Fifth and Sixth NRA Divisions to Jiangxi to attack the First and Third Red Army Corps of the First Front Red Army. His entire force consisted of two army corps, with one army in reserve, and one garrison army.[90] The entire force was estimated at 130,000.[91] In late June, the NRA forces moved into the Jiangxi Soviet. By the end of July, it had encircled the entire Jiangxi Soviet, occupying Futian, Baisha, Guangchang, and Ningdu.

Local Soviet citizens and the local militias mobilized to support the Red Army and prepare for another round of attacks from the NRA. The local Soviets reorganized its militia groups, ensuring that reconnaissance, guerrilla, and Red Guard units were equipped and manned. Chinese Soviets in border areas established "red" martial law to actively fight against enemy surveillance and subversion. The local populace also moved out to old battle sites to sweep the areas for equipment and supplies. The sweep not only provided additional supplies for the militia groups and the Red Army, it also denied the NRA any supplies as they moved through the area.[92] Even with the encirclement, the local populace continued to support the Red Army, providing supplies and food to the tired troops, though over time food had to be rationed due to limited supplies.[93]

The Red Army quickly moved back to the base area. The Red Army travelled through Ruijin, then moved west to Xingguo. By July 28, 1931, the Red Army had travelled more than 400 kilometers[94] to Gaoxing, northwest of Xingguo, without being detected. While back in the base area, the Red Army still needed to gain the initiative. On July 31, the Red Army conducted a daring breakthrough from Xingguo. The Red Army conducted a nighttime exfiltration, moving west to Wan'an before circling back to Futian to attack the KMT rear. The Red Army escaped the encirclement, but while it headed to Futian, the NRA discovered the Red Army's plans and reinforced the area with a division, as well as capturing Xingguo. On August 3, the Red Army stopped short of Futian and occupied areas near Laoyingpan and Gaoxing.[95]

To regain the initiative, the Red Army conducted a series of battles against the NRA near Liantang and Huangpi. The Red Army conducted a feint in the north with the Thirty-fifth Red Army, the Thirty-fifth Red Army Division, Twelfth Red Army, Fourth Independent Red Army Division, and Fifth Independent Red Army Division to draw the NRA focus towards the west in Wan'an. When the NRA forces moved, the First Red Army Corps, the Red Army's main effort, would attack along the seam in Liangtang, and assault through Longgang and Huangpi. On August 6, the Forty-seventh NRA Division entered Liantang as the Fifty-fourth NRA Division occupied nearby Huangpi, presenting the Red Army a great opportunity. With only a single NRA division in Liantang, the Red Army took advantage of the isolation and conducted an early morning attack. The Third, Fourth, and Twelfth Red Armies attacked the lone NRA division. One group was destroyed, with the remainder of the forces retreating to Longgang. With the momentum, the Red Army continued towards Huangpi and attacked the Fifty-fourth NRA Division. The division headquarters, unaware of the attack, walked straight into the attack, and was decimated. By the end of the August 7, two NRA brigades were destroyed. The two divisions suffered more than 1,000 casualties and more 3,500 POWs were taken; 3,000 weapons and fourteen canons were confiscated.[96]

The Red Army continued its attack on Huangpi. Originally, the plan included an attack on Longgang, but nine NRA brigades occupied the city, making it a hard target. Instead, the Red Army attacked the Eighth NRA Division in Huangpi. On August 11, the Third Red Army distracted NRA forces in Longgang by maintaining sporadic contact in order to prevent the unit from sending reinforcements. The Fourth and Twelfth Red Armies, the main effort, attacked the Eighth NRA Division in Huangpi, while the Third Red Army Corps and Seventh Red Division maneuvered to the east to cut off any escape route. In rainy, foggy weather, the Red Army destroyed four brigades, resulting in more than 1,000 casualties, 4,000 POWs, and capturing more than 3,000 weapons, eleven artillery pieces, one wireless communication set, and a large ammunition cache.[97]

These three victories in short succession gave Chiang Kai-shek a sense of urgency in the fight. The Red Army's victory at Huangpi revealed its main force location to the NRA. Almost immediately, Chiang deployed all his forces to surround the Huangpi area, effectively encircling the Red Army. For about one month, the Red Army was essentially under siege. In a report sent to the Central Committee after the Third Extermination Campaign, the Red Army leadership stated that the siege at Huangpi was the most difficult and trying time during the entire Extermination Campaigns to date.[98] Facing starvation and defeat, Mao and Zhu De hatched a bold plan to break out of the encirclement. The Red Army planned to split its force. First, disguising the Twelfth Red Army as the Red Army's main effort, the unit would sneak through the encirclement and move northeast to attack Le'an and Yihuang, which mirrored the NRA intelligence estimate. The remainder of the Red Army, and its main effort would instead move west and occupy Xingguo.

In the darkness of night on August 16, the First Front Red Army, minus the Twelfth Red Army, silently slipped through a 10-kilometer gap between the First NRA Army Corps and Second NRA Route Army, heading towards Xingguo. At the same time, the Twelfth Red Army began its march northeast towards Yihuang. An element of the Twelfth Red Army attacked Le'an in an attempt to erase any doubt that the Red Army's main effort was moving northeast. Seizing the chance to destroy the Red Army, Chiang ordered the Tenth NRA Division, and the First and Second NRA Route Armies to pursue and destroy the Red Army's main effort. For about two weeks, the NRA chased the Twelfth Red Army up and down mountain ranges and along narrow and winding passages, to no avail. The NRA forces just became more exhausted as they consumed their supplies and were subjected to constant guerrilla attacks along the route. In the meantime, First and Third Red Army Corps arrived in Xingguo undetected.[99] The Red Army forces refitted, reconstituted, and reorganized, taking a well-deserved, albeit temporary, respite from battle.

By the end of August, the NRA realized they had been duped, and that the Red Army's main effort was actually in Xingguo. The NRA forces turned around and headed west to attack the Red Army. Before the NRA could attack the Red Army near Xingguo, two Guangdong warlord factions rose against the KMT and established a rival government in Guangdong. Out of fear the warlord factions could attack Nanjing, or ally with former warlords, Chiang prematurely ended the Third Extermination Campaign.[100] With the NRA forces withdrawing, the Red Army attempted to exploit the situation for further gains, conducting a series of attacks on the retrograding forces. On September 7, the Third Red Army and the Fifth Independent Red Division attacked the Fourth NRA Corps at Laoyingpan, capturing 2,000 POWs, 2,000 weapons, and ten artillery pieces. On September 13, The Seventh Red Army encircled the Fourth NRA Corps at Fangshiling mountain ranges as the unit attempted to retreat north to Ji'an. The Red Army destroyed the Fifty-second NRA Division and one brigade of the Ninth NRA Division. The Red Army took more than 5,000 prisoners, 4,500 rifles, and 200 horses. These successes, however, were overshadowed by the Red Army's defeat at Gaoxing. On September 7, the

Fourth Red Army and the Third Red Army Corps conducted a coordinated attack against the First NRA Corps. Based on poor intelligence, the Red Army did not account for the relative strength of the NRA's Fifty-second, Sixty-first, and Sixty-second Divisions. The two sides engaged in a long bloody battle that ended in a stalemate.[101]

By the end of the Third Extermination Campaign, the NRA suffered huge losses. The Red Army destroyed seventeen NRA brigades, with more than 30,000 casualties. The Red Army's losses in comparison were as great. The loss at Gaoxing left the Red Army weak and unable to continue its attack. Yet, even in its compromised position, the Red Army made significant gains from their victory. At the end of the three campaigns, the Jiangxi Soviet doubled during that time, reaching almost 50,000 square kilometers, covering twenty-eight counties in Hunan, Jiangxi, and Fujian provinces.[102]

Analysis
Situational Assessment

During this two-year period, the Red Army continued to face similar external and internal threats to its existence. The NRA replaced the provincial and warlord forces as the primary external threat to the Red Army. With each Extermination Campaign, the numbers and quality of NRA soldiers increased dramatically, with Chiang Kai-shek personally leading the third campaign. The NRA also introduced more modern technology, such as wireless communications and air power to the battlefield. The NRA conducted its first air attack against the Communists during the Nanchang Uprising.[103] While the addition provided initial advantages, the Red Army was able to eventually turn the advantages into weaknesses. The NRA actually supplied the Red Army with the equipment and the operators to create its own wireless network system.[104] Besides increasing the size and technology of the military force, the NRA also adjusted its strategies. It took a slower, more deliberate approach to encircling and constricting the Jiangxi Soviet, with increasing success. By the Third Extermination Campaign, the NRA almost perfected its siege, nearly suffocating the Red Army in Jiangxi. These lessons learned would pay dividends in future campaigns.

Internal struggles continued to be the biggest threat to the Red Army. The Li Lisan line of 1930 highlighted the diverging factions within the Red Army. The Red Army split along a philosophical, military strategy, and power relations lines. Mao and his faction represented a peasant force that promoted a mobile defense strategy geared towards the rural areas. Li Lisan staked out a more conservative line with a proletarian force that adopted a more direct attack approach aimed at the urban centers. In an attempt to win the narrative, each side continued to leverage pejorative labels, such as "opportunism," "adventurism" or "retreatism," to gain the support of the populace.[105] While the political commissars at unit levels were split in their allegiances, military leaders instead were often stuck in the middle, attempting to hold a professional line. During the Futian Incident, the Twentieth Red Army vainly attempted to convince Zhu De and Peng Dehuai to turn on Mao and support the more conservative line. The divide caused by both the AB Corps purge and subsequent Futian incident led to an almost 20 percent reduction in combat strength and jeopardized the Red Army's western flank during the First Extermination campaign. Some Red Army leaders got caught up in the personal politics. During the first attack on Changsha, a disagreement between Peng and Mao supposedly caused Mao to limit Fourth Red Army Corps' support for the Third Red Army Corps.[106] Regardless of the political dimensions of the Red Army, the struggle for power and control negatively affected the Army's combat effectiveness.

Besides the internal political struggles, the Red Army still faced the same challenges it had faced since its inception. While the measures to increase the professionalism of the Red Army helped to improve combat readiness, problems of desertion, low levels of education, and unruly behavior remained prevalent in the Red Army, especially at the local militia level. Incidents of stealing from POWs and the local populace, as well as damaging private property were still unfortunate consequences of guerrilla operations.[107]

Another major issue was behavior inconsistent with the revolutionary ideal. Some local militia leaders continued warlord traditions, oppressing and exploiting the local populace and soldiers for profit and personal gain. Incidents of insubordination or failure to comply with orders were issues related to local militias' readiness. Compliance with CCP, Soviet government, or Red Army official orders was low among local militias, requiring that Red Army advisers to supervise operations. Personnel assigned to local militias took away from the combat strength and important experience level of frontline Red Army units. Lastly, the quality of life of militia soldiers, especially for units in the far flung rural areas remained quite low. Many of the soldiers in these units were treated poorly by leaders, received shoddy equipment and weapons, and received little if any training.[108]

These negative traditions had a double effect on the Red Army. First, the local militia was the reserve force for the Red Army, using combat ineffective units to fill key roles, which in turn, adversely affected the combat readiness of the entire Red Army. Second, the local militia was the recruiting ground for the Red Army, and the continued infusion of poor quality soldiers into the army also affected the combat readiness.[109]

Strategy

As the Red Army expanded and faced a stronger, more professional enemy, it adopted Mao's "lure the enemy in deep" strategy. The basic concept of the strategy is similar to General Matthew Ridgway's attrition strategy in Korea that would be employed on the Chinese Red Army almost twenty years later.[110] The strategy was based on a mobile defense; the goal was not to defend any specific territory, but rather to attack the enemy at an advantageous moment on favorable terrain. The Red Army ceded Soviet territory to the advancing NRA force, trading space for time. On a battlefield of their choosing, the Red Army conducted a massive counterattack to destroy the enemy.[111] This strategy was a logical transition from the guerrilla tactics embodied by Mao's "they advance, we retreat" philosophy.[112] It incorporated many of these tenets, specifically; it focused on how to effectively conserve its force in order to attack the enemy with the greatest amount of combat power.[113] In addition to the guerrilla warfare tenets outlined in the previous chapter, other key tenets of the "lure the enemy in deep" strategy were preparation, isolation, and concentration.

First, the Red Army's preparation for the "lure the enemy in deep" strategy exceeded the normal military preparation, and focused on political mobilization of the population. One major task in the preparation phase was fundraising in the Soviet areas. Through land reform and selective attacks on wealthy peasants and landlords, the Red Army raised the necessary revenues to pay for medicine, fuel, and other logistical and administrative costs. One expense that increased with each extermination campaign was pocket money for NRA POWs. The Red Army did not have the robust logistical structure to support itself, let alone POWs, and often freed POWs after battles. NRA officers and soldiers with intelligence value were often kept for interrogation; however, most NRA soldiers were allowed to leave. The Red Army gave each NRA soldier a small amount of money for travel expenses and sent them on their way.[114] The pocket money also doubled as positive propaganda for the Red Army, demonstrating the communists' magnanimity toward both its enemy and its own soldiers. Besides raising funds, the Red Army collected several months' worth of supplies to support its forces. The extermination campaign was basically a siege, and the Red Army had to prepare a large cache to survive the initial onslaught.

The second major task was mobilizing the people. While the Red Army may have adopted a "lure the enemy in deep" strategy, its success rested on the back of the local populace.[115] The Red Army leadership had to convince local residents to support a strategy that basically pulled away any military protection from their village. Additionally, the strategy called for local residents to actively resist NRA occupation of their village, at great risk to their lives. From this perspective, it is a bit easier to understand why there always was great trepidation in endorsing a mobile defense strategy. To alleviate the unease, the Red Army leveraged the democratic process to gain support and consensus for the strategy. For the Second Extermination Campaign, Mao could only initiate his strategy after two months of debate. The long debate process demonstrated how the Red Army gained the people's support for the plan. Once the people's support was secured, they were organized into different groups.[116] Many times, locals filled multiple roles in different communist organizations, providing logistical and guerrilla support, depending on the unit and operation. These local organizations were then integrated and synchronized with the main Red Army forces to ensure unity of action throughout the campaign.[117]

The second key tenet was isolation. As the NRA movement moved forward deeper into Soviet territory, its extended lines of communications became susceptible to a myriad of different attacks. Local militia groups constantly harassed the NRA, especially its rear areas during the night, increasing the confusion and instilling fear in the NRA units. Additional NRA forces had to be allocated to secure the rear areas, thereby decreasing the combat power at the front lines. The guerrilla attacks would draw NRA units into disadvantageous terrain or areas. Terrain was also used to isolate units. Many NRA units were usually separated from reinforcing units by mountain ranges or riverbeds, preventing the establishment of mutually supporting positions, and effectively shifting the advantage to the Red Army.[118]

The last tenet was concentration. Once the NRA unit was isolated in a battlefield of its choosing, the Red Army massed all its combat power to overwhelm its enemy. While the total NRA force consistently outnumbered the Red Army during each Extermination Campaign, the Red Army leveraged its strategy to create a three-to-one advantage over the NRA during battle.[119] Mao leveraged terrain to concentrate overwhelming power on the enemy, as the principle "ten engages one."[120] Zhu De believed in fighting at a location of his choosing, where he could leverage "concentration, surprise attacks, and dispersals, encircle and attack."[121] While massing combat power made tactical sense, it also had strategic implications. The Red Army needed to mass firepower in order to win a quick and decisive battle. The Red Army was incapable of sustaining contact for long period of times. The army remained critically short of logistical supplies, especially ammunition. Red Army units often lived from battle to battle, with each victory providing more supplies. Any sustained contact caused a severe strain on its logistical network, leaving the Red Army vulnerable. To protect against this weakness, the Red Army exercised patience and restraint when choosing battle. Only when the opportunity to engage in a quick, decisive battle did the Red Army concentrate its forces and overwhelm the enemy. The relative quickness of the actual battles fought during the Extermination campaigns demonstrates how the Red Army always chose quick battles for survival.

The "lure the enemy in deep" strategy gave the Red Army the advantage it needed to contend with numerically and technologically superior forces. Other than the above-mentioned tenets, the Red Army also used specific tactics in order to gain an advantage on the battlefield.

Tactics

The "lure the enemy in deep" strategy required the Red Army to apply certain tactics that focused on taking advantage of any and all favorable conditions for a weaker Red Army to emerge victorious. Through intelligence, deception, and local support, the Red Army exhausted, dispersed, and tripped up the NRA forces, and gave the Red Army the advantage on the battlefield.

One of the key strengths of the Communist defense against the Nationalist Extermination Campaign was its ability to collect intelligence. The communists would send scouts into the areas to conduct a thorough reconnaissance of the Nationalist-occupied villages and towns. A sample survey report from 1931 represented some of the thoroughness of these reconnaissance actions during that period.[122] The survey covered the following specific areas: (1) geographical land conditions; (2) waterways and river conditions; (3) ethnic minority populations; (4) road networks and trafficability, (5) local population and associated demographic information; (6) local government structure; (7) local militia structure; (8) local market and trade conditions; (9) manufacturing and production capabilities; (10) local living conditions; and (11) worker population and their living conditions. Key areas to highlight in the survey were the attention to details on the militia and workers conditions. The militia survey looked at not only government forces, but also "private" forces hired by wealthy land owners. It also looked to identify any cleavages or conflicts between these forces that could be exploited. For the workers, the focus on was the living conditions and status of land distribution. Intelligence reports also provided intricate details about NRA fortifications, to include how deep trenches and what building materials were used in fortifications.[123] All this information helped Red Army forces to analyze the weaknesses in these cities to gain the local populace support, defeat local militias, and create a Soviet government in the area.

Another key strength of the Red Army was its use of deception. It effectively used feints, cover and concealment, and mobility to deceive the NRA and create advantageous conditions to conduct an attack. During its deception, the Red Army demonstrated the tactical patience required for success. During the Second Extermination campaign, the Red Army remained concealed outside Donggu for twenty-five days waiting for the opportune moment to attack. The Red Army intelligence network also provided great insight into the NRA decision-making process that allowed it to conduct feints and deception plans that fooled the Red Army. Against a superior enemy, the communists leveraged their knowledge of the terrain and Nationalist forces tendencies, to develop an operational plan that they could mass firepower against an exposed weakness. Lastly, the Red Army also understood how to sell a feint to deceive the enemy.

During the Third Extermination Campaign, The Twelfth Army was very conspicuous, moving during the day, waving flags, leaving the First and Third Red Army Corps designations and markings along the route to trick the NRA.[124]

Guerrilla operations using local support remained very successful for the Red Army. The local populace was the first line of defense when the NRA came into Red areas. When the Red Army moved out of an area, the people would immediately spring into action. All grains, oil, and salt were hidden or shipped away so the NRA forces could not use them. The inability to forage caused the NRA forces to allocate more forces to transport and carry food, rather than conduct combat operations.[125] Local militia also conducted guerrilla attacks in order to disrupt the NRA. Their tasks included harassment, intercepting movement, wearing out the forces, conducting ambushes, infiltrating the units, luring the enemy, kidnapping, starving the enemy, blinding the enemy, and lastly, conducting surveillance on the enemy.[126] During the Third Extermination Campaign, guerrilla units conducted small-unit spoiling attacks on the flanks of the NRA, preventing it from establishing "stable footing." The attacks annoyed and frustrated the enemy, and prevent the NRA from establishing a rhythm or gain the initiative.[127] Local support was also the critical component in the Red Army's logistical network. Many locals foraged the battlefields for equipment. The skill and ability of the local populace to conduct resupply operations would pay dividends in the future for the Red Army, especially during the Huai Hai Campaign.

Organization

During this period, the Red Army conducted a series of reorganizations to centralize control of the Red Army. While the Li Lisan line has been panned for leading to the defeat of the Red Army at Changsha and Nangchang, some of his policies actually helped to reorganize the Red Army into a more professional military organization. Li Lisan's goal was to create large military units within the Red Army capable of conducting urban operations and press the revolution.[128] His strategy of attacking urban areas forced the Red Army to integrate smaller, and often scattered, independent units under a single military headquarters.[129] The reorganization of the Red Armies in 1930 helped to establish a single chain of command under the General Front Committee, controlled by the Central Committee, rather than Mao.[130]

In February 1930, the Red Army reorganized into two Red Army Corps. The Fourth Red Army, led by Zhu De and Mao, reflagged as the First Army Corps. Under the First Army Corps, its subordinate units reflagged as the Third Red Army, Fourth Red Army, Twelfth Red Army, Twentieth Red Army, and the Twenty-Second Red Army.[131] The Fifth Red Army, under Peng Dehuai, changed designations at the same time to the Third Red Army Corps. Its subordinate units included the Fifth Red Army and Eight

Red Army.[132] The First Front Red Army was established before the second attack of Changsha, combining the First and Third Red Army Corps, under the direction of Zhu De.[133] To accomplish this mass reorganization, the Red Army standardized many of these new units to establish a base level of training, equipment, and personnel. While this action hurt the communist movement in the short term by stripping the local areas of its militia, it helped to consolidate and organize the Red Army into a professional military structure.

Local forces organizations were also changed to streamline its operations. Two sets of organizational regulations were published in May 1930 and February 1931 to help standardize the units.[134] Before the First Extermination campaign, the Red Army held its first United Militia Conference. The command structure was set up with bureaus for each cardinal direction as well as the center, for a total five bureaus. Additionally, the conference divided southwest Jiangxi area into nine combat districts.[135]

As the scope of the extermination campaign grew, the First Front Army also saw an increasing need for a dedicated staff to conduct the necessary coordination and synchronization for combat. In 1931, the Red Army established a staff section at the First Front Army headquarters to coordinate operations, reconnaissance, administration, education, and mobilization. The staff also began to produce regulations standardizing reporting and orders production within the First Front Army.[136]

Other organizational changes served to insert political control at every military level to ensure compliance with party directives. By 1931, the Central Committee established three parallel governing structures that integrated with the Red Army. At the top of the structure was the Communist Party, which included the Central Committee of the CCP, its Central Military Committee, and the newly established Central Bureau of Soviet Areas. These organizations provided guidance to the General Political department within the Red Army, and helped to guide the Red Army's political mobilization actions. Next was the Soviet government level, with the Central Soviet Executive Committee and its Central Revolutionary Military Council, chaired by Zhu De, that assisted in guiding and directing Red Army actions. In between the Party and the Soviet stood the Red Army structure, with the First Front Red Army occupying the center stage within the Jiangxi Soviet.[137] The supreme headquarters was the Central Revolutionary Military Council, and it maintained military control over the Red Army.[138]

The structure built on the foundations of Mao's concepts and the agreements reached at the Gutian Conference reinforced the superior role of political power within the Army. Li Lisan then added an additional layer in both the government and military by consolidating and funneling power to the Central Committee. Most of the Red Army leadership sat on two or more committees, and provided their own input to the direction of the Army. The difference in the makeup of each specific committee, however, changed the dynamic, as some leaders, especially Mao, could not monopolize control of every committee. The consolidation of power also helped to tamp down any perceived wayward movements or plans. Fear of "guerrillaism," militarism, and the other erroneous ideologies placed a large strain on the Central Committee.[139] By consolidating power, and leveraging the political commissars at each military level, deviations could theoretically be stopped.[140]

Overall, the series of organizational changes helped to establish effective central control over the Red Army, and helped in its overall professionalization. However, these changes would also lead to the diminishment of Mao's influence over the Red Army in the future.

Training

During this period, the Red Army continued to employ the same training techniques from the previous period. After each Extermination Campaign, the Red Army conducted an after-action review to identify key lessons. Zhu De attempted to attend many of these meetings, and found these conferences of the "greatest technical and educational value for our army."[141] After the First Extermination Campaign, the First Front Army conducted a series of conferences, and identified areas of improvement in logistics and medical care. It also identified training tasks in marksmanship and more rehearsals for pursuit operations.[142] Additionally, many of the Red Army soldiers and leaders learned from doing, especially in combat during the first three Extermination campaigns. The number of combat veterans helped to populate the training cadre of the Red Army schools, and ensured that the training remained relevant and practical. Many officers continued to travel abroad for training, especially to the Soviet Union. Starting in 1931, Yeh Qianying, Zuo Zhuan and Xiao Qingguang and Liu Bocheng returned from military training, adding greater military expertise needed to professionalize the force.[143]

Building on that experience, the Red Army continued to expand and professionalize its military education system. The Red Army's transition from training units to a professional military school system occurred just before its departure from Jinggangshan. Its flagship institution, the Red Academy, had a complicated beginning because it had to adapt to the changing environment. The first Red Army School initially started in the middle of 1929, when the Fourth Red Army established it at Jinggangshan. Before it could start its first class, NRA forces besieged Jingangshan and forced the Red Army School to become an accompanying training school. The school staff eventually escaped with the Fourth Red Army. Upon its arrival at Western Fujian, the Fourth Red Army, using the accompanying school as the foundation, reestablished the Red Army School on December 1929 at Longyan. Two months later, The Fourth Red Army headquarters left western Jiangxi, and the Twelfth Red Army and Western Fujian

Soviet government assumed responsibility for the school in March 1930, changing the name to the Western Fujian Red Army School.

With the initial success of the Jiangxi Soviet expansion, the need for military training in the Red Army increased. To meet this demand, the Central Committee used the Western Fujian Red Army School to establish two centrally controlled Red Army Officer Schools in April 1930.[144] The First Branch of the Red Army Officer School remained at Longyan, and the Third Branch of the Red Army Officer School was opened in Ji'an.[145] The first class of the Red Army Officer School at Longyan finally started in August 1930 with more than 300 students. The curriculum covered both military and political training topics, with two-thirds of training focused on military affairs. About 40 percent of the first class of students actually passed the final examinations and graduated from the three-month course. After graduation, the majority of the students went to serve at the platoon and company level within the Red Army, while some graduates went to local militia units.[146] The second class was selected, but never started class because of the First Extermination Campaign, forcing the First Branch of the Red Army Officer School to relocate to Hugang. The school was designated the Fujian-Guangdong-Jiangxi Border Red Army School.

While this military school system provided a basic level of education, the Red Army leadership still continued to work toward developing a professional military academy. Its first attempt was the Chinese Workers and Peasants Red Army School, created in September 1931 out of the Fujian-Guangdong-Jiangxi Border Red Army School, the First Front Red Army Central Training Unit, and the Third Red Army Corps Accompanying School Unit.[147] In October, Mao pushed for something even greater, a professional military academy that would develop Red Army leaders competent in military and political matters. Using Republican China's Huangpu Military Academy as a model, the Red Army created the Chinese Workers and Peasants Red Army Central Military and Political School, known as the Red Academy, in Ruijin, Jiangxi Province.[148] The school's curriculum expanded the scope of training, and incorporated basic education into the military and political training. The academy's primary student population was still lower-level Red Army officers and cadre members, developing the basic leadership skills to lead soldiers and mobilize the population. While the first class at the Red Academy started in December 1931, the school flourished under the guidance of Liu Bocheng when he took over in 1932, which will be discussed in more depth in the following chapter.

Besides the Red Academy, each Soviet created its own military training school to provide training for local cadre and military leaders. The push for the localized training began in April 1930, when the Central Military Council authorized the creation of local military schools to develop and train its leaders.[149] By December, the Red Army had five branches of the

Red Army Officer School and two base-area military schools spread out in the western Jiangxi Soviet, Hunan-Hubei-Jiangxi Soviet, northeast Jiangxi Soviet, Hunan-western Hubei Soviet, and Hubei-Henan-Anhui Soviet.[150]

Some of the demand for more professional training was a result of the Red Army's victories on the battlefield. The demand for low density skill sets, such as medical and communications, increased as the Red Army confiscated modern equipment from the NRA. Wireless communications and medical supplies were some of the most valuable caches found after battle, and helped to increase the combat effectiveness of the army. In response to the new equipment, the Red Army developed specialty schools for low-density skills sets. The first two specialty schools developed in 1931 were the Red Army Communications School and Red Army Medical School.

The communication school started as the First Front Red Army Wireless Communication Unit in Donggu in January 1931. The unit was built on soldiers and officers with experience on wireless communication equipment, along with wireless communications equipment and operators captured from the NRA during the First Extermination campaign. The inaugural class had twenty soldiers and they were sent straight to the field during the Second Extermination Campaign, moving with political mobilization teams to establish the Red Army's communication network within the Jiangxi Soviet. By January 1932, three classes had graduated, and the Red Army used the graduates to establish the Red Army Wireless Communications School.[151]

The Red Army Medical School stood up alongside the Red Academy in Ruijin in November 1931. The first class graduated twenty-five soldiers. Initially, the facilities and equipment for the medical school were sparse and elementary. The school had very few experienced instructors. The students' educational backgrounds were also very low, making teaching difficult. The school lacked books and diagnostic equipment. Given the lack of equipment and facilities, many of the students received their education out in the field because they were attached to field units during class. Despite the initial difficulties, the medical school began to develop and expand in the following years.

Other specialty training was also conducted, though the results were uneven. A demand for artillery training grew after the Red Army captured cannons during the Second Extermination Campaign. However, scarcity of artillery ammunition and mobility challenges of the equipment rendered much of the training and units ineffective.[152] Engineering training and units were a bit more successful. Engineering forces were created around a cadre of former miners, who helped establish air shelters against the new air NRA threat.[153] Engineering training remained limited, leveraging existing mining technology to create simple defensive structures.

The Red Army also trained its soldiers and leaders through the publication and distribution of periodicals. The Red Army Political Department and the Red Academy both led the production of military periodicals. The expansion in much of the printing can be attributed to the capture of KMT printing presses.[154] One example is *Wuku*, a periodical published by the General Political Department of the Third Red Army. While the magazines still provided a propaganda value, it also was a great medium for professional exchange. Peng Dehuai publicly addressed some challenges within his unit in the periodical in order to promote awareness and help other units defend against these problems.[155] One of the major topics during this period was issues of professionalization of the military. Issues included commanders shirking training responsibilities for their units, or political training, to include reading classes, not being done to standard.[156] To address these problems, some authors recommended a renewed focus on political training for soldiers, commissars, and officers to reinvigorate the revolutionary spirit and eradicate this problem from the Red Army.[157]

Training of the local militia was also critical during this period. The Communist Youth (CY) organizations trained on offensive and defensive tactics, as well air defense. In addition to traditional warfare, the training also focused on identifying counter-revolutionary personnel, especially in light of the Futian Incident. Another task for the CY was developing ways to win over POWs. Specific training focused on developing proselytizing techniques to convert NRA soldiers to join the communist fight. Political education was part of the curriculum. The CY used plays and newspapers to strengthen revolutionary spirit and increase courage. Lastly, the CY made sure training was fun, making a big push for playing sports and activities in order to both increase physical fitness as well as improve morale of the soldiers.[158]

Conclusion

By 1931, the Red Army had a string of victories over the numerically and technologically superior NRA. Leveraging its strengths of mobility, intelligence, and deception into Mao's "lure the enemy in deep" mobile defense strategy, the Red Army gained territory, equipment, and most importantly confidence with each victory. The Jiangxi Soviet spanned three provinces and claimed more than a million citizens. These gains were not without costs. The Red Army luckily survived a bitter intraparty struggle between two factions on the philosophical, militarily, and political ends of the spectrums. The Li Lisan line embodied the urban-centric, conservative communist approach that dominated the Central Committee in Shanghai. Its plan to incite the revolution through a series of urban insurrections failed, and Mao's rural Soviet strategy prevailed. Remnants of the leftist movement still remained in the Red Army, and the AB Corps purge and the Twentieth Red Army's mutiny almost led to the Red Army's defeat.

The Red Army's thorough political mobilization of the local peasant areas, however, tilted the odds in its favor, as the peasant support helped the Red Army beat the NRA in three extermination campaigns. During this time, the Red Army continued to adopt professionalization measures, even creating its "Red" version of the Huangpu Military Academy. All these measures helped to professionalize the main Red Army force. Yet, the local militia groups that supported, and often augmented the Red Army were still filled with problems. Discipline issues, corruption, and issues with compliance were more common than acknowledged. Even worse, the future for the Red Army looked more difficult. The KMT had not given up on defeating the communists; they simply took a break and would be back even stronger. Additionally, unbeknownst to him, Mao's influence within the Red Army and the party was waning. A new group of left-leaning communists, known as the Twenty-Eight Bolsheviks, were rising to the top of the Communist Party, and would, once again, change the strategy for the Red Army and Communist China.

Notes

1. John P. Harrison, *The Long March to Power: A History of the Chinese Communist Party, 1927-72* (New York: Praeger Publishing, 1972), 162.

2. Harrison, *The Long March to Power*, 161.

3. William W. Whitson, *The Chinese High Command: A History of Communist Military Politics, 1927-71* (Westport, CT: Praeger Press, 1973), 28.

4. John E. Rue, *Mao Tse-tung in Opposition: 1927-1935*. (Stanford: Stanford University Press, 1966), 138.

5. Harrison, *The Long March to Power*, 171.

6. Harrison, *The Long March to Power*, 168.

7. Rue, *Mao Tse-tung in Opposition*, 143.

8. Robert C. North, *Moscow and Chinese Communists* (Stanford: Stanford University Press, 1963), 127.

9. North, *Moscow and Chinese Communists*, 128-129.

10. Saich, *The Rise to Power,* 400-407; North, *Moscow and Chinese Communists*, 130-131.

11. North, *Moscow and Chinese Communists*, 127.

12. Harrison, *The Long March to Power*, 169.

13. Agnes Smedley, *The Great Road: The Life and Times of Chu Teh* (New York: Monthly Review Press 1956), 275.

14. Rue, *Mao Tse-tung in Opposition*, 144.

15. Rue, *Mao Tse-tung in Opposition*, 122-124. In April 1929, the Chinese Police conducted a raid on Soviet consulates in Northern China, finding documents and evidence that the Soviet Union was planning to subvert and overthrow the Nationalist government. The incident was part of a greater battle for control of the Chinese Eastern Railway, which was a lucrative venture for both the Soviets and the Chinese. The veracity of the documents seized in the raid is debated. Nevertheless, the Nationalist government expelled key Soviet diplomats, and both sides cut relations. On November 16, 1929, the Soviet Union invaded Manchuria to reestablish its dominant role. During this time, Li Li-san used the slogan "Protect the Soviet Union," to demonstrate his hardened support for the Russians.

16. Rue, *Mao Tse-tung in Opposition*, 133.

17. Rue, *Mao Tse-tung in Opposition*, 134.

18. Harrison, *The Long March to Power*, 169.

19. North, *Moscow and Chinese Communists*, 126.

20. Rue, *Mao Tse-tung in Opposition*, 205.

21. Rue, *Mao Tse-tung in Opposition*, 206.

22. *Di fang wu zhuang de ce lue zu zhi gong zuo lu xian* [Strategy, Organization, and Working Line of the local Armed Forces], CBSA Circular,

No. 10, February 1931, SSC, Reel 7:9.

23. Smedley, *The Great Road*, 274.

24. Wuhan, and three surrounding cities of Hankou, Wuchang, and Hanyang, was a regional industrial center on the Yangtze River. Its concentration of factories and industries made it essential launching point for the proletariat-led urban insurrection. Rue, *Mao Tse-tung in Opposition*, 206.

25. North, *Moscow and Chinese Communists*, 133.

26. North, *Moscow and Chinese Communists*, 131-132.

27. Mao, Tse-Tung, *Selected Works, Vol. 1* (New York: International Publishers, 1954), 201.

28. Rue, *Mao Tse-tung in Opposition*, 145.

29. Mao, *Selected Works, Vol. 1*, 122.

30. Mao, *Selected Works, Vol. 1*, 122-123.

31. Smedley, *The Great Road*, 275.

32. Smedley, *The Great Road*, 277.

33. Smedley, *The Great Road*, 275.

34. The reorganization of the Red Army will be discussed later in this chapter.

35. Rue, *Mao Tse-tung in Opposition*, 213.

36. Some scholars stated that Peng Dehuai was designated as the chairman. See Rue, *Mao Tse-tung in Opposition*, 215.

37. North, *Moscow and Chinese Communists*, 140.

38. Smedley, *The Great Road*, 277.

39. Whitson, *The Chinese High Command*, 265.

40. Smedley, *The Great Road*, 278.

41. Shaoqun Huang, *Zhong qu feng yun: Zhong yang Su qu di yi zhi wu ci fan "wei jiao" zhan zheng shi* [Zhong qu Feng yun: the History of the First through Fifth Extermination Campaigns in the Central Soviet] (Beijing: Zhong gong zhong yang dang xiao chu ban she, 1993), 27. Hereafter cited as *ZQFY*.

42. Smedley, *The Great Road*, 280.

43. Smedley, *The Great Road*, 279.

44. Some scholars see little evidence of the existence of the AB Corps to the extent first portrayed by Mao and the CCP. Subsequent examination by the CCP concurred that the AB threat at the time was exaggerated. See Stephen C. Averill, "Origins of Futian Incident," in *New Perspectives on the Chinese Revolution*, Tony Saich and Hans J. van de Ven, eds. (Armonk: M.E. Sharpe, 1995); Robert Suleski "Futian Incident Reconsidered," *The China Quarterly* 89 (1982): 97-104.

45. Stephen Uhlaney, *History of the Chinese Communist Party* (Stanford: Hoover Institution Press, 1988), 44-45.

46. Averill, "Origins of Futian Incident," 105.
47. Averill, "Origins of Futian Incident," 106.
48. Uhlaney, *History of the Chinese Communist Party*, 45.
49. *ZQFY*, 13-14.
50. North, *Moscow and Chinese Communists*, 142.
51. Stephen Averill argued that one of the factors leading to the Futian incident was the local power dynamics in the greater Ji'an area. See Averill, "Origins of Futian Incident." Ronald Suleski also examined the Futian incident in Ronald Suleski and Daniel Bays, *Early Communist China: Two Studies* (Ann Arbor: University of Michigan Press, 1969); Ronald Suleski, "The Futian Incident Reconsidered," *The China Quarterly* 89 (1982): 97-104.
52. *ZQFY*, 31.
53. Harrison, *The Long March to Power*, 217.
54. Chi, "The Chinese Red Army and the Kiangsi Soviet," 129. For a more detailed discussion on discrepancies with Red Army numbers, refer to Appendix A.
55. *ZQFY*, 32.
56. *ZQFY*, 33.
57. *ZQFY*, 33-34.
58. Whitson, *The Chinese High Command*, 268.
59. *ZQFY*, 43.
60. *ZQFY*, 44.
61. *ZQFY*, 45-47.
62. *ZQFY*, 47.
63. *ZQFY*, 51.
64. *ZQFY*, 51-52.
65. *ZQFY*, 52.
66. *ZQFY*, 53.
67. *ZQFY*, 53-54.
68. *ZQFY*, 56.
69. Whitson, *The Chinese High Command*, 270.
70. Zhongguo ren min ge ming jun shi bo wu guan, *Zhongguo zhan zheng fa zhan shi* [History of the Development of War in China] (Beijing: Ren min chu ban she, 2003), 831. Hearafter cited as *History of the Development of War in China*, 853. Smedley reported the NRA force at 150,000, Smedley, *The Great Road*, 295.
71. *Zhongguo jun dui shi zhan shi lu: Zhong ri liang jun xue zhan, guo gong liang jun xue zhan, zhong Mei liang jun xue zhan* [Record of China's Military Combat: First and Second Sino-Japanese War; the Chinese Civil

War; and First and Second Sino-American Wars (Korean War and Vietnam War)], (Beijing: Guo fang da xue chu ban she, 1993), 9-10. Hereafter cited as *ZGJDSZSL*.

72. *History of the Development of War in China*, 853.

73. This portion was based off the research presented in *ZQFY*, 96-101.

74. Smedley, *The Great Road*, 298.

75. *ZQFY*, 98.

76. *ZQFY*, 102-105. Among the captured was the division commander, Gong Bingfan, who wore an enlisted soldier's uniform to conceal his identity, and successfully escaped. See Smedley, *The Great Road*, 297.

77   There is still debate over why the Nineteenth Route NRA Army never reinforced the area. Pingfeng Chi argued lack of coordination in NRA operations. See Chi, "The Chinese Red Army and the Kiangsi Soviet," 133. Wheras others believed it was personality conflicts between the commanders that prevented any reinforcement. See *ZQFY*, 105-106.

78. *ZQFY*, 105-106.

79. *ZQFY*, 106.

80. *ZQFY*, 106-107.

81. *ZQFY*, 107-108.

82. *History of the Development of War in China*, 853.

83. *ZQFY*, 108.

84. Whitson, *The Chinese High Command*, 272.

85. Whitson, *The Chinese High Command*, 272.

86. *ZQFY*, 123.

87. *ZQFY*, 120-121.

88. *ZQFY*, 124-125.

89. *ZQFY*, 124.

90. Chi, "The Chinese Red Army and the Kiangsi Soviet," 134; *ZGJDSZSL*, 13-14.

91. Snow, *Inside Red China*, 179. For more information on the differences of numbers for the Red Army, see Appendix A.

92. *ZQFY*, 122.

93. *ZQFY*, 127.

94. Mao stated that the Red Army travelled more than one thousand *li*. Mao, *Selected Works*, Vol. 1, 230.

95. *ZQFY*, 126-128. During the Third Extermination Campaign, most Chinese sources called the Gaoxing area *Gaoxingwei*, meaning the embankment area near Gaoxing. In terms of geographical proximity and ease of understanding, this study uses the city proper name of *Gaoxing* to describe the area.

96. *ZQFY*, 129-130.

97. *ZQFY*, 130-131.

98. *ZQFY*, 131-132.

99. *ZQFY*, 132-133.

100. *ZQFY,* 134. Pingfeng Chi's research corroborates this theory that the threat from the Guangdong warlord factions prematurely ended the Third Extermination Campaign. See Chi, 137. Other scholars argued that the September 18, 1931, Japanese invasion of Manchuria, known as the Mukden Incident, prematurely caused the end of the Third Extermination Campaign. See Chong Kun Yoon, "Mao, The Red Army, and the Chinese Soviet Republic," Ph.D dissertation (The American University, 1968), 144. Either way, external factors caused Chiang Kai-shek to cease operations and return to Nanjing.

101. Some scholars argue the battle of Gaoxing was a loss for the Red Army, blaming Mao and Zhu De for being overzealous in the attack and not sticking to its original principles. See Helen Foster Snow, *Inside Red China* (New York: Da Capo Press, 1979), 254. However, Mao and Zhu's action, taken into context, makes more sense. The Red Army had recently refitted, while the NRA conducted a fruitless two-week search for the Twelfth Red Army. Additionally, the Red Army's intelligence reports had a history of accurate findings. The Red Army also had a history of success conducting pursuits on familiar terrain as well.

102. *History of the Development of War in China*, 854.

103. Nym Wales, *Red Dust* (Stanford: Stanford University Press, 1952), 124.

104. The development of the Red Army wireless communications systems will be discussed further in this chapter under training.

105. Retreatism is a pejorative term used to describe a conservative military strategy that adopts withdrawal in the face of challenge. See Snow, *Inside Red China*, 168.

106. Peter Donovan, "The Chinese Red Army in the Kiangsi Soviet, 1931-1934" (Ph.D dissertation, Cornell University, 1974), 54.

107. *Di fang wuzhuang de celue zuzhi gongzuo luxian* [Strategy, Organization, and Working Line of the local Armed Forces], CBSA Circular, No. 10, February 1931, SSC, Reel 7:9.

108. *Jiangxi di yi ci gong nong bing su wei ai da hui dui di fang wu zhuang wen ti de jue yi an* [Jiangxi Provincial Workers and Peasant Army First Plenum Conference on the Local Militia question], December 1931, SSC, Reel 7:6.

109. *Jiangxi di yi ci gong nong bing su wei ai da hui dui di fang wu zhuang wen ti de jue yi an* [Jiangxi Provincial Workers and Peasant Army First Plenum Conference on the Local Militia question], December 1931, SSC, Reel 7:6.

110. For more information on the use of attrition warfare in the Korean War, see Carter Malkasian, *A History of Modern Wars of Attrition* (Westport: Praeger Publishing, 2002), 119-186.

111. Jin, Yuguo. *Zhongguo zhan shu shi* [History of Military Tactics in

China] (Beijing: Jie fang jun chu ban she, 2003), 304. Hereafter cited as *History of Chinese Military Tactics*.

112. *History of the Development of War in China*, 853.

113. *History of the Development of War in China*, 858.

114. Smedley, *The Great Road*, 289. While many NRA soldiers were released, soldiers with specialized skills, such as advanced weapons or communications training, were often coerced to join the Chinese Red Army and fill in training positions for the Red Army. One method employed by the Chinese Red Army was leveraging the CY to subtly persuade captured NRA soldiers to join the Red Army.

115. *Seventy years of the PLA*, 70.

116. Refer to chapter 3 for a more in-depth description of the different military organizations within the Red Army.

117. *History of Chinese Military Tactics*, 304.

118. Whitson, *The Chinese High Command*, 270.

119. *History of Chinese Military Tactics*, 304.

120. Yoon, "Mao, The Red Army, and the Chinese Soviet Republic," 134.

121. Smedley, *The Great Road*, 288.

122. See *Chi bai qu yu she hui qing kuang diao cha baogao da gang* [An Outline of a Survey Report on the Social Conditions in the Red and White Areas], Front Committee of the Third Group Army, CWPRA, January 1931, SSC, Reel 6:21, as a sample report of a Nationalist area.

123. Smedley, *The Great Road*, 295.

124. *ZQFY*, 132.

125. *ZQFY*, 94.

126. *ZQFY*, 95.

127. *ZQFY*, 119.

128. *Seventy Years of the PLA*, 75.

129. Donovan, "The Chinese Red Army in the Kiangsi Soviet," 29.

130. The General Front Committee measure did not meet its expectations, as Mao became the Chairman of the General Front Committee, consolidating his power under the new organization. See Rue, *Mao Tse-tung in Opposition*, 204-237. The General Front Committee was dissolved in 1931, and replaced by the Central Bureau of Soviet Areas.

131. *ZQFY*, 372. Donovan's organizational analysis differed slightly. He mentioned the Eleventh Red Army as part of the First Army Corps. Additionally, he cited the Twelfth, Twentieth, and Twenty-second Red Armies as attached units, rather than organic to the First Red Army Corps. See Donovan, 172-174. Rue's organizational chart maintained the Third, Fourth, Twelfth, Twentieth, Twenty-first, and Thirty-fifth Red Armies. See Rue, *Mao Tse-tung in Opposition*, 212.

132. *ZQFY*, 372. The designations changed for the Third Army Corps subordinate units throughout the first three campaigns. By the Second Extermination campaigns, the Corps subordinate units were the First Red Division, Third Red Division, Fourth Red Division, and Sixth Red Division. See *ZQFY,* 374, 376. Donovan presented different subordinate units. Instead of the Eighth Red Army, the Seventh Red Army was directly subordinate to the Third Red Army Corps. The Eight Red Army was an attached unit, rather than an organic unit. See Donovan, "The Chinese Red Army in the Kiangsi Soviet," 173-174. Rue only included the Eight Army under the Third Army Corps, See Rue, *Mao Tse-tung in Opposition*, 212.

133. Snow, *Inside Red China*, 175.

134. Yoon, "Mao, The Red Army, and the Chinese Soviet Republic," 164.

135. The First district contained Ningdu, Guangchang, Nanfeng, and Le'an; Second District contained Ji'an and the eastern bank of Jishui; Third District contained Yongfeng county; Fourth district contained was Xingguo county; Fifth District contained Western Bank of Gan River; Sixth District contained Eastern Bank of Gan River; Seventh District contained Taihe, Wan'an, and Zhuchuan; Eighth District contained Hexi District; and Ninth District contained Southeast Hunan. *ZQFY,* 95.

136. *Seventy Years of the PLA*, 77.

137. Donovan, "The Chinese Red Army in the Kiangsi Soviet," 58-61; Harrison, *The Long March to Power*, 202-203; Rue, *Mao Tse-tung in Opposition* 206-214.

138. Donovan, "The Chinese Red Army in the Kiangsi Soviet," 58; *History of the Development of War in China*, 864.

139. According to Gregory Benton, "guerrillaism" is seen as a "pejorative term used to describe a military style characterized by indiscipline, a lack of strategy or system, and the pursuit of 'individual heroism' above corporate interest, a way of fighting characterized as 'peasant.'" See Gregory Benton, *New Fourth Army: Communist Resistance Along the Yangtze and the Huai, 1938-1941* (Berkeley: University of California Press, 1999), 666.

140. Donovan, "The Chinese Red Army in the Kiangsi Soviet," 76.

141. Smedley, *The Great Road*, 292.

142. *ZQFY,* 90.

143. Whitson, *The Chinese High Command*, 54-55.

144. *Chinese Military School History*, 334.

145. The "Futian Incident" prematurely ended the Ji'an Red Army Officer School. Most of the teachers were transferred back to the First Front Army training unit. See *Chinese Military Education History*, 276.

146. During the same time, the Red Army School held a two-week Political Commissar Training course and Communist Youth Training course for approximately 50 students in order to help local cadre members conduct political mobilization tasks. See *Chinese Military School History*, 335.

147. *Chinese Military Education History*, 278; *Chinese Military School History*, 337.

148. The nickname for the new Chinese Workers and Peasants Red Army Central Military and Political School was actually *hongpu* (translates to "red harbor"), which was a play on words in Chinese, incorporating the character for "Red" in the name, making the name sound very similar to Huangpu Military Academy. See *Chinese Military School History*, 337. In Jane Price's *Cadres, Commanders, and Commissars,* she called the school Red Army School, and called the 1933 Red Army military school for high level leaders Red Academy. See Jane L. Price, *Cadres, Commanders, and Commissars* (Boulder, CO: Westview Press, 1976), 121-127.

149. *Chinese Military School History*, 332.

150. *Chinese Military Education History*, 276-277.

151. *Chinese Military School History*, 352-353.

152. *Seventy Years of the PLA*, 86-87.

153. Smedley, *The Great Road*, 293.

154. Smedley, *The Great Road*, 292.

155. "Kuo da hong jun" [Red Army Expansion], *Wuku* [Weapon Depository], No. 7 (General Political Department of the CWPRA Third Group Army, December 31, 1931), SSC, Reel 7:3.

156. "Yi shi dang nei de yanzhong de cuowu" [Serious mistakes in the First Division CCP], *Wuku* [Armory], No. 7 (General Political Department of Third Group Army, CWPRA, December 31, 1931), SSC, Reel 7:3.

157. "Fan dui fu" [Fight against Corruption], *Wuku* [Weapon Depository], No. 8 (General Political Department of Third Group Army, CWPRA, January 12, 1932), SSC, Reel 7:3.

158. *Hong jun zhong shuo gong gong zuo da gang* [Red Army Communist Youth Training Outline], June 20, 1931, SSC, Reel 7:17.

Chapter 5
Twenty-Eight Bolsheviks and Final
Extermination Campaigns (1932-1934)

External influences began influencing the KMT-Communist conflict. Japanese expansion into China threatened Soviet interests, and Moscow looked to the Chinese Red Army as a potential bulwark against Japanese interests. From 1930 to 1931, the Red Army was successful in defending the Soviet areas against the NRA Extermination Campaigns; however, it still suffered from problems with discipline, compliances, and overall professionalism. Under the leadership of the new Central Committee, led by the Twenty-Eight Bolsheviks, and a new COMINTERN representative, Otto Braun, the Red Army adopted a series of initiatives starting in 1932 to expand and professionalize the Red Army. All Red Army units were standardized to establish better command and control. Political indoctrination and military training also became more standardized as a wave of new manuals was distributed among the Red Army force. The Red Army expanded the Red Academy with the creation of the Red Army War College for mid-grade and senior officers. Branch schools and specialty schools were also established in other Soviet areas to increase competency and training level of Red Army soldiers. Political mobilization still remained an important part of the Red Army, with the focus remaining on the recruitment of new soldiers, though there was a renewed emphasis on the urban proletariat in the revolution. The biggest change to the Red Army operations was the adoption of Soviet offensive tactics to seek decisive battle. CCP leaders mistakenly believed that simply the élan from revolutionary fervor would give the Red Army the silver bullet. However, these professionalization efforts were not met with commensurate investment in weapons and equipment. Coupled with the NRA's adoption of effective counterinsurgency tactics in the Fifth Extermination Campaign, the Red Army suffered severe casualties and was forced to conduct a long retreat, known as the Long March, for survival. In the end, the new strategy failed to deliver the decisive victory sought by the CCP but at the same time, the strategy helped to institutionalize key initiatives within the Red Army that allowed it to become a more professional fighting force.

Twenty-eight Bolsheviks

As the Red Army was defeating the NRA in the Third Extermination Campaign, another intraparty power struggle was growing within the Communist party, with new leadership taking charge of the party. After the fall of Li Lisan, a group of students returning from studies in the Soviet Union began a systematic operation to gain control of the CCP. This group of "Returned Students," also known as the Twenty-eight Bolsheviks, was a group of twenty-something Chinese students, who returned to China with the new COMINTERN adviser, Pavel Mif, in 1931. Two key members of the group,[1] Qin Bangxian, known as Bo Gu, and Chen Shaoyu, known as Wang Ming, would later assume key positions of influence within the CCP. Many of them had attended Moscow's Sun Yat-sen University, and become acquainted with Mif, then the head rector of the university. The school was a breeding ground for ultra-orthodox Stalinist communist doctrine.[2] The students of the group were heavily influenced by the Soviet models and coalesced around the strict conservative Moscow view. Mif saw the group as a "well-disciplined force" and used them to help purge out divergent groups within the university.[3] This partnership continued in China after they arrived in Shanghai in late 1930.

The Rise of the Bolsheviks

The initial push into power began in September 1930, with the Third Plenum. Mif attempted to use the forum to denounce Li Lisan's plan as running counter to the COMINTERN policies, but failed to convince the majority of the Central Committee.[4] Mif's opportunity rose after the COMINTERN condemned Li Lisan and recalled him back to Moscow in November. At the Fourth Plenum in January 1931, Li Lisan and at least eleven of his supporters were ousted from the Central Committee, and their positions were filled by Moscow-aligned Communist Party members.[5] For the next year, the Twenty-Eight Bolsheviks were engaged in a brutal intraparty struggle with other Communist factions, often using coercion and violence. Some Communist party members even leveraged the KMT to eliminate the opposition and consolidate power.[6] By late September 1931, the Bolsheviks had effectively destroyed most of the opposition and incorporated the surviving members into a Central Committee loyal to the Soviet Union. Bo Gu assumed the head of the Central Committee from Wang Ming, who returned to Moscow.

Once the Twenty-eight Bolsheviks gained control of the CCP within Shanghai, their next target was Mao and the Red Army in the Soviet areas. They saw the First All-China Soviet Congress held in November 1931 as a perfect opportunity to launch their first attack. Mao, however, was well prepared for the initial assault to his power, having gotten word about actions in Shanghai from loyal supporters. Before the Central Committee arrived in Ruijin, Mao had already emerged victorious from the extermination campaigns, suppressed dissension among his own ranks, and established a delegation of loyalists within the Soviet Congress.[7] The Bolsheviks failed to gain majority within the Congress, gaining only two seats in the Central Executive Committee. On the other hand, Mao was elected Chairman of the Central Executive Committee of the Soviet, Zhu De was selected as the Commissar of War, and other Mao loyalists filled other positions in the Soviet government.[8] While the Bolsheviks attempted to gain political control over the Red Army, they also employed Zhou Enlai[9] to help break Mao's monopolistic control over the Red Army.[10]

In early 1932, the CCP pushed the Red Army to expand the Soviet territory to a greater scale than ever before. During this period, the Red Army was also expanding. The successful defense against the Extermination Campaigns brought in many former NRA soldiers, some voluntary, others forced. One of the biggest reasons for growth came in December 14, 1931, when the NRA Twenty-sixth Route Army rebelled against the KMT and joined the Red Army. These rebel forces were integrated into the Red Army, and were designated the Fifth Red Army Corps. This addition along with other recruits increased the First Front Red Army's strength to around 70,000.[11] With the Red Army growing so large, the Soviet area needed to expand in order to support itself and the revolution.

Changes to Red Army Strategy

On January 9, 1932, the Central Committee issued "Resolution of the CCP Central Committee on Winning Initial Revolutionary Successes in One or More Provinces" outlining a new strategy for the CCP and the Red Army.[12] The resolution started with an assessment of the current situation in China, stating that the combination of an international depression negatively affecting the Chinese economy, the Red Army's growth and string of victories from the Extermination Campaigns, and the increase in imperial aggression embodied by the Mukden Incident presented a great opportunity for the CCP to advance the Chinese revolutionary struggle.[13] The resolution then reasserted the primacy of the urban proletariat in the revolution, and outlined the strategy for the future.[14] Foremost, the party must "expand the territory, link up the separated Soviet areas to form an integrated Soviet area, and take advantage of the present favorable political and military conditions to seize one or two important central cities so as to win an initial victory of the revolution in one or more provinces."[15] Based on the new strategy, the Red Army conducted a series of offensives to expand the Soviet territory and connect the Soviets starting in early 1932, targeting southern Jiangxi, to include Ganzhou, Nanchang, and Jiujiang, as well Fujian's Zhangzhou, Fuzhou, and Xiamen.[16]

The resolution also pushed for a "positive and offensive line,"[17] characterizing the former "lure the enemy in deep" strategy as "no longer right because circumstances have changed."[18] It directly attacked Mao's strategy as being "right opportunism" that "underestimated" the situation and maintained a "pessimistic attitude," and called upon the party and army to must actively guard against these incorrect mindsets.[19] It cemented the divide between the left-leaning Bolshevik "positive and offensive line" and the right-leaning Maoist "lure the enemy in deep" strategy.

The first target city was Ganzhou, Jiangxi Province. The city linked the Hunan-Jiangxi border areas with the Fujian-Jiangxi borders areas, and provided a launching station north to Ji'an.[20] During a meeting on January 1932 at Ruijin to discuss preparations, Mao expressed reservations about the attack, stating the Red Army did not have the necessary weapons or supplies necessary to seize the city.[21] Zhu De supported Mao's view, but the Central Military Committee vetoed his measures and continued to plan for the Ganzhou attack.[22] On January 10, the Revolutionary Military Committee finally issued the order to the First Red Army Corps, Third Red Army Corps, Fifth Red Army Corps, and Jiangxi Soviet Military Regional forces to conduct the attack on Ganzhou in February. The KMT was well prepared for the attack and conducted preparations for the assault.[23] Around February 3, 1932, the Red Army arrived at Ganzhou and encircled the city. The next day, the Fifth Red Army Corps, about 20,000 strong, conducted the main attack on the East Gate, puncturing the defenses, but were repelled. On February 17 and 23, the Red Army conducted two additional assaults, expanding the attack to the West Gate and South Gate as well, but the Red Army could not gain a foothold. During the siege, two NRA brigades reinforced the distressed garrison in Ganzhou just two days before the final assault. On March 4, the Red Army conducted its fourth assault, and again was repelled. Three days later, the Red Army retired to Jiangkou to reorganize after suffering about 3,000 casualties.[24]

The CCP was undeterred by the loss at Ganzhou, believing that the strategy was still correct. The CCP was also bolstered by Japan's occupation of Manchuria, as it signaled the revolution was near.[25] At a March 18, 1932 meeting, Mao again attacked the strategy as being overly ambitious, failing to understand the current conditions of the Red Army. He argued that it was still premature to use the Red Army to attack the cities. His argument fell on deaf ears, and the CCP reorganized the Red Army into two route armies. The West Route Red Army, made up of the Third Red Army Corps, was responsible for expanding the Soviet areas west of the Gan River in the Hunan-Jiangxi area with a focus around Zhuchuan, Taihe and Wan'an. The First and Fifth Red Army Corps formed the Central Route Red Army. Taking Mao's recommendations, the Central Route Army targeted Southern Fujian for expansion operations, with Xiamen as the final target.[26] On March 26, the Central Route Red Army occupied the Changting area and under Mao's guidance, conducted the political mobilization of the local populace. Seeing little progress in actual military action, Zhou Enlai pushed hard for Mao to stop the political mobilization and actually engage the enemy by moving south to Zhangzhou.[27] The Red Army moved its operations south, and attacked the Forty-Ninth NRA Division in Fujian province. On April 10, the Red Army seized Longyan and destroyed one brigade of the Forty-ninth NRA Division. The Fifth NRA Corps attempted to reinforce the Forty-ninth Division, but lost two brigades to the Red Army. The Red Army continued its march south, and on April 20 took Zhangzhou by defeating the Forty-ninth NRA Division. At Zhangzhou, 1,675 prisoners were taken, 2,000 rifles, a couple of artillery pieces, 13,000 rounds of ammunition, two airplanes, and more than one million yuan. Additionally, supplies of food, salt, and oil were also confiscated for the Red Army.[28]

After the success of Zhangzhou, Mao sent a telegram in late April to

Zhou Enlai requesting the Red Army move back to Jiangxi to focus on consolidating and improving operations in the Soviet area. Mao believed that the Red Army had made great gains at Zhangzhou, but did not have the manpower or support in the area to establish a strong defense against a determined NRA force. Instead, the Red Army should conduct minimum operations in the Fujian area, such as establishing local militia and guerrilla units.[29] The CCP ruled against Mao's recommendation, and on June 5, 1932, ordered the Red Army to conduct offensive operations against the Guangdong military forces near Southern Jiangxi.[30] Once completing operations in Guangdong, it would move north up the Gan River valley, and attack Ganzhou, Ji'an, Zhangshu, and Nanchang, in order to gain the initial revolutionary success in Jiangxi province.[31] The Red Army reorganized its forces, placing the First, Third, and Fifth Red Army Corps under the First Front Red Army banner, and then moved into Guangdong. From late June into early July, the Red Army conducted offensive operations and seized Nanxiong and Shuikou, defeating fifteen Guangdong NRA brigades and expanded the Chinese Soviet into Guangdong.[32]

Even with the string of offensive victories, Mao remained a vocal opponent to the plans, constantly submitting his recommendations to the Central Military Committee to adjust the attack. On July 25, Mao and Zhu De sent a joint communique to the CCP requesting a change to the current strategy. Instead of immediately attacking the Gan River cities of Ji'an and Zhangshu, the Red Army should conduct clearing operations on the eastern part of the valley, focusing on Le'an and Yihuang. Initially, the Central Committee was against Mao's proposal since he represented the erroneous "right line." However, Zhou Enlai intervened and pushed for Mao's proposal given his military experience on the ground.[33] In August, the First Front Red Army held a conference and confirmed the plan to attack Le'an and Yihuang. Shortly after, the Red Army seized the city, and defeated the Twenty-seventh NRA division near Le'an, taking 5,000 prisoners, 4,000 rifles, twenty machine guns, twenty artillery pieces, and three wireless communication sets.[34]

After the victory, the Red Army leadership contemplated its next attack to Ji'an. However, after some consideration, Mao sent a communique on September 25, 1932, stating that an attack on Ji'an was not prudent given the strong enemy presence in the Ji'an area, and instead his units would conduct political mobilization operations in the Le'an-Yihuang area.[35] The Central Committee had had enough of Mao's insubordination. By this time, the Twenty-eight Bolsheviks had gained enough power and began stripping Mao of key positions within the Red Army. He was first removed from the Military Committee of the Central Bureau of the Soviet Areas. Later, in October 1933, an emergency conference was called at Ningdu to discuss future Red Army operations, especially as word came of another impending KMT campaign.[36] Conference attendees, who included Zhou

Enlai, Zhu De, Peng Dehuai, Chen Yi, and Liu Bocheng, all confirmed that the new offensive line was the Red Army strategy and viewed the Red Army as fully capable to switch to offensive operations outside the Soviet. Additionally, the party condemned Mao's conservative military strategy as inappropriate and outdated.[37] Zhou Enlai saw the Red Army's inaction as procrastination and a sign of Mao's obstinate attitude toward CCP-directed operations. Zhou continued to push for "expanding Soviet territory swiftly, engaging the enemy on KMT territory, bringing Jiangxi and its neighboring Soviet areas together by force, taking key cities in the Gan valley, including Nanchang, Ji'an, Ganzhou, and Pingxiang, so as to achieve preliminary successes in one or more provinces."[38]

After the Ningdu conference, the Red Army continued its offensive operations, expanding its attack on Jianning, Lichuan, and Taining in October. In November, the First Front Army seized the Jiangxi county seats of Jinxi and Zixi. In the short term, the battlefield successes helped the CCP expand the Soviet in the eastern Gan valley, yet at the same time, it took away from the Red Army's ability to prepare for the upcoming Fourth Extermination Campaign.[39]

During these expansion operations, the KMT's suppression of the communists in Shanghai drove the Bolsheviks and other CCP members to the Jiangxi Soviet in late 1932.[40] Intermittent and insufficient financial support from the COMINTERN was another factor driving many of the urban communists to the rural areas.[41] Their arrival in the Jiangxi Soviet added tensions to the command and control of Red Army forces during the Fourth Extermination Campaign. The presence of the Central Committee also changed the tide of the communist movement, turning many members of the party and Red Army toward the left-leaning line. The Maoist adaptation of Marxist-Leninist theory was replaced by a more orthodox line following COMINTERN policies focused on the greater good of the Soviet Union.[42] Many of the Twenty-eight Bolsheviks moved to different Soviets almost soon after their arrival in the Jiangxi Soviet,[43] marking the beginning of a new phase of Central Committee leadership of the CCP.

Extermination Campaigns
Fourth Extermination Campaign

Before the start of the Fourth Extermination Campaign in 1933, the Red Army from the Jiangxi Soviet conducted expansion operations into Fujian and Guangdong. Other Red Army units in other communist base areas conducted similar operations in Hunan, Hubei, and Sichuan. The Soviet expansion became a large enough threat that Chiang Kai-shek refocused his military operations on the Red Army. In April 9, 1932, he created the Bandit Suppression Headquarters in Wuhan, placing He Yingqin as the commander.[44] Starting in June 1932, He Yingqin and a force of 500,000 soldiers conducted a brutal encirclement and suppression

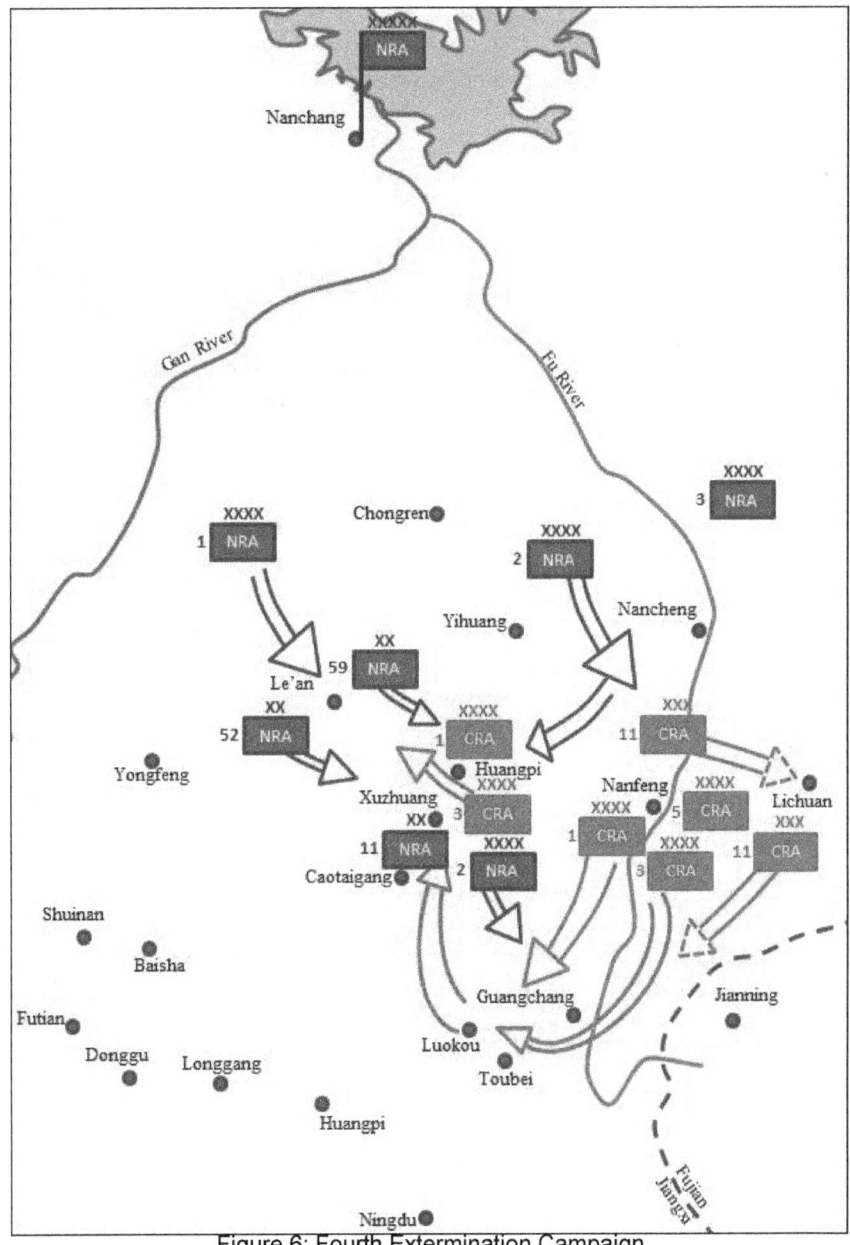

Figure 6: Fourth Extermination Campaign
Source: Created by author

campaign against the Hubei-Henan-Anhui and western Hubei-Hunan Soviet areas.[45] By November 1932, both the Hubei-Henan-Anhui and the western Hubei-Hunan Soviet fell. With these two areas completely cleared of communist insurgent forces, Chiang ordered He to shift operations to the Jiangxi Soviet.

In December 1932, Chiang Kai-shek shifted 400,000 soldiers and thirty divisions to the Central Soviet operation.[46] He even personally moved down to Nanchang to supervise the operation, with the forward headquarters in Fuzhou. The main force consisted of three columns, approximately 150,000 soldiers in twelve divisions, led by Chen Cheng.[47] The plan was to build a series of blockhouses as part of an effort to establish an economic blockade around the Soviet. Approximately 240,000 soldiers were allocated for the blockade, in addition to the main force, which brings the total force package to 400,000. Each flank was assigned 70,000 soldiers, approximately six divisions, to conduct blocking operations in the Jiangxi-Guangdong border area and the Fujian-Jiangxi Border area. Another 100,000 soldiers were used to conduct anti-guerrilla operations in northwest and northeast Jiangxi as well the southeast Hunan-southwest Jiangxi border area.[48] Once the blockade was set, the NRA would deploy the three columns south along separate routes converging on the Red Army's rear for a concentrated attack.[49] On the other side of the battlefield, the Red Army had expanded its size, and was currently at 70,000 strong.[50] The Red Army was based near Lichuan, and consisted of the First, Third, and Fifth Red Army Corps, along with the Eleventh, Twelfth, Twenty-first, and Twenty-second Red Armies.[51]

The Fourth Extermination Campaign coincided with the Red Army urban offensives. In December 1932, the next target city for the Red Army was Nancheng. The Central Committee gave orders to attack, but due to NRA reinforcements, the Red Army had to withdraw from the outskirts of Nancheng.[52] The next closest city for an attack was Nanfeng. Under pressure from the Central Committee to continue the urban offensive, the Red Army moved south and reached Nanfeng on February 1, 1933 and began encircling the city. On February 7, the Red Army besieged the city. For approximately one week, the Red Army faced stiff resistance as it attempted to break the city's defenses.[53] The NRA quickly dispatched the Central Route Army to reinforce the city and conduct a counterattack. With the stronger NRA force in the area on February 13, Zhou Enlai ordered the Red Army to finally withdraw from the area and moved to Luokou, near Huangpi, to reorganize and wait for an attack.[54]

During the withdrawal, the Red Army set a diversion to allow the main body to safely exfiltrate. Using a similar tactic from the Third Extermination Campaign, the Eleventh Red Army, pretending to be the Red Army's main force, deceived the NRA by attacking Lichuan.[55] Reacting to the attack as expected, the NRA moved its three columns to Lichuan in order to concentrate fires on the Red Army main effort. While moving to Lichuan, the first column, which included the Fifty-second and Fifty-ninth NRA divisions, became separated from the other two columns. On February 25, the two divisions moved west towards Huangpi along two routes separated by a mountain ridge. As they moved, their distance from the NRA Second and Third Columns became larger, making any mutual support ineffective. On February 27, the First and Third Red Army Corps and the Twenty-first Red Army used the rainy conditions to conduct a surprise attack on the Fifty-second NRA Division. The next day, the Fifth Red Army Corps and the Twenty-Second Red Army attacked the Fifty-ninth NRA Division in Huangpi. The unit was destroyed, with the commander of the Fifty-ninth NRA Division being captured.[56] After the victory, the Red Army moved back to Luokou to reorganize and prepare for another assault.

After the devastating loss, the NRA reorganized its forces into two columns and changed its strategy. Instead of moving in three separate columns, the NRA instead concentrated its forces in the center area to penetrate the Soviet.[57] On March 16, the two NRA columns began its advance. The Red Army moved swiftly around, using the Eleventh Red Army again for deception operations. The Eleventh Red Army executed a feint towards Guangchang, attracting the front column of NRA units in pursuit.[58] The action separated the two columns by 50 kilometers and isolated the rear column's Eleventh NRA Division near Caotaigang. On March 20, the First Front Army conducted a vicious attack near Xuzhuang, decimating the division, as well as a unit from the Ninth NRA Division.[59]

After the battle of Caotaigang, no other major battles occurred in the Fourth Extermination Campaign. For the remainder of March 1933, the Red Army conducted political operations near Le'an until NRA forces moved to Le'an to secure the city, forcing the Red Army to withdraw to the base areas.[60] In April, NRA forces began to withdraw from the Jiangxi Soviet area, ending the Fourth Extermination Campaign.[61] The NRA losses in the campaign were quite significant. The NRA lost three divisions, and 10,000 POWs were captured.[62] The Red Army collected 10,000 rifles, 300 new German machine guns and forty artillery pieces.[63] Another important result of the victory was the apparent validation of the Bolshevik-led Central Committee strategy, which silenced Mao and his many supporters, who were the strategy's biggest critics.

Bolshevik control of the Jiangxi Soviet

With effective control of the Red Army after the Fourth Extermination Campaign, the CCP adopted a series of measures to reform the Red Army so it could seize large cities in China. First, the CCP attempted to expand the Red Army's overall personnel strength. Starting in February 1933, the CCP launched a large recruiting drive to expand the Red Army. In addition, it incorporated all local militias into the main Red Army force. To pay for the expansion, the CCP adopted a sweeping change to the land distribution policy to generate revenue.[64] Under the guise of a land investigation, the CCP conducted political operations in the Soviet areas to complete land distribution in 80 percent of the Soviet area. During the distribution, the CCP attempted to raise almost one million yuan.[65] Throughout the summer of 1933, the CCP also focused on suppressing any dissidents and counterrevolutionaries, finding and arresting many of its opponents, effectively ending any resistance.[66]

One of the most famous critics to the Twenty-eight Bolshevik's policies was Luo Ming. In the spring of 1933, Luo Ming, then sectratary of the Fujian-Guangdong-Jiangxi Soviet Committee,[67] requested an exception to the policy. In his letter, Luo outlined the issues in his local area. The revolutionary attitude in the Fujian area was low, and the recent heavy recruiting drives and large tax collection had whittled away at the morale of the local people. He agreed to continue to support expanding the Red Army, but he did not want those units to leave the local area, and instead thought that they should stay for local defense. Given these issues, he proposed avoiding battle with the NRA forces unless they were forced and looked to scale back mobilization operations in his area.[68] While Luo Ming's request may have seemed reasonable, his position was similar enough to Mao's "retreatist," "lure the enemy in deep" strategy, that it gave the Bolsheviks an opportunity to leverage the situation. At the time, Mao's influence was still too great, and attacking Luo Ming was in essence a tangential approach to weakening Mao's power.[69] The CCP used the pejorative term "Luo Ming line" to describe any non-offensive strategy, and began a systematic purge of the Fujian-Guangdong-Jiangxi Soviet leadership.[70] The "Luo Ming line" became the slogan and term to describe any "right" leaning member who was against the Central Committee's strategy.

In the summer of 1933, the Red Army continued to experience many different changes. The Central Committee felt vindicated by the successful defeat of the Fourth Extermination Campaign, and continued to press the offensive line. The arrival of the Bolsheviks and Otto Braun, the COMINTERN military adviser, at the Jiangxi Soviet increased central oversight over the Red Army as they began to directly control military strategy. On May 8, the CCP passed a resolution separating the Central Military Council and the Red Army leadership. Zhu De and Zhou Enlai remained in charge of the Red Army; however, Bo Gu gained greater control of the military council and controlled the Red Army's strategy and its employment of the military.[71] Otto Braun would also play a large role in the strategy, leveraging his experience at Frunze Academy to push for the offensive.

The Red Army also reorganized its units to facilitate the execution of its new strategies. In June, the CCP divided the First Front Red Army into the Eastern Front Red Army and Central Red Army. Bo Gu and Braun believed the Red Army forces had sufficient firepower and strength, that it no longer needed to have mutually supporting operations, and instead the Red Army units could conduct independent operations in separate areas.[72] The Eastern Front Red Army consisted of the Third Red Army Corps, and was deployed to western Fujian. The Central Red Army, created from First

Red Army Corps, remained in the Central Soviet area.⁷³

Under the direction of the new Central Military Committee, the Eastern Front Red Army conducted expansion operations into Fujian after the NRA left the area. Peng Dehuai's force conducted a three-month expedition in Fujian, expanding the Soviet territory, collecting supplies – especially salt – and raising funds that helped the Red Army and the CCP meet many of its deficiencies.⁷⁴ Before the Fifth Extermination Campaign, the Central Soviet boasted having 60,000 square kilometers covering parts of three provinces.⁷⁵ Focused on the expansion of the Soviet, the Red Army did not keep its eye on the KMT as it prepared for another extermination campaign.

Fifth Extermination Campaign

In the late winter and early spring of 1933, the advance of the Japanese Kwantung Army deep across northern China temporarily diverted the attention of Chiang and the KMT military forces to the north. However, they still remained focused on the internal struggle with the Communists. Starting in July 1933, the KMT established a review team to examine the problems with the previous campaigns in order to identify key lessons and areas of improvement. The KMT also established division level training units to retrain its units, using the lessons from its assessments on how to properly attack the Red Army.⁷⁶ Additionally, they continued to integrate foreign advisers, especially from Germany, to improve tactics and strategies. The Germans proposed a more deliberate strategy to attrit the Communists in the Soviet. The first step was to establish an economic blockade. Raw materials and durable goods could not enter or leave the Soviet areas. Rice and salt were two commodities expressly banned from transportation. The second step was establishing a series of fortifications, basically blockhouses made of concrete, to provide fire support to offensive operations in nearby cities. As the NRA cleared areas and moved forward, the previous set of blockhouses was abandoned and new ones were built. Additionally, along lines of operation, roads were built in the rear areas to expedite logistical transports to the front. Some of these strategies had been used individually in previous campaigns with varying success. Now, the KMT also introduced political reforms that complemented the military strategy. Under the slogan, "Thirty Percent Military, Seventy Percent Political," the KMT, with the assistance of NRA forces, revived the *baojia* system to create local security teams and new village administrations.⁷⁷

To accomplish this strategy, the KMT increased the NRA forces deployed to Jiangxi. The new force strength was 700,000 broken into four areas supported by five air corps.⁷⁸ The NRA deployed its Northern Route NRA Army, consisting of thirty three divisions, along the Jishui, Jinzhi, Nangeng, and Le'an front.⁷⁹ The Southern Route NRA Army, made up of eleven Guangdong divisions and one independent regiment, established a blocking position along a line connecting the cities of Wuping, Anyuan,

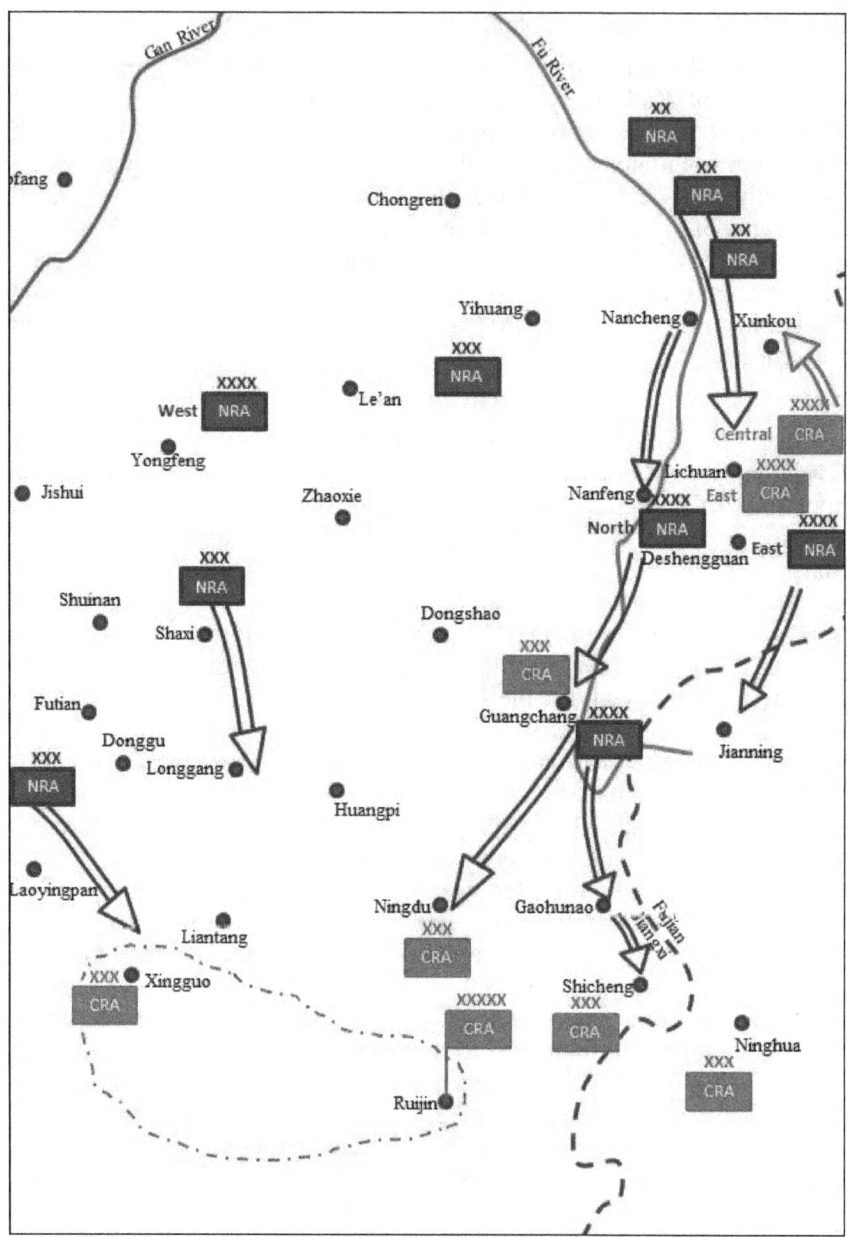

Figure 7: Fifth Extermination Campaign
Source: Created by author

Ganxian, and Shangyou.[80] On order, the Southern Route NRA Army would move the blocking positions north in coordination with other NRA forces to squeeze the Red Army. The Western Route NRA Army controlled nine Hunanese Divisions and three independent regiments that were responsible for blocking enemy forces from moving west of the Gan River.[81] The Fujian-Zhejiang-Jiangxi Region Headquarters was assigned eleven divisions and four security regiments to block any Red Army units from escaping to Northeast Jiangxi. With all these changes instituted, the NRA launched the Fifth Extermination Campaign.

When the NRA was ready to attack, it was too late for the Red Army to begin to prepare for the encirclement. The only positive area of improvement was the size of the Red Army. During the summer, the Red Army touted the slogan "Million Man Army" to recruit soldiers during its mobilization operations. By late October, the Red Army had reached 100,000.[82] However, with that many soldiers, the Red Army required even more supplies and equipment. With the Eastern Front Army in Fujian, the Central Front Army and the local populace did not start raising revenues and hoarding supplies, especially rice and salt, until late August. The lack of preparation would have deleterious effects in the future.

On September 25, 1933, the NRA sent three divisions south from Nanchang and attacked Lichuan. Within three days, the city fell, which surprised the CCP. The Central Front Red Army fell back and waited for the Eastern Front Red Army to rush back from Fujian to reinforce their position. On October 6, the Central and Eastern Front Red Armies combined forces and conducted a counterattack. The initial attack near Xunkou was successful, with the Red Army destroying three NRA brigades. However, future attempts were less successful. For two months, the Red Army attacked NRA blockhouses at Xiaoshi, Zixi, Huwan Bajiaoting, Yuangai Mountain, and Daxiongguan, but each attempt to break the line was unsuccessful. Using the concrete blockhouses as pillboxes, the NRA concentrated fires from new German machine guns, German artillery pieces, and aerial bombs on Red Army formations as they assaulted the line. In November 1933, the battles took a tactical pause as the Fujian Incident temporarily diverted the KMT's attention from the Jiangxi Soviet.[83]

On November 20, 1933, the KMT Nineteenth Route Army, in conjunction with the Fujian provincial government, rebelled against the KMT and set up an independent government.[84] The renegade unit had initially made a military alliance with the CCP in October. The initial agreement included a cease fire between the two sides, opening of economic and political dialogue, and the release of political prisoners.[85] However, after the revolt, both sides failed to meet any of the agreed points. The Fujian renegade government did not achieve any of the reforms or requests either.[86] Members of the Central Committee attacked the Fujian rebels as being fakes.[87] Other communists, including Mao and Zhu De, maintained a more positive outlook towards the rebels. The Red Army even pushed forces from the First Front Army to the outskirts of western Fujian, but no material support was ever sent to the rebels. The KMT moved quickly to Fujian and put down the rebellion by January 20, 1934. In response to Mao's alleged support for the alliance, The CCP punished him during the summer of 1934, placing him on probation, and effectively terminating his influence on the Red Army until the Long March.[88]

During this same time, the Revolutionary Military Council held a meeting to discuss its plan of attack. Braun took to the stage and pushed for a strong offense to defeat the KMT. Stating that the golden age of guerrilla warfare in China was over, the Red Army must now conduct a full offensive against the NRA's positions. The "lure the enemy in deep" strategy was replaced by "defending against the enemy outside the Soviet" and the holding of every inch of territory.[89] In January 1934, the Second All Soviet Congress was held and the Congress passed a series of resolutions to focus the Red Army on its upcoming tasks during the Fifth Extermination Campaign. The resolutions reiterated Braun's offensive strategy, and attacked the previous Maoist line of "active defense." The CCP adopted a new strategy for the Red Army. Building on the original strategy of attacking outside the Soviet, Otto Braun proposed using "short, swift thrusts," which employed repeated infantry assaults to overwhelm and defeat the NRA line of blockhouses. He also pushed for the continued recruitment of the "million men Red Army" and discussed system of conscription to fill its ranks.[90]

After the Fujian Incident, the NRA restarted operations from the Northern Front. The NRA established a line of blockhouses from Lichuan to Le'an, and began a methodical clearing operation south towards Ruijin with thirty-five NRA divisions.[91] Its first target was the city of Guangchang, which was halfway between Nanchang and Ruijin. The NRA's Eastern Front also began its movement west. The Fujian incident actually benefited the NRA, forcing it to reorganize and move forces to the east. The Eastern Route NRA Army was reorganized with the remnants of the Nineteenth Route NRA Army, making it a total of fourteen divisions, to conduct operations from Western Fujian.[92] By March 1934, the NRA Northern and Eastern Fronts linked up by Deshengguan, Jiangxi Province, and began a coordinated movement towards Guangchang.

In response to the NRA movement towards Guangchang, the Red Army built a series of fortifications and trenches to defend the territory. On April 9, the NRA began its attack on Guangchang, deploying Third Route NRA Army's ten divisions from Nanfeng, with artillery and aircrafts providing covering fire. The NRA forces moved south along both sides of the Xu River leading up to Guangchang. The Northern Route NRA Army established blockhouses on one side of the river, before advancing and clearing the other side, alternating on each bank as it moved south. The operation took about two weeks for the NRA to push down the river and reach Guangchang.[93] By April 23, 1934, the NRA broke through the Red Army's lines of defense and occupied the high ground surrounding

Guangchang. The Red Army retreated to the city and constructed more fortified defenses and trench lines. On April 27, 1934, the NRA conducted artillery and air bombardments, breaking the Red Army's wooden fortifications and trench lines. The next day, the NRA invaded the city and Guangchang fell, forcing the Red Army to retreat south.[94] The Red Army lost 5,093 soldiers, approximately 20 percent of the fighting force at Guangchang, whereas the NRA only sustained 2,000 casualties.[95]

After Guangchang, the NRA continued its march from all four directions. From the west, Western Front NRA forces occupied both Shaxi and Longgang by May 1. On the eastern front, Eastern Route NRA forces continued to push through and seized Jianning on May 16. By June the CCP felt the pressures of the attacks. The combination of the blockade and *baojia* worked to drain away local support for the CCP. The attrition style battle also began to decrease the quality of leadership and the level of experience in the Red Army. The lines were increasingly filled by inexperienced soldiers who, under pressure, often deserted, further degrading the Red Army's effectiveness. The lack of supplies and food further reduced the Red Army morale and support for the offensive line among the public. Support for the offensive line slowly ended, even within military and party publications.[96] Magazines began promoting the expansion of guerrilla operations to conserve resources. Recruitment campaigns to replenish losses made little difference as the superior NRA strategy continued to slowly strangle the Soviet and shrink it from seventeen counties to ten.[97]

In the summer of 1934, the Red Army began to look at new strategies. It established a new defensive perimeter from Ninghua to Ningdu to Xingguo. In May, the Central Committee held a meeting and decided the current offensive strategy was not working, which most likely would require the Red Army to evacuate the Soviet. The Committee requested permission from the COMINTERN to change strategy, which was approved a few days later with the emphasis that the CCP's main task was to protect the combat strength of the Red Army. While the COMINTERN approved the strategy, Braun and Bo Gu had a different plan of accomplishing it.[98] Instead of planning for the immediate withdrawal of the Soviet, they pushed for a final struggle, calling for everyone to give their maximum effort to defend the Soviet and achieve victory. Besides the change in slogan, the Red Army also continued its strong positional defensive strategy, creating wooden blockhouses and trenches to defend the territory. The CCP also authorized the expansion of guerrilla warfare on all fronts to defeat the NRA.[99]

The NRA conducted another offensive in July, targeting the city of Shicheng, set between Ninghua and Ningdu as its penetration point. The two sides engaged in a bitter struggle along this final defense line for about a month. In early August, the Red Army delivered a strong counterattack against the NRA at the battle of Gaohunao, causing more than 4,000 NRA casualties. However, the Red Army also suffered large losses and was forced to withdraw to the final defensive line just north of Shicheng. At Shicheng, the Red Army held the NRA to a stalemate. Finally, the NRA brought up twelve large howitzers to assist in the siege and finally broke through the line in August. The city of Shicheng ended up falling in October. The defense of Shicheng cost the Red Army 5,000 casualties, severely wounding it and forced the leadership to contemplate some drastic measures.[100] The Jiangxi Soviet was reduced to a small area surrounding Ruijin and Xingguo. Given all the casualties and the looming NRA attack on Ruijin, the Red Army executed a daring retreat from Jiangxi on October 10, 1934, ending the Fifth Extermination Campaign, and starting the Long March.

Analysis
Situational Assessment

During 1932 to 1934, the Red Army continued to adopt measures to expand and professionalize its forces. While its actions did improve the overall effectiveness of the unit, the Red Army was defeated by the NRA and forced to retreat from its home base as a result of the Fifth Extermination Campaign. Chinese Communist sources continue to blame the defeat of the Red Army on the Twenty-Eight Bolsheviks and Otto Braun's faulty strategy; however, the KMT and NRA deserve credit for their own adaptation and innovations during this period.[101] First, they conducted a series of after-action reviews to identify areas of improvement within the NRA from the Fourth Extermination Campaign. These lessons were incorporated into a greater reform plan led by German advisers, such as Hans von Seeckt and Alexander von Faulkenhausen.[102] The German advisers helped to reform the NRA by focusing on improving the training of its general staff, employment of modern military tactics, and acquisition of modern military equipment. While the primary goal was to create a force able to defeat Japanese aggression,[103] these reforms also helped to increase the combat effectiveness of the NRA against the Chinese Red Army.

Second, the NRA employed a counterinsurgency strategy that complemented its conventional warfare strategy. Starting in 1928, the KMT instituted the *baojia* system which stressed local responsibility for security and administration. Similar to other counterinsurgency strategies later used in Malaya and Dhofar, the NRA first cleared "Red" areas, and then established local administrations loyal to the KMT that were protected by a local militia.[104] The NRA was able to hold these cleared areas and block any Red Army or Chinese Communist infiltration. Many residents actually began to provide information and intelligence for NRA operations.[105] The *baojia* system also supported the economic blockade by providing sentries at the entrances of all the villages, which placed tremendous pressure on the Red Army and the local populace. Chiang and the KMT government also instituted political reforms under the "seventy percent political, thirty percent military" strategy to incorporate many of the disenfranchised Chinese during the Civil War and take support away from the communists. These efforts all helped to erode the local support necessary for the Red Army to conduct its "peoples' war."

Lastly, the NRA adopted a methodical, patient approach that attacked the biggest weaknesses of the Red Army. The Red Army did not have the necessary weapons to neutralize the NRA's consecutive lines of blockhouse fortifications. The Red Army also did not have the resources necessary to sustain a prolonged battle which the NRA worked to its advantage by conducting prolonged operations. The long campaign wore on the Red Army much more than it did on the NRA. Additionally, the NRA did not fall for any Red Army feints or ruses, and instead when threatened, withdrew back to the fortification lines where it held the advantage. Lastly, the NRA had a decisive advantage by having its largest deployment of forces to date in support of the Fifth Extermination campaign of close to a million soldiers. With that said, its adaptation and innovation in the Fifth campaign propelled it over the Red Army.

During the same period, the Red Army continued to face its own internal challenge during this time of uncertainty. While the Red Army continued to implement measures to reform and professionalize the Army, especially under the leadership of the Twenty-eight Bolshevik-controlled Central Committee, the basic challenges of soldier quality still pervaded the military. Increased political and military training, which will be discussed later in the chapter, were for the most part successful at addressing many of these issues. However, the gains were quickly neutralized by the crippling effects of Red Army expansion and high rate of casualties. The "Million Man Red Army" push enlisted mostly uneducated peasant recruits who needed intense political training and guidance. Red Army leaders continued to deal with low levels of effort and commitment to the political cause, and general lack of political understanding of the mission.[106] At the same time, the new offensive strategy was decimating Red Army units, and many new recruits were sent to the line immediately without much training. The lack of training and guidance inevitably lowered unit morale, and desertions increased. One report argued that the main cause for desertion was homesickness.[107] By the end of the Fifth Extermination Campaign, the Red Army was in a downward spiral where it could not generate the proper forces to fill its demand, and instead began sending untrained peasants to the line to fight, further degrading its combat effectiveness.[108]

Strategy

The arrival of the Twenty-eight Bolsheviks into the CCP brought about many changes to the overall Red Army military strategy. Much of the new CCP leadership's views were influenced by Stalinist Soviet ideology. This ideological view greatly differed from both Li Lisan and

Mao, though its differences with Mao were more profound and influenced by political factors. The ideological differences also created a large divide with the application of military tactics. However, the Bolsheviks and Mao maintained a similar line on the expansion and training of the Red Army, with both sides espousing the critical role of political training in developing a strong party army.[109] Ultimately, the CCP believed that the Red Army's success depended on the professionalization of the force, as this would ensure unity of command, a common understanding of the mission, and a strengthened ability to execute its mission.[110]

The biggest supporter of the Red Army's professionalization strategy was the Soviet Union. Stalin's interest in the Red Army was motivated by both external and internal factors. The Soviet Union perceived a looming threat from the Japanese as well as the Germans. Japan, Russia's long-time enemy, increased its presence in China, especially after the 1932 Japanese occupation of Manchuria, which directly threatened Russia's southern flank and its national security. The Soviets believed a large, professional Red Army, loyal to the Soviet Union, would be a strong bulwark against Japanese, and later on, German aggression. The Russian even reopened dialogue with the Nationalist government after years of silence to help ensure their Chinese flank remained secured.[111] For Stalin, the fight for control of the Chinese Communist Party was also part of a greater Soviet intraparty power struggle with Trotsky. Stalin's internal struggles with Trotsky hardened his communist views, which translated to a hard line within the COMINTERN and the new CCP. Through the COMINTERN and Bolsheviks, Stalin looked to consolidate his power by purging any Trotskyites in China. These Soviet political dynamics inevitably influenced the selection of Chinese political and military strategies that would negatively affect the Red Army.

On the surface, the Twenty-eight Bolshevik policies were very similar to Li Lisan. The two sides placed the urban proletariat as the pivotal character in the center of the communist revolution. Both believed that the combination of the proletarian revolutionary spirit and modern tactics would enable the Red Army to seize victory. They also believed that the conditions for the revolution were ready for expansion into the urban cities, and that the Red Army must move into the cities to help students and workers in the movement.[112] Wang Ming even stated that while the attack on Changsha in 1930 was a mistake, he did not believe the failure disproved the correct line of attacking urban centers.[113]

However, after further examination, the differences between the two sides were quite stark. Disagreements between the two factions began early. In June 1930, Li Lisan censured Wang Ming and Bo Gu and two other members of the group for attacking his plan.[114] Yet the differences were even deeper than simple political warfare. From an ideological perspective, the Bolsheviks disagreed with Li Lisan's definition of the bourgeois. In Wang Ming's *The Two Lines*, he believed all "capitalist bourgeois reformers were counterrevolutionary."[115] This interpretation expanded the definition to include the rich and middle-class peasants to be targeted during land reforms.[116] Another difference was the approach to attacking the urban centers. The two sides also viewed the role of the Red Army differently. Li Lisan maintained that the Red Army would assist the urban proletariat uprisings to overtake the cities, whereas the Bolsheviks viewed the Red Army as the sole force in seizing the metropolis.[117]

The differences between Mao and the Bolsheviks were great. Unlike Mao, the Bolshevik-led CCP rejected any alliance, pressing for the defeat of both the Nationalists and the Japanese.[118] In their eyes, there was no difference between the two; both were imperialists and an equal threat to the Soviet Union and the communist cause.[119] At the time, the Mukden Incident drove many nationalists and communists to pursue a new united front against Japanese Aggression. However, the CCP was expressly against it, as it pushed "for the overthrow of the agent of imperialism—the Guomindang."[120] Even when the Chinese Soviet government declared war on the Japanese on April 5, 1932, the party was very particular in its handling of the situation, issuing multiple policies denouncing Japanese aggression and Nationalist partnerships individually.[121]

The Bolsheviks also maintained a strong stance against Maoist military policy. They believed that an erroneous line of guerrillaism pervaded the Red Army, embodied by the "lure the enemy in deep" strategy. Wang Ming equated the strategy to an act of "retreat" or "escape."[122] The Bolsheviks pushed for a large expansion and professionalization of the Red Army to move away from the peasant mindset.[123] With the larger force, the Red Army could take the offensive, using Soviet offensive tactics to seize the urban centers and expand the Soviet.[124] Guerrilla warfare was not fully disavowed, though it was a task for the local militias in the rear and flank areas. Mao had a more pragmatic view on the ability of the Red Army soldier.[125] He understood that the Red Army did not have the technology to conduct these types of battles. Mao also believed that victory in itself was not necessarily the most important objective. He saw that the force must be sustainable after the victory, and second, spoils must greatly exceed the losses.[126]

In retrospect, the positional warfare and offensive strategy, promoted by Otto Braun and the Returned Students, was a poor strategy against the NRA. However, at the time, support for the strategy over Mao's "lure the enemy in deep" is quite understandable. The new offensive military strategy was based on the assumption that the Red Army was strong and capable of conducting attacks against the NRA. While the assessment may have been exaggerated, the victories against the Extermination Campaigns did bolster the self-esteem of the Red Army. The later success of the Red Army in opposing the Fourth Extermination Campaign further proved the capability of the Communist military forces.

The offensive strategy also moved away from the tactic of ceding territory, which was always a difficult proposition for the local populace. The CCP gained more support for its strategy by stating that the Red Army was strong enough now to defend the land and take the fight to the enemy, which allowed the locals to stay at home. That simple change engendered more support for their cause. On the flip side, Mao had a firm grasp on the local conditions and understood the negative impact of the Bolshevik policies on land redistribution. The Bolshevik position increased the burden on a larger share of the local populace and upset the delicate support necessary for conducting "people's war."[127] Mao and his supporters also sought to delay and obstruct large recruitment drives, arguing that the expansion was not and would be an unnecessary distraction to the local populace, who were already busy tending to the fields.[128]

The Bolshevik offensive strategy was also a more conventional strategy than Mao's mobile warfare concept. At the time, Mao's "lure the enemy in deep" and other mobile warfare strategies were revolutionary in China and still had many critics and skeptics. Even after the sound defeat of the Li Lisan line, the ability of the Bolsheviks and Otto Braun to resurrect a similar platform two years later shows the amount of support for a more conventional strategy.

Tactics

Within the new strategy, the Red Army incorporated old and new tactics to attack the enemy. In terms of old tactics, the Red Army still relied heavily on its strengths in intelligence collection and deception operations to gain an advantage over the NRA. However, with the arrival of the Twenty-eight Bolsheviks and Otto Braun, the Red Army shifted from its mobile defense strategy and began using "short, swift thrusts" as an offensive tactics against the NRA blockhouses in the Fifth Extermination campaign.

The Red Army continued to leverage some of its advantages from previous campaigns. Advances in signal intelligence, especially from collecting more wireless communication devices and the establishment of training schools, provided the Red Army with detailed knowledge of the NRA's movement during the Fourth Extermination Campaign.[129] The Red Army also continued to incorporate tactical intelligence into its operations. The Red Army continued to use plain-clothed soldiers, and even sent double agents into KMT units to collect intelligence and subvert units.[130] The level of detail during collection also was a strength of the Red Army. An example of the thoroughness of the Red Army tactical intelligence is an intelligence report on the KMT Seventy-ninth NRA Division. The report analyzed the origin and motivation of the NRA soldiers, and saw that many of the soldiers originated from the same area as their commander, which resulted in strong loyalties.[131] This discovery made the unit a less attractive target for subversion given the traditional Confucian hierarchal loyalty. The Red Army continued to conduct feints and deception operations during its operations. The Eleventh Red Army played the main effort on two separate occasions, with great effect. Additionally, the Red Army also sent fake communications to deceive NRA forces. While near Huangpi, NRA scouts "intercepted" a Red Army message, stating that the Red Army main forces were in Nanchang. The division units put down their guard while in the city, and were ambushed.

The biggest change to Red Army tactics was the introduction of Otto Braun's "short, swift thrusts. " Lin Biao defined the tactic as "those sudden fast raids launched against the enemy who comes out of their blockhouses to advance the line of fortifications by a small distance (specifically a distance of between 2½ to 5 kilometers or even less). These thrusts are launched to wipe out the main enemy forces at a time when the enemy has not yet stabilized its foothold."[132] While the tactics seemed straightforward, there were key differences in its application, especially between Braun's theoretical concept and Lin Biao's application.

First, the end goal of the tactics was very different. Braun's version was used as part of a greater strategy to protect Soviet territory. Instead of attempting to gain a decisive victory over the superior-numbered NRA forces, the Red Army would defend territory and gain small tactical victories that could be transformed into operational and strategic gains.[133] Lin Biao, on the other hand, viewed the tactic as one method to "annihilate the enemy, or win a victory in the entire battle."[134] His focus and goal was enemy-focused, and looked for a method to gain a decisive victory.

Second, Braun advocated a more deliberate strategy, with the Red Army establishing strong points with small groupings of fortifications. These zones provided defensive cover from artillery and air, and helped to set the conditions for the Red Army to conduct quick attacks against the NRA when they were away from the blockhouses.[135] During the actual attack, Braun believed the Red Army should first fix the NRA on its rear, flank, or even front, then conduct an attack to weaken the force in order disintegrate it.[136] Lin Biao had a very different take on the attack, seeing mobility and movement paramount for the Red Army during the thrusts. The Red Army's main defense was its secrecy.[137] It would move quietly and occupy high ground, only establishing hasty defensive structures for air and artillery defense.[138] Once the enemy moved into its area, the Red Army would encircle the forces, blocking its retreat, and quickly attack the enemy flanks before they could builds their fortifications.[139]

The last major difference was in its view of the pursuit. Braun advocated the pursuit, believing that it was the best way to translate a tactical victory into an operational or strategic success. On the other hand,

Lin Biao did not believe in the pursuit, because if his tactic was done effectively, the enemy would have no avenue to retreat, negating any need for a pursuit.[140]

Overall, the differences in interpretation of the tactics highlighted the difficulties in translating theoretical military concepts into application. Otto Braun's offensive concept was based on his own experiences and knowledge of Western military traditions. When applied to the Chinese battlefield, Lin Biao applied his own experiences to create his own version of "short, swift thrusts," which followed some of Mao's tactical points. Given the Red Army's situation, Lin Biao pursued a short, decisive victory that avoided any protracted battle with the NRA. He leveraged intelligence and terrain, especially through reconnaissance, to gain an advantage over the enemy. Lastly, his focus remained on the enemy, rather than on securing territory, allowing his unit to conduct battle on the best terrain. While the localization of the "short, swift thrusts" did not give the Red Army the decisive advantage it needed to defeat the NRA, it demonstrated how the Red Army continued to adapt ideas to the local conditions to succeed in battle.

Organization

During this period, the Red Army continued to consolidate the organization in order centralize control under the Central Committee. The Red Army leadership saw some issues with professionalism within the Army and insisted that party control was lacking, which led to breakdowns in discipline.[141] To correct these issues, the Red Army standardized unit structures across both the regular Red Army forces and local militia units to ensure uniformity across all ranks. These measures were critical in supporting the rapid expansion of the Red Army as it raised additional forces to fight the NRA in the Fifth Extermination Campaign.

The major reorganization occurred in the summer of 1933. To accommodate the push to create the "Million Man Red Army," the Revolutionary Military Committee passed a reorganizational plan for its forces. Under the new task organization established in June 1933, the Red Army had a total of five Red Army Corps: First, Third, Fifth, Seventh, and Ninth Army Corps. First Red Army Corps had the First Red Army Division, Second Red Army Division, and Third Red Army Division. The Third Red Army Corps had the Fourth Red Army Division, Fifth Red Army Division, and Sixth Red Army Division. The Fifth Red Army Corps had the Thirteenth and Fourteenth Red Army Divisions.[142] In October 1933, the Seventh and Ninth Red Army Corps stood up as Red Army units.[143] A sixth Red Army Corps, the Eighth Red Army Corps, was added in September 1934.[144] Additionally, independent provincial armies were designated as Red Army units to increase the ranks. The Fujian Military Region's Nineteen Army and Twelfth Army became the Thirty-fourth Red

Army Division (later attached to Fifth Red Army Corps) and First Red Independent Brigade, respectively. The South Jiangxi Military Region's Twenty-third Army became the Twenty-second Red Army Division.[145]

Besides changes to the organizational chart, the Revolutionary Military Committee pushed standardization of units across the Red Army. Building on the three-three-three system first introduced in 1930, the Red Army established complete standardization of its unit structures. From the corps level down to platoon level, each headquarters maintained three subordinates. In other words, a corps had three divisions, which had three brigades, all the way down to platoon level.[146] The standardization of the unit structure required a cross-leveling of equipment and personnel, and during the summer of 1933, the Red Army transferred equipment and personnel to ensure each unit was at the prescribed strength. While the action helped to establish an equal standard across military units, it also served to enforce central control over units. Before 1933, some units had more personnel and equipment than other units, giving the commander more influence and power. Additionally, certain commanders and commissars were able to hide within these units and exert influence while remaining out of the Central Committee's purview.[147] By establishing a standardized unit structure, the Revolutionary Military Committee and Central Committee had greater control and authority over the units by breaking old traditional relationships within Red Army units.

The lack of uniformity also pervaded local militia units within the Red Army which resulted in some large disparities. Formations, equipment, commands, organizational structures, and regulations were uneven among units, which often led to problems with compliance to superior orders. In 1932, the Revolutionary Military Committee began standardizing independent regiments and local guerrilla units. Some independent regiments became Red Army main force units, and were issued Red Army equipment and uniforms. Their original equipment was handed down to the local militia units, increasing the combat effectiveness of both the independent regiments and local militia forces.[148] The Red Army also established a standard table of organization for the guerrilla units and vanguard youths. Guerrilla units also adopted a 3-3-3 organizational structure, with each company maintaining three platoons of three squads. The vanguard youths used a more flexible structure, where there could be three to five platoons in a company, and three to five squads in a platoon.[149] All these changes helped to integrate the local militia, guerrilla units, CY units, and independent regiments into the Red Army, and make the transition into the Red Army main force quicker and easier.

One of the biggest changes in organization was the formalization and standardization of logistical units within the Red Army. The drive for standardization and professionalization of logistical units became more acute after the Third Extermination Campaign. The sheer size of the Jiangxi Soviet required the Red Army to improve its supply depots and supply route operations. The Red Army created three types of supply depots: central, large, and medium size, with transportation units assigned to each depot to help move freight and supplies. Additionally, the Red Army established categories for supply routes, designating certain routes as main, supplementary, and temporary routes for transport.[150] Many of the transportation units were either local citizens or local militia units. For the battle of Zhangzhou against the NRA's Fourth Extermination Campaign, the Red Army hired more than 10,000 workers to transport more than one million kilograms of food and salt.[151] The Red Army also developed its own weapons and supplies factories within the Soviet. The main factory was in Xingguo, which produced weapons and ammunition for the Red Army. From 1931 to 1934, the Xingguo factory produced more than 40,000 rifles, 200 machine guns, 100 artillery pieces, more than four million rounds of ammunition, and six million grenades.[152] The Red Army also created an import and export business and traded local commodities such as bamboo, wood, paper, tobacco, tea oil, tungsten ore, and coal in exchange for kerosene, salt, cotton, cloth, and medicine. The trade helped raise revenue for the Red Army and provided the Red Army with ample supplies of necessary goods. With all these developments, the Red Army recognized the importance of logistics, and in June 1933, the Revolutionary Military Committee established the Logistics Departments at the Central and Front Army level to specifically manage all supplies and transportation.[153]

Training

From 1932 to 1934, the Red Army expanded its military education system, providing basic, advanced, and specialty training for its forces. Its flagship institution, the Red Academy, led by Liu Bocheng, was a strong force in professionalizing the Red Army through its training programs. Under Liu's lead, the Red Academy established a comprehensive curriculum to address the educational needs of the junior-level Red Army leader.

The curriculum was a three-month program that ran every day from six in the morning to nine at night, covering military, political, and cultural classes. Sixty percent of the Red Army officers' coursework was military classes; conversely, 60 percent of political commissars and bureaucrats' coursework was political classes, ensuring both groups received a focused education.[154] The military classes taught at the Red Academy were designed to be a comprehensive overview of key basic tasks that connected theory into practice.[155] Much of military theory taught in the Red Academy was based primarily on Soviet doctrine, though influences from Japan and Germany were also present. Specialty classes in communications, engineering, and logistics were also created at the Red Academy. Political classes at the Red Academy covered topics such as Imperialism in China, the Chinese Communist Party and the Chinese Revolution, the class struggle, land reforms, military reforms, Soviet reforms, and political work.[156] Besides classes, the Red Academy used the school newspapers,[157] singing, political discussion groups, speeches, and reports for political training and propaganda. The cultural classes were basic education classes intended to increase the literacy and competency of the students. About one-third of the Red Academy students were illiterate when they arrived at the school, forcing the Red Army to conduct an intensive educational training program. The classes focused on recognizing simple characters, progressing to geography and science, then to mathematics. The purpose of these classes was to develop within each student the skills to properly write letters, formal notes, orders, and reconnaissance surveys.[158] An example of the development in literacy training is a comparison between basic character readers from 1932 and 1934. The reading book used initially in 1932, as described in a previous chapter, was mainly focused on political slogans and propaganda as a way to indoctrinate new recruits. The 1934 edition not only covered political slogans, but also had basic characters and classes, such as numbers, cardinal directions, seasons, and time. The 49 lessons also covered hygiene, discipline, and government organizations. These books were directed at a more basic level training the soldiers how to act at the most elementary level, rather than providing abstract communist concepts.[159]

The Red Academy also pushed its curriculum to the greater Red Army through publications. In summer 1932, the Red Academy published more than 6,000 copies of nine manuals that were distributed across the Red Army.[160] The Political Department published at least six books for distribution.[161] It also published periodicals that covered military and political topics, giving key Red Army leaders ways to discuss tactics and strategies.[162] One example in particular is the collection of articles published in the *Red Battlefield* dated June 1933. In the collection, there were five translated articles from Germany, Russia, and Japan discussing mountain warfare tactics. Zhu De wrote an article covering how to study mountain warfare. Other topics in articles included attacking forces in defense, pursuit and attacks, withdrawals, feints, and cavalry raids.[163]

Given the educational background of the students, the Red Academy faculty employed different pedagogical methods to gain the highest comprehension from the students. Some of its methods were influenced by the Soviet Union as the instructors tried to maintain students' interest in the material.[164] In May 1932, the Red Academy published guidance for teachers. All teachers were required to publish a syllabus and outline before class. Teachers were to encourage students to discuss topics during review time at night to increase comprehension. Key points on certain lessons were to be repeated multiple times to help students remember. Class materials should connect theory with current practice. Teachers were encouraged to use visual aids and models to aid their instruction. Before conducting exercises, the class should conduct rehearsals on sand tables. During practice, teachers should ask questions to students to stimulate thought and test comprehension. Lastly, teachers were directed to help students connect all the lessons and practices along the common theme of training to ensure maximum comprehension.[165]

One of the key pedagogical methods of the Red Academy was its practical exercises. The employment of practical exercises was twofold. First, they helped link the theoretical material taught in class with practical application in the field. Second, they also helped to retain the students' attention by maintaining their interest through action. The scope of the practical exercises increased over time. Starting with the second class, Red Academy students participated in four large military exercises. The third class increased the training by conducting platoon level offensive and defensive operations, even conducting mock battles. The fourth class conducted exercises that incorporated local militias into the operations. By the sixth class, the Red Academy students were working Front Army level exercises, incorporating military maneuvers, logistics, and intelligence into the exercises.[166] Another instruction method was using guest instructors and lecturers. The Red Academy invited Red Front Army and Red Army Corps leaders to discuss their experiences and training to help add relevance to the course. Additionally, key Central Committee leaders visited the school, to include Mao Zedong, Zhou Enlai, and Zhu De, to name a few.[167]

Like the previous training schools, the Red Army Academy students and faculty were always prepared to conduct combat operations at a moment's notice, especially during the Extermination Campaigns. The Red Army counted on the students and faculty to bolster their combat ranks when needed. The school maintained a military organizational structure of platoons, companies, and battalions to facilitate command and control outside the school.[168] The conditions at the Red Academy were similar to other schools. The combined deleterious effects of sustained combat operations, enemy economic blockades, and few revenue sources kept teaching materials and supplies in low supply. With that said, morale at the school was reported to be quite high. The Red Academy maintained social programs with singing, dancing, games, and performances to make up for any material inadequacies.[169]

By October 1933, the Red Army had graduated six classes with more than 11,000 graduates.[170] Approximately two-thirds of the graduates returned to the Red Army, and about one-third went to local base areas to assist in training and administration. Around the same time, the NRA's Fifth Extermination Campaign pushed the demand for more trained officers as part of its greater "Million Man Red Army" drive. The CCP increased its requirements for the Red Academy, pushing the school to train and graduate 10,000 officers each year, a tall order given its meager resources. To help the Red Academy meet these requirements, the Revolutionary Military Council issued "Order Regarding Changes at the Red Academy" on October 17, 1933. The order authorized a complete reorganization of the Red Army military education system to help meet the training demand. First, the Red Academy's advanced program was changed to create the Red Army War College, a school focused on training and developing leaders at the brigade and division level. Some members of the sixth class and all the students from the Red Academy's seventh class formed the cadre for two new infantry schools.[171] The artillery, engineer, machine gun, air defense, and anti-armor training units were also detached from the Red Academy to create the Specialty Branch School. Lastly, the guerrilla training unit within the Academy created its own Guerrilla Training School.

The Red Army War College opened its doors at Ruijin in October 1933. Its mission was to develop upper echelon Red Army leaders. The Red Academy had done a good job at developing lower and middle level leaders, and the Red Army wanted to expand to the higher levels in order to create a leadership able to meet both present and future challenges. The college had three major departments: training department, political department, and economics department. Besides these three departments, the Red Army War College also maintained a high-command department, advanced politics department, general staff department, logistics department, advanced marksmanship unit, and survey and map making department.[172]

Initially, the Red Army War College had difficulties in its operations. The teaching staff was unprepared for classes, and the curriculum they used sometimes was irrelevant to the current fight. Students complained that the teachers were often slow to respond to students' questions, and some teachers did not even supervise training. Students were also guilty of poor behavior, with many of them arriving tardy or unprepared for class.[173]

The school graduated three classes during its one year of operation with approximately 200 students per class.[174] Each class of students attended core courses in military and political activities, similar to the Red Academy. The military classes included infantry combat regulations, squad to brigade level training and basic knowledge, and marksmanship.[175] The political classes included how to create political parties, the history of social development, and political work within the Red Army.[176] Some of these classes were taught by senior leaders. Mao Zedong, Zhou Enlai, Zhu De, Liu Bocheng, Liu Shaoqi, and Deng Xiaoping came to the Red Army War College to teach classes.

By August 1934, the pressures from the Fifth Extermination Campaign had taken a toll on the college and the fourth class did not start. With the Long March looming near, the faculty of the Red Army War College was transferred to the Red Army Cadre Unit, and moved with the forces out of the Jiangxi Soviet in October, effectively ending the short tenure of the Red Army War College.

At the same time it established the Red Army War College, the Red Army created the Specialty Branch School for its engineers, artillery, and machine-gun unit leaders. The instructors came from either of two backgrounds. Some instructors received their training from the Red Academy and gained practical experience in Red Army units. Other instructors were former NRA soldiers who possessed technical and tactical knowledge on the specialized equipment.[177] Initially, the Revolutionary Military Council viewed the program as a very elite school, and started in February 1934 to restrict admissions to only the most qualified students. However, because of low number of qualified students, the Revolutionary Military Committee lowered the standards in June 1934 to gain a wider pool of students.[178] Because of the overall low educational background of the students, the Red Army Specialty Branch School adopted a more hands-on instructional approach to overcome any illiteracy obstacles. Many of the classes were done outside where the soldiers learned the tasks while doing them, in order to keep them engaged, and increase comprehension. Specialty equipment was also on short supply, since most of it was being used on the front line. The Specialty Branch School did, however, have a Krupps artillery piece confiscated during the first attack on Changsha. The weapon piece doubled as not only the only artillery weapon system available for training, but also as a historical example of the Chinese revolution and the Red Army's path towards modernization.[179]

In 1934, the Red Army began feeling the strong effects of the Nationalist's new strategy. The Red Army's ranks increased with new recruits as causalities mounted. To ensure that new recruits stayed loyal and in place, the Red Army paired old veterans with new recruits. The purpose of the policy was twofold. First, the veteran could mentor and train the new recruit on tactics he had learned on the field. Second, the veteran soldier also filled supervisory role to ensure the new recruit would not desert or turn on the Red Army.[180]

Conclusion

From 1932 to 1934, the Red Army reached its peak in terms of size and professionalization, only to be defeated by a superior NRA force. With the rise of the Twenty-eight Bolsheviks to power, the Red Army adopted a more aggressive, offensive strategy. While the strategy would later prove to be a poor choice, the strategy pushed a series of reforms that helped to professionalize the Red Army. During this period, the Red Army almost doubled in size to six army corps. Within the corps and even to the local militia groups, all Red Army units were standardized to ensure uniformity and centralize command and control. The Red Army also established the Red Academy and Red Army War College, as well as specialty schools to train and develop its officers. These changes helped the Red Army achieve victory over the NRA in the Fourth Extermination Campaign and expand the Soviet into four provinces. Yet, the NRA also adapted and innovated after its loss, and applied a superior strategy against the Red Army. Without the necessary heavy weapons or supplies, the Red Army was unable to stop the methodical encirclement of the Jiangxi Soviet during the Fifth Extermination Campaign. In October 1934, the Red Army made a daring escape, retreating from the Jiangxi Soviet to protect its forces and started the Long March. While the Red Army was defeated, it was not broken, for the foundations for a professional military force were established during this time. It was now up to the leadership to survive and live to fight another day.

Notes

1. There is debate on the actual twenty-eight members of the group. Price cited the following names: (1) Qin Bangxian (Bo Gu), (2) Chen Shaoyu (Wang Ming), (3) Zhang Qinqiu (Madam Shen Zemin), (4) Zhang Wentian (Luo Fu), (5) Chen Changhao, (6) Chen Yuandao, (7) Zhu A'gen, (8) Zhu Zishun, (9) He Kechuan (Kai Feng), (10) He Zishu, (11) Xia Xi, (12) Xia Tefu, (13) Li Zhousheng, (14) Li Yuanjie, (15) Meng Qingshu (Madam Chen Shaoyu), (16) Shen Zemin, (17) Sun Jimin, (18) Song Panmin, (19) Du Zuoxiang (Madam Chen Changhao), (20) Wang Jiaxiang, (21) Wang Baoli, (22) Wang Shengdi, (23) Wang Shengyong, (24) Wang Yuncheng, (25) Yang Shangkun, (26) Yin Jian, (27) Yuan Jiayong, and (28) Yue Sheng, See Jane L. Price, *Cadres, Commanders, and Commissars* (Boulder, CO: Westview Press, 1976), 100. Rue contended that no comprehensive list existed, and only identified sixteen members of the twenty-eight. See John E. Rue, *Mao Tse-tung in Opposition: 1927-1935* (Stanford: Stanford University Press, 1966), 7-8.

2. The two-year program included classes in Russian language and history, along with Marxist, Leninist, and Stalinist communist theories. Price, *Cadres, Commanders, and Commissars*, 89-93.

3. Price, *Cadres, Commanders, and Commissars*, 95-96, 100.

4. The majority of the Central Committee disagreed with Li Lisan's policies, but other political considerations and intraparty dynamics prevented the wholesale condemnation of the Li's leftist deviation. Rue, *Mao Tse-tung in Opposition*, 239-240.

5. Rue, *Mao Tse-tung in Opposition*, 242.

6. Rue gave some anecdotal stories of betrayal between two factions within the CCP. One story was that Wang Ming alerted the British Police of a secret meeting in Shanghai. Key Li Lisan supporters and enemies of the Twenty-eight Bolsheviks were arrested, turned over to the KMT, and executed. Rue, *Mao Tse-tung in Opposition*, 243.

7. Rue, *Mao Tse-tung in Opposition*, 247.

8. Rue, *Mao Tse-tung in Opposition*, 249.

9. Zhou Enlai's role in the fight between Mao and left leaning Communist party members remains uncertain. Almost all western scholarship viewed the Zhou-Mao relationship as antagonistic, with Zhou leading the charge to push forward the "offensive" line and the removal of Mao from positions of power. See Pingfeng Chi, "The Chinese Red Army and the Kiangsi Soviet" (Ph.D dissertation, George Washington University, 1977), 145-146; John P. Harrison, *The Long March to Power: A History of the Chinese Communist Party, 1927-72* (New York: Praeger Publishing, 1972), 229; Chong Kun Yoon, "Mao, The Red Army, and the Chinese Soviet Republic" (Ph.D dissertation, The American University, 1968), 219. This argument is most likely based on Gong Chu's autobiographic account of the time in *Wo yu Hongjun* [The Red Army and I]. The other perspective is more conciliatory, seeing Zhou Enlai as a mediator and middleman between the two sides during the offensives, with Zhou often supporting Mao's position once presented with the realities of the situation. See Rue, *Mao Tse-tung in Opposition*,

251; Shaoqun Huang, *Zhong qu feng yun: Zhong yang Su qu di yi zhi wu ci fan "wei jiao" zhan zheng shi* [Zhong qu Feng yun: the History of the First through Fifth Extermination Campaigns in the Central Soviet] (Beijing: Zhong gong zhong yang dang xiao chu ban she, 1993) (referred to as *ZQFY*), 175-189.

10. Ilpyong J. Kim, *The Politics of Chinese Communism: Kiangsi under the Soviets* (Berkeley: University of California Press, 1973), 97.

11. Yoon, "Mao, The Red Army, and the Chinese Soviet Republic," 160.

12. See Tony Saich, ed. *The Rise to Power of the Chinese Communist Party* (Armonk, NY: M.E. Sharpe, 1996), 558-566.

13. Saich, *The Rise to Power*, 561.

14. Saich, *The Rise to Power*, 560.

15. Saich, *The Rise to Power*, 563. The targeted cities were Nanchang, Fuzhou, and Ji'an. The areas needing to be connected were the Jiangxi Soviet, Fujian-Guangdong-Jiangxi, northeast Jiangxi, Hunan-Hubei-Jiangxi, and Hunan-Jiangxi areas. The other Soviet areas to be linked were Henan-Hubei-Anhui Soviet, northeast Anhui, east Hubei, Huei-Henan border, upper and lower reaches of the Yangtze River, and the Beijing-Hankou Railway. Saich, *The Rise to Power*, 564.

16. Harrison, *The Long March to Power*, 229.

17. Saich, *The Rise to Power*, 515.

18. Saich, *The Rise to Power*, 563.

19. Saich, *The Rise to Power*, 566.

20. *History of Development of War in China*, 869.

21. *ZQFY*, 178.

22. According to *ZQFY*, Zhou Enlai was empathetic to Mao's view. He even expressed his own reservations when he arrived at the Jiangxi Soviet in December, but was overruled by the Central Committee. They ordered the Red Army, at a minimum, to attack one city, in accordance with the new strategy. See *ZQFY,* 177-178.

23. *ZQFY*, 178. Ganzhou city walls were bordered on three sides from the Gan River, providing a strong defensive perimeter for the peninsula city. Within the walls, the NRA Twelfth Division had two divisions of 3,000 men protecting the city, augmented by local and private militias, bringing the total military force to about 8,000. Reinforcements of two NRA divisions in Ji'an and twenty NRA regiments in Nanxiong were not far away either.

24. *History of Development of War in China,* 869; *ZQFY,* 177-181.

25. Peter Williams Donovan, "The Chinese Red Army in the Kiangsi Soviet, 1931-1934" (PhD dissertation, Cornell University 1974), 94.

26. Yoon, "Mao, The Red Army, and the Chinese Soviet Republic," 220.

27. *History of Development of War in China*, 870; *ZQFY*, 183.

28. *History of the Development of War in China*, 870; *ZQFY,* 184.

29. *ZQFY*, 185.

30. *ZQFY*, 187. Yoon argued that the deployment of the NRA Nineteenth Route Army to defend Fujian pushed the Red Army to abandon plans of seizing Fujian, and instead conduct offensive operations in Guangdong. See Yoon, "Mao, The Red Army, and the Chinese Soviet Republic," 220.

31. *History of the Development of War in China*, 870; *ZQFY*, 187. Harrison attributed this quote to Zhou Enlai, prefacing it with, "Chou En-lai charged Kiangsi leaders with procrastination in carrying out the Party line and reaffirmed the call for [attack]," to support the argument of a Zhou-Mao conflict. See Harrison, *The Long March to Power*, 229. However, the above Chinese Mainland sources do not mention any sort of conflict on this specific issue. Rue took a more balanced approach, arguing that both sides assisted each other in planning operations, but still were divided on the basic strategy. See Rue, *Mao Tse-tung in Opposition*, 251.

32. *History of the Development of War in China*, 870; *ZQFY*, 187-189.

33. *ZQFY*, 190.

34. *History of Development of War in China*, 871.

35. *History of Development of War in China*, 871.

36. There is a discrepancy on the date of the Ningdu Emergency Conference. According to Harrison and Rue, the conference occurred in August, 1932. See Harrison, *The Long March to Power*, 230; Rue, *Mao Tse-tung in Opposition*, 253. However, Saich and mainland sources cite October 1932 as the date of the conference. See *History of Development of War in China*, 871; Saich, *The Rise to Power*, xxv.

37. Harrison, *The Long March to Power*, 230.

38. Harrison, *The Long March to Power*, 229.

39. *History of Development of War in China*, 872.

40. Some of the urban communist party members began leaving Shanghai as early late 1931. See Harrison, *The Long March to Power*, 222. Harrison cited that the KMT arrested 24,000 Communists and 155,525 radicals during the ten-year civil war. They also had penetrated almost one-third of the Communist cells in Shanghai in the 1930s. See Harrison, *The Long March to Power*, 220.

41. Harrison, *The Long March to Power*, 222.

42. Rue, *Mao Tse-tung in Opposition*, 257.

43. Zhou Enlai, Bo Gu, and Zhang Wentian remained in Ruijin. Xia Xi went to the Hunan-Hubei-Sichuan-Guizhou Soviet. Chen Changhao and Shen Zemin went to the Henan-Hubei-Anhui Soviet. Robert C. North, *Moscow and Chinese Communist*. (Stanford, CA: Stanford University Press, 1963), 159.

44. Yoon, "Mao, The Red Army, and the Chinese Soviet Republic," 220. May 1932 is the date quoted in mainland sources for the start of the Bandit Suppression Headquarters. See *History of Development of War in China*, 872.

45. *History of Development of War in China*, 872. The force included provincial KMT forces from Jiangxi, Fujian, Guangdong, and Hunan.

46. *History of Development of War in China*, 874; Yoon, "Mao, The Red Army, and the Chinese Soviet Republic," 229. *ZQFY* quoted 500,000 as the total strength of the NRA force. See *ZQFY,* 208.

47. Chi, "The Chinese Red Army and the Kiangsi Soviet," 151. The first column had three divisions, the second and third column had four divisions each. One division was placed in reserve. See *ZQFY,* 208.

48. Chi, "The Chinese Red Army and the Kiangsi Soviet," 151; Yoon, "Mao, The Red Army, and the Chinese Soviet Republic," 230.

49. Chi, "The Chinese Red Army and the Kiangsi Soviet," 151-152, Yoon, "Mao, The Red Army, and the Chinese Soviet Republic," 231.

50. *History of Development of War in China*, 874. Refer to Appendix A for discussion on Red Army numbers.

51. *History of Development of War in China*, 874; *ZQFY,* 219. Chi maintained a slightly different task organization, identifying the First, Third, Fifth, and Seventh Red Army Corps as the units within the Red Army in Jiangxi Soviet. See Chi, "The Chinese Red Army and the Kiangsi Soviet," 151.

52. To support the theory that Zhou Enlai did not completely believe in the Braun's offensive plan, Zhou Enlai exchanged telegrams with the Central Committee, from December 16, 1932 to February 4, 1933, expressing his reservations in attacking Nancheng and Nanfeng. According to this research, Zhou Enlai requested to conduct mobile warfare operations in the area, instead of attacking the cities; however, he was rebuffed multiple times by the Central Committee and forced to attack Nanfeng. See *ZQFY,* 220-225.

53. Chi, "The Chinese Red Army and the Kiangsi Soviet," 153.

54. *ZQFY,* 225.

55. *History of Development of War in China*, 874.

56. There are two versions to the story of the commander's capture. The first story is that Chen Shiqi, the Fifty-ninth Division commander, and about 100 of his men attempted to escape the Red Army after the battle, and became disoriented. They found a local guide to help navigate them out of the area. Instead, the guide brought the group directly to the Red Army and they were captured. See Chi, "The Chinese Red Army and the Kiangsi Soviet," 154. The other version stated that Chen attempted to contact Li Ming, the Fifty-second NRA Division commander, but his telegram was intercepted. His group attempted to flee to Le'an but was captured by the Red Army. *ZQFY*, 230.

57. *ZQFY*, 231.

58. *ZQFY*, 231.

59. *History of Development of War in China,* 874.

60. Chi, "The Chinese Red Army and the Kiangsi Soviet," 154.

61. The reason for the NRA's withdrawal from the Fourth Extermination Campaign is not certain. One theory is that the losses of three combat divisions, especially units especially loyal to Chiang, caused him to end the campaign and reorganize. See Yoon, "Mao, The Red Army, and the Chinese Soviet Republic,"

232. The other theory is that Japan's takeover of Manchuria and subsequent crossing of the Great Wall forced Chiang to focus his efforts on the Japanese, rather than the communists. See Chi, "The Chinese Red Army and the Kiangsi Soviet," 155.

62. *History of Development of War in China,* 875.

63. *ZQFY,* 233.

64. Rue, *Mao Tse-tung in Opposition,* 259.

65. Harrison, *The Long March to Power,* 231.

66. Rue, *Mao Tse-tung in Opposition,* 260.

67. Gregor Benton, *Mountain Fires: The Red Army's Three-Year War in South China, 1934-1938* (Berkeley: University of California Press, 1992), 132. Harrison stated Luo Ming was the acting secretary of the Fujian committee. See Harrison, *The Long March to Power,* 230. Rue identified him as an old Red Army commander based in Fujian. See Rue, *Mao Tse-tung in Opposition,* 258.

68. Benton, *Mountain Fires,* 132-133.

69. Benton, *Mountain Fires,* 133.

70. The purge took down not only Luo Ming, but also Mao's brother, Mao Zetan. Benton, *Mountain Fires,* 133; Harrison, *The Long March to Power,* 231.

71. *ZQFY,* 262-263.

72. *ZQFY,* 263.

73. *History of the Development of War in China,* 876.

74. *ZQFY,* 265-266.

75. *History of the Development of War in China,* 876.

76. *History of the Development of War in China,* 875-876.

77. Chi, "The Chinese Red Army and the Kiangsi Soviet," 163; *History of the Development of War in China,* 876. *Baojia* is a Chinese form of counterinsurgency strategy. Used multiple times during the Song, Ming, and Qing dynasties to prevent internal revolt, the *baojia* system leveraged community relationships to create local security forces and civil administrations loyal to the government. For more information on the *baojia* system in Imperial China, see Phillip Kuhn, *Rebellion and its Enemies in Late Imperial China: Militarization and Social Structure, 1796-1864* (Cambridge: Harvard University Press, 1970). For a detailed study of the counterinsurgency techniques employed by the KMT, see William Wei, *Counterrevolution in China: the Nationalists in Jiangxi during the Soviet period* (Ann Arbor: University of Michigan Press, 1985).

78. According to Chi, the main body strength was considered to be at 400,000. See Chi, "The Chinese Red Army and the Kiangsi Soviet," 162. Other sources have quoted the NRA size to be at one million, with a main body attack force of 500,000. The five air corps also consisted of approximately 200 airplanes, total. See *History of the Development of War in China,* 876. Another source stated there were fifty-four aircraft in each unit, for a total of 270 aircraft. See *ZQFY,* 260. More research is needed to verify the size of the NRA forces during the

Fifth Extermination Campaign, especially how it conducted logistical operations to sustain such a large force.

79. *History of the Development of War in China*, 876. The Northern Force included the First, Second, and Third Route NRA Armies, led by Chen Cheng. See *ZQFY*, 260.

80. *History of the Development of War in China*, 876; *ZQFY*, 260.

81. *ZQFY*, 260.

82. *History of the Development of War in China*, 876. Refer to Appendix A for more discussion on troop strength in the Red Army.

83. *History of the Development of War in China*, 877.

84. One of the reasons for the revolt was that Cai Tingkai, commander of the Nineteenth Route NRA Army, and Fujian native and Nationalist leader, Chen Mingshu, were upset at Chiang Kai-shek accepting the Tanggu Truce Agreement with the Japanese in May 1933. They were against any appeasement of the Japanese, and established their own People's Revolutionary Government. Yoon, "Mao, The Red Army, and the Chinese Soviet Republic," 257-258.

85. Harrison, *The Long March to Power*, 233.

86. Harrison, *The Long March to Power*, 233.

87. Rue, *Mao Tse-tung in Opposition*, 261. Harrison pointed out that history of disagreements between Fujian leaders and the Communists, dating back to the 1920s may have contributed to the mistrust between the two groups. Harrison, *The Long March to Power*, 234.

88. Rue, *Mao Tse-tung in Opposition*, 263.

89. *ZQFY*, 269.

90. Yoon, "Mao, The Red Army, and the Chinese Soviet Republic," 263.

91. Chi, "The Chinese Red Army and the Kiangsi Soviet," 165.

92. Chi, "The Chinese Red Army and the Kiangsi Soviet," 165.

93. In October 1933, the NRA had developed a construction plan to establish blockhouses on the river banks within nine to fifteen days using four divisions. *ZQFY*, 260.

94. Chi, "The Chinese Red Army and the Kiangsi Soviet," 167.

95. *History of the Development of War in China*, 878. Chi stated that the NRA lost 4,000 soldiers during the fight for Guangchang. Chi, "The Chinese Red Army and the Kiangsi Soviet," 167.

96. Chi, "The Chinese Red Army and the Kiangsi Soviet," 165.

97. Yoon, "Mao, The Red Army, and the Chinese Soviet Republic," 265.

98. *ZQFY*, 335.

99. *ZQFY*, 335.

100. *History of the Development of War in China*, 878.

101. Harrison, *The Long March to Power*, 239; Kim, *The Politics*, 200.

102. For more information on the German advisers to the KMT, see F. F. Liu, *A Military History of Modern China: 1925-1949* (Princeton: Princeton University Press, 1956).

103. Hans J. van de Ven, *War and Nationalism in China* (New York: RoutledgeCruzon, 2004), 156.

104. For more information on local administration as part of COIN in Dhofar, see Walter Ladwig III, "Supporting Allies in COIN: Britain and the Dhofar Rebellion," *Small Wars and Insurgencies* 19, No.1 (2008), 62-88; Ian Beckett, "The British Counter-insurgency Campaign in Dhofar, 1965-1975," in *Counterinsurgency in Modern Warfare*, Daniel Marston and Carter Malkasian, eds. (Oxford: Osprey Publishing, 2010), 175-190. For Malaya, see Riley Sutherland, *Army Operations in Malaya, 1947-1960* (Santa Monica: RAND, 1964), 112-164; Simon Smith, "General Templer and Counter-insurgency in Malaya: Hearts and Minds, Intelligence, and Propaganda," *Intelligence and National Security* 16, No. 3 (2001), 60-78; Richard Stubbs, "From Search and Destroy to Hearts and Minds: The Evolution of British Strategy in Malaya 1948-60," in *Counterinsurgency in Modern Warfare*, Daniel Marston and Carter Malkasian, eds. (Oxford: Osprey Publishing, 2010), 101-118.

105. van de Ven, *War and Nationalism in China*, 144.

106. *Dang tuan sheng wei wei kuo da hong jun zhi ge ji dang tuan bu xin* [A Letter from the CCP and CY Provincial Committess to all CCP and CY Headquarters Concerning Expansion of the Red Army], (CCP and CY Jiangxi Provincial Committee, July 28, 1932), SSC, Reel 6:74.

107. The report outlined that most soldiers returned home rather than joining another cause. Many of them left their weapons at their fighting position and simply walked away. *Zhengzhi Gongzuo* [Political Work], No. 1, April 12, 1932, SSC, Reel 9:55.

108. Many of the peasants who went on the line fought valiantly, and were seen as heroic martyrs for the Red Army. With that said, their élan did not make up for their lack of training and military skill and did lower the combat effectiveness of the Red Army.

109. A more thorough discussion on these topics will be covered later in the chapter.

110. *Zhongguo gong nong hong jun* [The Chinese Worker and Peasant Red Army], (General Political Department, CWPRA, July 1932), SSC, Reel 7:1.

111. Harrison, *The Long March to Power*, 227, 232.

112. *Zhongyang su qu zhongyang ju gei zhonggong Jiangxi sheng wei xi*, [a Letter from the CBSA to the CCP Jiangxi Provincial Committee], February 7, 1932, SSC, Reel 6:82.

113. Rue, *Mao Tse-tung in Opposition*, 256.

114. Rue, *Mao Tse-tung in Opposition*, 238.

115. Rue, *Mao Tse-tung in Opposition*, 254.

116. *Zhongguo gong nong hong jun.*

117. Rue, *Mao Tse-tung in Opposition*, 256.

118. Rue, *Mao Tse-tung in Opposition*, 246.

119. *Zhongguo gong nong hong jun.*

120. Harrison, *The Long March to Power*, 232.

121. Rue, *Mao Tse-tung in Opposition*, 253.

122. Rue, *Mao Tse-tung in Opposition*, 257.

123. *Zhongguo gong nong hong jun.*

124. Rue, *Mao Tse-tung in Opposition*, 248.

125. Shanti Swarup, *A Study of the Chinese Communist Movement* (Oxford: Clarendon Press, 1966), 103.

126. Mao Tse-Tung, *Selected Works, Vol. 1* (New York: International Publishers, 1954), 239.

127. Rue, *Mao Tse-tung in Opposition*, 251.

128. Rue, *Mao Tse-tung in Opposition*, 251.

129. Yoon, "Mao, The Red Army, and the Chinese Soviet Republic," 231.

130. *Hong se zhan chang* [Red Battlefield], SSC, Reel 9:23.

131. *Bai jun qi shi jiu shi de gai kuang* [Situation report on the White Seventy-Ninth Division], October 26, 1933, Reel 9:17.

132. Saich, *The Rise to Power*, 629.

133. Chi-hsi Hu, "Mao, Lin Biao, and the Fifth Encirclement Campaign," *The China Quarterly* 82 (1980), 255.

134. Saich, *The Rise to Power*, 635.

135. Hu, "Mao, Lin Biao, and the Fifth Encirclement Campaign," 257.

136. Hu, "Mao, Lin Biao, and the Fifth Encirclement Campaign," 257.

137. Saich, *The Rise to Power*, 634.

138. Saich, *The Rise to Power*, 630.

139. Saich, *The Rise to Power*, 633.

140. Hu, "Mao, Lin Biao, and the Fifth Encirclement Campaign," 258.

141. *Hong jun wen ti jue yi an* [Decision on the Red Army question], April 18, 1932, SSC, Reel 7:20.

142. *ZQFY*, 263. Donovan cited that the Fifth Red Army Corps had, in addition to its two divisions, a third division, the Fifteen Red Army Division. Donovan, "The Chinese Red Army in the Kiangsi Soviet," 178.

143. *ZQFY*, 263. According to Donovan, the Seventh Red Army Corps had the Nineteenth Red Army Division, Twentieth Red Army Division, and Twenty-first Red Army Division. No subordinate units were identified for the Ninth Red Army Corps in either source. Donovan, "The Chinese Red Army in the Kiangsi Soviet," 178.

144. Donovan, "The Chinese Red Army in the Kiangsi Soviet," 181.

145. *ZQFY*, 263.

146. Donovan, "The Chinese Red Army in the Kiangsi Soviet," 104.

147. Donovan, "The Chinese Red Army in the Kiangsi Soviet," 104.

148. *Tong yi bian zhi du li tuan you ji dui wen ti* [The Question of Unified Organizational System for Independent Regiments and Guerrilla Detachments] (Political Department of the Jiangxi Military District, March 22, 1932), SSC, Reel 6.95.

149. *Tong yi bian zhi du li tuan you ji dui wen ti*.

150. Jun shi li shi yan jiu bu. *Zhongguo ren min jie fang jun de qi shi nian* [Seventy Years of the PLA] (Beijing: Jun shi ke xue chu ban she, 1987), 82.

151. The original amount was 20,000 *dan*. *Dan* is a Chinese weight measurement that is equal to approximately 50 kilograms. *Seventy Years of the PLA*, 83.

152. *Seventy Years of the PLA*, 83.

153. *Seventy Years of the PLA*, 82.

154. *Chinese Military School History*, 338.

155. *Chinese Military School History*, 338. The classes focused on six areas: (1) tactical training, including individual, squad, platoon, and battalion tasks; (2) marksmanship and employment of weapon systems; (3) fortifications and camouflage; (4) unit staff and administrative work; (5) simple surveying and communications; and (6) command and control/leadership classes, which covered unit training, discipline, military etiquette, unit sanitation, and unit culture.

156. *Chinese Military School History*, 338-339.

157. Price discussed the use of the school newspaper as a strong propaganda and training tool within the Red Academy. Called the "wall newspaper," the publication published news of upcoming events and announcements. It also had a "red" and "black" list of good and bad students, to promote or curb certain behaviors. Price, *Cadres, Commanders, and Commissars*, 120.

158. *Chinese Military School History*, 339.

159. *Hong jun ren zi ke ben* [Red Army Character Reader], March 1934, SSC, Reel 8:60.

160. The manuals included *The Infantry Course, the Artillery Course, Tunnel Operations Course, Essentials of Defensive operations, Bayonet Manual, Military Weapons Abstract, Explosives Abstract, Employment of Machine Gun Squads and Platoons, Summary of Planning Training, Night Warfare*, and *Handouts on Mortars*. See *Chinese Military School History*, 338.

161. The books included *Compendium of Red Army Communist Youth Training, The Chinese Workers and Peasants Red Army, Red Army Education and Management, Political Questions and Answers, Land Reforms*, and *Imperialism and China*. See *Chinese Military School History*, 338.

162. The titles included *Red Academy Weekly* (in 1933, it changed to *Red*

Academy Life), *Revolution and War*, and *Red Battlefield Collection*. See *Chinese Military School History*, 338.

163. *Hong se zhan chang hui kan* [Collection of the Red Battlefield], June 1933, SSC, reel 9.23.

164. Price, *Cadres, Commanders, and Commissars*, 118.

165. *Chinese Military Education History*, 279.

166. *Chinese Military School History*, 340.

167. *Chinese Military School History*, 341.

168. *Chinese Military School History*, 340.

169. *Chinese Military School History*, 343.

170. The first class had approximately 780 students which grew exponentially, reaching almost 4,000 with the sixth class. See *Chinese Military School History*, 342-243.

171. The infantry schools were called the First Infantry School, known as Pengyang Infantry School, and the Second Infantry School, known as Gonglüe Infantry School. See *Chinese Military School History*, 345.

172. *Chinese Military School History*, 349. Price stated there were only four departments: a command class, an advanced command class, a senior political class, and a staff class. Price, *Cadres, Commanders, and Commissars*, 121.

173. "Yi yue lai de the hong jun da xue," [The First month of the Red Army war College], *Ge ming yu zhan zheng* [Revolution and War], No.2, SSC, Reel 16:2.

174. *Chinese Military Education History*, 280.

175. *Chinese Military School History*, 349. Price differentiated the military classes to the specific command class, which focused on military history, strategy, staff operations, study of arms, command of unified fighting with various types of forces, and building fortifications. Price, *Cadres, Commanders, and Commissars*, 124.

176. *Chinese Military School History*, 349. Price added the following topics into the political training: basic tactics, with regulations on irregular skirmishing, and basic military knowledge and training from squad to regimental level, including skills such as firing a gun, stabbing with a bayonet, and some civil engineering. Price, *Cadres, Commanders, and Commissars*, 124.

177. *Chinese Military School History*, 355.

178. The initial requirements were for applicants to be between the age of 18 and 30, who were physically fit, politically strong, literate, and self-motivated. Each applicant needed to have combat experience, with experience as a squad leader in a machine gun unit for a minimum of a year. The new standard deleted the literacy requirement. Additionally, if there were not enough applicants, the school lowered the combat experience time requirement to six months. Recently promoted or inexperienced platoon leaders were also considered. *Chinese Military School History*, 355.

179. *Chinese Military School History*, 356.

180. *Hong se she shou* [Red Marksman], No. 35, (Political Department of the Min-Kan Military District, Provisional Central Government of the Chinese Soviet Republic, July 1, 1934), SSC, Reel 6:70.

Chapter 6
Epilogue

By late September 1934, the Chinese Red Army was at the brink of destruction. The NRA had effectively encircled its base area and had inflicted heavy damage on the Communist military force. To avoid complete defeat, the First Front Red Army escaped through a gap in the NRA encirclement in October 1934 and conducted a year-long strategic relocation through China's mountainous interior. During the travels, the Red Army had a battle within its ranks, as Mao Zedong struggled to consolidate power over the party and the Army. At the same time, the Red Army survived under the most arduous conditions, travelling thousands of miles to finally arrive in northwest China in late 1935. There they established a new Soviet base area and mounted a Japanese resistance propaganda campaign that caught the nationalist undercurrent sweeping across China. A strong desire for a united front with the communists against the Japanese instead of continued war with a fellow Chinese led Zhang Xueliang to kidnap Chiang Kai-shek in Xi'an in December 1936, and demand the creation of the Second Chinese United Front against the Japanese forces. To gain his freedom, Chiang agreed to the united front, effectively ending the hostilities against the Communists and ensuring the survival of the Chinese Red Army.

The Long March

As the stranglehold of the NRA encirclement became stronger and stronger, the Red Army and Central Committee of the CCP looked for new strategies to counter the KMT. Some argue that the first discussions began in May 1934 after the defeat at Guangchang.[1] With the offensive strategy no longer viable, the Red Army entertained alternatives to save it from its predicament. One broad strategy was to co-opt the NRA by leveraging nationalistic fervor to create a united front against the Japanese. The Red Army leadership hoped that by having a common enemy they could gain a temporary reprieve from war with the KMT. In July 1934, the Red Army attempted this new strategy by deploying the Seventh Red Army Corps to western Fujian to join the Tenth Red Army, led by Su Yu.[2] This force was designated as the Anti-Japanese Vanguard Column to gain Nationalist support; however, the propaganda did not work. The NRA destroyed the Red Army Column, killing or executing most of the forces. About 800 survivors escaped the area and banded together as a guerrilla group under Su Yu. They would fight independently until the Second United Front was established in 1937 and eventually link up with the New Fourth Army in 1938.[3] Another breakout occurred on July 23, 1934 when the Sixth Red Army Corps, based out of the Hunan-Guangdong border area, moved through Hunan and linked up with the Third Red Army, creating the Second Front Red Army, led by He Long on October 22, 1934.[4]

It is unknown if either operation had any effect on the KMT. However, any diversionary effect had already dissipated by the time the Long March started. Mounting costs and continued casualties increased the burden on the Red Army, making it difficult to survive in its current location. The Red Army needed a new secure location to reorganize, refit, and recruit forces. In August 1934, Bo Gu and Otto Braun made the decision in secret to abandon the Jiangxi Soviet.[5] The original plan was to move southwest toward Hunan to more friendly territory, and link up with the Second Front Red Army.[6] While the exact location of the Second Front Red Army was unknown, the leadership saw Hunan as the most likely location, and planned a route to the area. The rest of the Red Army continued its frenzied recruiting campaign, as well as raising money and collecting equipment. On the night of 10 October 1934, the Red Army leadership gave marching orders to the First Front Red Army. The units moved southwest in two columns, with First, Third, Fifth, Eight, and Ninth Red Army Corps.[7] The total force was approximately 87,000.[8] For many soldiers, they did not know it would be the last time they would see the Jiangxi Soviet. Instead, many believed they were on another maneuver to outflank the KMT and attack its rear. A force of 16,000, including many injured soldiers such as its leader, Chen Yi, was left behind in Ruijin to defend against and delay the KMT forces, giving the First Front Red Army enough time to escape unnoticed. With this movement, the Long March began.

The initial few days of the Long March were quite peaceful. The Red Army avoided any major engagement with NRA forces and navigated through a gap in the encirclement quite easily. Earlier, Zhou Enlai had negotiated a truce with the Guangdong and Guangxi warlords participating in the Extermination campaign, helping the Red Army gain safe passage through the area.[9] Meanwhile, the remaining Red Army forces in Ruijin fought tenaciously against the NRA, which helped conceal the reality that the main body had already absconded. Up until November 8, Nationalist newspapers reported the Red Army had been all but destroyed.[10] The First Front Red Army moved at night, travelling along small trails to avoid aerial detection and attack. The formation of forces was the First and Ninth Red Army Corps on the left flank, the Third and Eighth Red Army Corps on the right flank, the leadership and logistical units in the center, and the Fifth Red Army Corps providing rear guard.[11] The Red Army hired porters to help carry its heavy equipment, to include printing presses, X-ray machines, and its money. Other porters helped transport litters that carried the injured and key leaders. Some of the Red Army leaders, to include Zhou Enlai, were sick or injured during this time, though others, like Mao, rode in litters to rest during the day after long night-planning sessions.

By mid-November 1934, the NRA discovered the Red Army had escaped the encirclement to the west and began its pursuit. From the Red Army's movement, Chiang and the NRA leadership deduced that southern Hunan was the Red Army's most likely destination and deployed troops in pursuit. The Red Army continued to rapidly move west, hoping to cross the Xiang River before the NRA forces arrived. On November 27, 1934, the Red Army arrived at Daoxian and attacked the NRA blockhouses protecting Xiang River crossings. The Red Army was able to quickly reduce the blockhouses, and began flowing forces across the river. However, its central column, bogged down by heavy equipment and injured soldiers, did not keep pace with the rest of the Red Army, and lagged behind. On November 28, the NRA attacked the rear elements of the Red Army before it made it to the Xiang River. For five days, the Red Army fought a ferocious rear-guard action as it attempted to disengage its forces from the NRA and cross the river. By December 2, 1934, all the Red Army forces had made it across the Xiang River, though at a cost. The Red Army lost more than two divisions from the Third and Fifth Red Army Corps. After the Xiang River crossing, just over 30,000 soldiers remained in the force.[12] Additionally, much of the Army's heavy equipment and books were abandoned along the route in order to lighten its load.[13]

After the Red Army made it across the Xiang River, it continued to avoid any pitched battles with the NRA. The difficult battle at the Xiang River changed the Red Army in different ways. Desertions increased as soldiers realized the movement was an exodus from Jiangxi. Porters for the heavy equipment were leaving at night as well, especially after carrying all the equipment up and down the mountains along muddy trails.[14] The Red Army attempted to move north multiple times to link up with He Long and the Second Front Red Army, only to find the routes blocked by the NRA. The Red Army switched plans instead, and continued west to Guizhou in order to reach Sichuan and link up with the Fourth Front Red Army and set up a new Soviet.[15] Once at Liping, Guizhou province, the Red Army leadership decided on December 18 to head north towards Zunyi in order to reach Sichuan.[16] Guiyang, the provincial capital of Guizhou, was the original target destination, but the city was reinforced by seven NRA divisions. Zunyi, on the other hand, seemed like a better target. It was the second largest city in the province, and only guarded by Guizhou provincial forces. On January 1, 1935, the Red Army began movement to Zunyi, crossing the Wu River under heavy fire from Guizhou provincial forces. Within the three days, the Red Army completed the river crossing and moved toward Zunyi. On January 7, the Red Army attacked Zunyi, which fell two days later. Once Zunyi was captured, the Red Army began its normal recruiting drive, gaining 30,000 recruits to expand its ranks. It also buried or abandoned much of its heavy equipment to make it more mobile. The Red Army originally hoped to stay in the area for an extended period of time to refit, reorganize, and recruit forces. The Central Cadre Unit's Red Army Medical School staff took advantage of the break and held a one-week course to help train soldiers on basic first aid.[17] However, local conditions prevented any long-term stay. The major crop in the area was opium, which was good for bartering but could not sustain the Red

Army. The city's location along a bend in the river also limited the Red Army's escape routes if the NRA were to attack the area.[18] Given these conditions, the Communist leadership held a conference to discuss its military strategy.

The conference, which convened on January 15, 1935, became a critical turning point in Communist history.[19] In attendance were members of the Politburo: Mao Zedong, Zhu De, Chen Yun, Zhou Enlai, Luo Fu, and Bo Gu. Liu Bocheng, Liu Shaoqi, Lin Biao, Nie Rongzhen, Peng Dehuai, and Otto Braun were in attendance as well.[20] The main discussion of the meeting was the failed military strategy used against the Fifth Extermination Campaign. Bo Gu and Zhou Enlai first spoke and both apologized for the poor strategy, and accepted blame for the problems. Mao followed with a blistering attack against the strategy's "leftist" deviation, denouncing the use of the "short, swift thrusts" tactics and the failure to unite with the Fujian Nineteenth NRA Army. The meeting went on for a three more days, with most of the Red Army leadership denouncing Bo Gu and Otto Braun's failed strategy and throwing their support towards Mao. By the end of the meeting, most of the key CCP and Red Army leaders effectively distanced themselves from the Twenty-eight Bolsheviks. Mao became the CCP's de facto leader, even though he was not elected to any new leadership post in Zunyi.[21] A major change was the dissolution of the triumvirate leadership council of Bo Gu, Otto Braun, and Zhou Enlai. Zhu De and Zhou Enlai were placed in charge of the Red Army and then the Red Army began moving towards Sichuan to link up with the Fourth Front Red Army.[22]

The Red Army departed Zunyi with its four army corps: the First, Third, Fifth, and Ninth Red Army Corps, though all dramatically smaller than before. The First Front Red Army's total strength was approximately 35,000 soldiers.[23] It moved north through Tongzi, picking up gold and opium to help it purchase food and supplies later in the journey.[24] The First Army Corps, led by Lin Biao, continued ahead as the Red Army's lead unit searching for a pass to cross the Yangtze River. As the First Army Corps attempted to secure a crossing near Chishui, the remainder of the Red Army became engaged in a pitched battle with a Sichuan NRA army force near Tucheng. The battle became so intense that Mao recalled Lin Biao and his First Army Corps to help with the fighting. The Red Army eventually broke contact on January 29, 1935 and abandoned its plans to cross the Yangtze River. Instead the Red Army moved west to Zhaxi, Yunnan province, to escape NRA forces. The Red Army gained only a temporary reprieve as more NRA forces moved west into Sichuan covering all possible river crossing sites along the Yangtze. With few options available, Mao proposed a daring new plan on February 7. The Red Army would split up and head back east into Guizhou as separate columns to confuse the NRA. It would then reunite its forces and head southwest into Yunnan and find a safer crossing point over the Yangtze.[25]

In accordance with this plan, the Red Army executed a series of feints, diversionary attacks, and other deception operations that confused the NRA leadership and even some of its own leadership. Mao sought to confuse the NRA in order to create an opening where the Red Army could escape into Yunnan and cross the Yangtze River in the Jinsha river area. The Red Army began moving east and gained victories over the NRA, such as at Loushan Pass where the Red Army gained about a division's worth of personnel and equipment from the NRA. The Red Army continued east and captured the city of Maotai, picking up even more gold and opium for bartering.[26] In March 1935, Mao was appointed political commissar of the Red Army, with Zhu De as the commander in chief. Mao's leadership position was further reinforced when he was selected to the triumvirate Military Council with Zhou Enlai and Wang Jiaxiang.[27] Mao now began a deception operation, deploying the Ninth Red Army Corps north as a feint to the Yangtze River to reinforce NRA intelligence estimates. Chiang believed that all this erratic movement signaled the Red Army was ready to make its final fight. He moved his NRA headquarters to Guiyang and deployed almost all the Guizhou NRA forces up to the Yangtze River area to encircle and destroy the Red Army. The NRA deployment opened a north-south corridor in Guizhou for the Red Army to turn south toward Guiyang. With most of the NRA forces along the Yangtze, Guiyang was defenseless. Mao preyed on these fears, sending more Red Army units on a feint toward the provincial capital. Chiang scrambled NRA forces from Yunnan to help defend Guiyang, opening yet another corridor for the Red Army to escape. The Red Army exploited the corridor, moving with lightning speed into Yunnan. The Red Army employed a similar feint tactic used in Guiyang, deploying units from the First Red Army Corps to threaten Kunming. Since the Yunnan main force was still in Guiyang, this forced the Yunnan government to divert its frontier and militia forces to secure the capital, which opened one last corridor for the Red Army to escape through a crossing at the Jinsha River.[28]

By April 1935, the Red Army had completed one of its boldest maneuvers, escaping the NRA forces by conducting an end around into Yunnan. Even with the maneuver, the Red Army still needed to cross over the Yangtze. One segment of the Yangtze River that flows from Tibet through Yunnan to Sichuan is known as the Jinsha River, and provided excellent crossing points for the Red Army. On April 29, Mao designated three crossing spots for the Red Army. The First Red Army Corps was to cross in the north at Longjie. In the center, the Third Red Army Corps was to cross at Hongmen. The Central Cadre Unit was to take the south crossing point at Jiaopingdu. Meanwhile, the Fifth and Ninth Army Corps were to conduct rear-guard operations and cross at the closest crossing point. While the First and Third Red Army corps had trouble securing the crossing spots, the Central Cadre Unit secured seven boats, established security on both sides of the river, and began a ferrying operation that would take nine days. The First and Third Red Army Corps abandoned their crossing points and also moved to Jiaopingdu. The Third Red Army Corps crossed on May 7 and the First Red Army Corps crossed the next day. The Fifth Red Army Corps continued its rear guard, and then sped across the Jiaopingdu crossing on May 9.[29]

Once in Sichuan, the haggard troops of the Red Army began questioning what was next. The Red Army had been travelling for almost nine months, with little rest and at an enormous cost. The Red Army now numbered about 25,000 soldiers, and much of its heavy equipment lay abandoned and scattered along its western retreat route. The Red Army attempted to take Huili, but failed as the Twenty-fourth NRA Division mounted a strong defense against the invasion.[30] Outside the city, the Red Army leadership held a conference on May 12 and decided to continue moving north through Sichuan and cross the Dadu River in order to link up with the Fourth Front Red Army.[31]

The Red Army began moving through the Yi minority area. The Yi people despised the Han, and attacked Red Army stragglers, stealing their weapons and clothes, and left many to die. Fortunately, Liu Bocheng and his vanguard unit of the First Red Army Corps negotiated a truce with the Yi, gaining safe passage in return for equal land rights and treatment after the war was won.[32]

On May 23, the Red Army reached Anshunchang along the Dadu River. The initial attempt to cross the river by ferry was thwarted by a strong NRA defense on the far shore. The Red Army only mustered three boats which were insufficient to support a crossing. The Red Army leadership decided on May 27 to take a risk and sent troops north to seize the Luding Bridge, an iron-chained suspension bridge along a relatively inaccessible trail in the mountain passes that crossed the Dadu River. In a daring feat, the Fourth Regiment, Second Division, First Red Army Corps, led by Yang Chengwu, marched almost 100 miles in less than three days to secure the bridge. Fighting against a defending NRA brigade along sheer cliffs, the Fourth Regiment moved quickly and seized the bridge under constant fire. Only eighteen of the eighty-two men who made the final assault survived.[33] Because of their actions, the Red Army was able to avoid the main KMT force and crossed the Dadu River, finally settling in Hualingping for refitting operations.

The trials for the Red Army continued after crossing the Dadu. The leaders of the First Front Red Army still did not know where the Fourth Front Red Army was located. One possible area was directly north behind the Jiajin Mountains. Mao decided to avoid the more convenient eastern and western routes to avoid detection from NRA forces or ambushes from Tibetans, and instead moved the Red Army along a central walking trail through the Jiajin Mountains. For most Long March survivors, the Jiajin leg of the Long March was the most grueling and difficult.[34] The Red Army soldiers fought the hunger, cold, thirst, avalanches, and the altitude as they attempted to traverse the snow-capped mountain tops with little more than the clothes on their back. On June 12, the first units of the Red Army arrived at Danwei at the northern foot of the Jiajin Mountains. On June 14, the rest of the Red Army came down from the mountain and linked up with Li Xiannian, a liaison officer from the Fourth Front Red Army. Approximately 10,000 soldiers survived the cold and made it down the mountain. [35] Fortunately, they had linked up with fellow Red Army comrades and could take another well-deserved rest.

The First and Fourth Front Red Armies finally linked up at Lianghekou on June 18, 1935. The Fourth Front Red Army faired remarkably better than the First Front Red Army. The Fourth Front Red Army had originated in the Hubei-Henan-Anhui Soviet, and moved to the Shaanxi-Sichuan border before finally resettling in northwest Sichuan in March 1935.[36] Its forces were at almost 80,000, well above the First Front Red Army. Some First Front Red Army soldiers looked with awe and envy at how fat the soldiers and horses were in the Fourth Front Red Army.[37] On June 26, the two front armies' leadership met to discuss the future movements of the Red Army.[38] Mao proposed that the Red Army move north to Gansu, and then head east toward Ningxia, with the eventual destination of Mongolia to establish communications with the Soviet Union. Zhang Guotao had a different plan, proposing to go west instead of east, toward Xinjiang and connect with the Soviet Union through the Central Asian Republics. Underneath the debates of military direction, there was also political maneuvering as both Mao and Zhang attempted to assert control over the Red Army. In the end, both sides were cordial, and a unified strategy and command were established. The Red Army would move north to southern Gansu to establish a Soviet along the border areas. Zhang Guotao was also appointed vice-chairman of the Military Council. On June 30, the First Front Red Army moved north into the Grasslands, with Zhang Guotao and the Fourth Front Red Army following one day behind.[39]

The Lianghekou meeting never settled any political disputes between the Zhang and Mao factions, and the conflict grew with time. On the surface, Zhang continued to press for the Red Army to move west to Xinjiang. At the same time, Zhang worked hard to recruit key leaders from the First Front Red Army to his side, to no avail. Mao remained resolute with the agreed plan to go to Gansu and took precautionary measures against any Zhang subversion. The conflict came to a head at a conference in Maoergai on August 6. The Red Army arrived at Maoergai the day before to rest and refit the troops, and discuss the future of the Red Army. One version of the story states that Mao held the meeting in the adjacent town of Shawo, and secured the meeting location before Zhang's arrival. As the only representative from the Fourth Front Red Army on the Politburo and Central Committee, Zhang planned to introduce more representatives to the council in order to increase his influence, but they failed to get past security.⁴⁰ Zhang became furious at the political power play. Another version stated the exact opposite. The meeting occurred at Zhang's own Eleventh Red Army Division headquarters under the watchful eye of his loyalist soldiers to ensure no subversion by Mao and his loyal First Front Army. Either way, no known agreements were brokered at the meeting. A second meeting was held on August 20 at Maoergai and a brokered settlement was made. The Red Army remained under the command of Zhu De, but was divided into two columns. The Right Column consisted of the First and Third Red Army Corps, led by Lin Biao and Peng Dehuai respectively. It also received the Thirteenth and Fourth Red Armies from the Fourth Front Army. Mao, Zhou Enlai, Bo Gu, and Otto Braun would travel with the Right Column. The Left Column had the rest of the Fourth Front Army, with the addition of the Fifth and Ninth Red Army Corps. Zhang Guotao and Liu Bocheng were in charge of the Left Column, and Zhu De travelled with the force. The two columns would travel north, skirting the Grasslands, with the Left Column moving toward Aba and the Right Column moving toward Baxi. Once both sides agreed on the plan, they began movement on August 23 into the Grasslands.⁴¹

In the Grasslands, the Red Army faced conditions as arduous as those in the mountains. This was another minority area and this time the Tibetans were as unforgiving as the Yi had been, attacking and killing many of the stragglers. There was limited food to forage for in the Grasslands and many of the Red Army soldiers did not know which plant species were edible. Water supplies were limited because much of the water sources were stagnant and polluted. The Red Army ended up eating wheat kernels, which wreaked havoc on the soldiers' digestive systems. The situation was worse for the trailing elements as vanguard troops turned the dirt trails into muddy pits and left no food behind for foraging. The Right Red Army Column made it to Baxi on August 27. The week-long trek took its toll; the Third Red Army Corps lost 400 soldiers on the march through the Grassland.⁴² The Left Column moved a bit slower, and arrived at Aba about a week later.

Once outside the grasslands, the Red Army faced another internal struggle that jeopardized its retreat. On September 3, Zhang Guotao sent a wireless message to Mao and the Right Column stating that his forces were stationed at Aba and the White River, north of Aba, was impassable. Mao pressed Zhang to abide by the Maoergai decision, and he even offered more troops to help cross the river. Zhang politely refused the aid. On September 9, Mao found out about a secret message Zhang sent to his aide in the Right Column. Zhang wanted the Right Column to move back south through the Grasslands to reunite the two columns and convene a meeting to discuss a new strategy, with intentions to begin an intraparty struggle for power.⁴³ Out of fear that Zhang would use his superior numbers to force his strategy on the rest of the Red Army, the First and Third Red Army Corps left Baxi undetected and continued north to Gansu. The approximately 8,000 strong force arrived at Ejie, and held an emergency conference. The Red Army consolidated and reorganized its forces as the Anti-Japanese Vanguard Force of the Red Army to help garner support from the local populace. It also published a "Resolution Concerning the Mistakes of Comrade Zhang Guotao" that reprimanded his actions, but did not expel him from the Communist party.⁴⁴ On September 14, the Red Army continued its movement north and seized the Lazikou Pass, defeating two entrenched battalions guarding the pass.

Zhang Guotao and his Fourth Front Army went the opposite direction, moving south toward Chengdu. Zhang was furious once he discovered Mao and his loyal Red Army forces left unannounced. However, he did not pursue them, and instead turned his troops around and pushed toward Chengdu. The Fourth Front Red Army gained initial victories in October 1935 over the NRA at Baoxing and Tianquan, and was within 60 miles of the Sichuan provincial capital. Chiang Kai-shek responded to the threat by pouring more than eighty NRA regiments to defend Chengdu. The NRA launched a counterattack at Baizhang, decimating the Fourth Front Red Army. Its forces retreated in disarray all the way back to Ganzi, western Sichuan province, and would remain in the area until it linked up with the Second Front Army in June 1936.⁴⁵

While the Fourth Front Army moved south to Sichuan, the Red Army made the final leg of its difficult journey. On September 21, 1935, Mao and the Anti-Japanese Vanguard arrived in Hadapu, a Han city in Gansu province. The soldiers at rejoiced being surrounded by their own ethnic group and took a few days of rest. While in the city, Mao and other Red Army leaders discovered that a Soviet led by Liu Zhidan, a friend of Mao Zedong, actually existed in northern Shaanxi, and supported the Twenty-fifth and Twenty-sixth Red Armies. Ten days later, the Anti-Japanese Vanguard departed Hudapu and quickly moved west to avoid NRA Muslim cavalry units and link up with its comrade units in Shaanxi. On October 19, 1935, Mao linked up with the Twenty-fifth and Twenty-sixth Red Armies, and settled near Wuqi.⁴⁶ The remnants of the First Front Red Army had survived its year-long, 6,000-mile journey with approximately 4,000 soldiers.

Xian Incident

Once in the relative security of Shaanxi, the Red Army returned to its old political mobilization strategy to gain resources, recruits, and spread the communist revolution. The First Front Red Army moved east on February 5, 1936 to conduct political mobilization operations. During the next two months, the Red Army defeated seven provincial divisions, capturing more than 4,000 soldiers. It also recruited 8,000 new soldiers, collected $300,000 in new revenue, and added twenty Shanxi counties to the new Soviet.[47] In May, the First Front Army moved west for a two-month operation, collecting more than 2,000 rifles and 400 horses. The operation expanded the Soviet into Gansu and Ningxia. However, these operations were eventually defeated by the NRA forces, forcing the Red Army to relocate from Wuqi to Bao'an in June 1936.[48] In October 1936, the Second and Fourth Front Armies finally reached Bao'an and completed the Long March for the Red Army. With all three Red Army units united again, the Red Army War College reopened and resumed teaching operations in Dengjiaqiao, with Liu Bocheng eventually returning to head the College.[49] The Red Army military school also opened its doors for training in Tai'erwan.[50]

During this same time, the Red Army began to focus on the growing Japanese aggression. In late December, the Red Army received word from the Soviet Union that Stalin wanted a United Front with the Nationalists to fight the Japanese forces. On December 15, 1935, the CCP Politburo held a meeting and issued the Wayaopao Resolution, effectively calling for a united front with the Nationalists to resist to Japanese aggression.[51] From December 1935 forward, the Red Army leadership began reaching out to different nationalist groups to gain support for the united front against the Japanese. In January, the Red Army established communications with the warlord militias in Northeast China. They gained the interest of Zhang Xueliang, the commander of the Northeast Army and son of the famous warlord Zhang Zuolin. The two sides continued discussions and by late summer 1936, the Red Army had established an informal nonaggression pact with the Northeast Army leader.[52] Coincidently, Chiang Kai-shek also appointed Zhang Xueliang in charge of the next Extermination Campaign. The new Extermination Campaign was headquartered out of Xi'an, and Chiang flew up to the city twice to discuss the strategy. At the first meeting in October, Zhang Xueliang refused to attack the Communists. The second meeting was set for December 7, 1936. During the interim, public sentiment supporting Japanese resistance and anger at the Nationalist government continued to grow more fervent.

Chiang Kai-shek arrived in Xi'an on December 4, 1936 and met with Zhang Xueliang. Zhang again requested that Chiang stop attacking the Communists and focus on the Japanese. Chiang refused, and stated that if Zhang did not comply with orders to begin the Sixth Extermination Campaign on December 12, he would be removed as commander.[53] On December 12, Zhang Xueliang's bodyguard kidnapped Chiang Kai-shek and held him as a prisoner for two weeks. During the two weeks, intense negotiations circled around what to do with Chiang. Zhang presented Chiang with eight demands for governmental reform, cessation of attacks again the Communists, and a united front against the Japanese.[54] Mao and

Zhu De initially pressed for Chiang's execution, though the COMINTERN pushed for a more moderate stance, calling for the release of Chiang in exchange for agreement on the United Front.[55] On December 25, Chiang Kai-shek was released, and in exchange he agreed to the creation of the Second United Front, ending the ten-year civil war within China between the Communist Red Army and the Nationalist Revolutionary Army.

From 1934 to 1936, the Red Army escaped extinction by enduring the most difficult of conditions and travelling across some of China's most difficult terrain to escape the NRA and provincial forces. Mao Zedong maneuvered the politics within the Red Army, coming out of the conflict as the supreme leader of the CCP and the Red Army. The Communists also benefited from the difficulties within the NRA and KMT leadership. The Red Army leveraged Chiang's inability to fully control his subordinate warlords and their military units to avoid unnecessary battles. When the Red Army finally reached Shaanxi in late 1935, the Long March survivors were not only hardened by the harrowing experience, but also carried all the lessons and experiences from the successes of the previous campaigns. In the relative security of the new Soviet, the Red Army expanded its forces and resumed its training and mobilization operations. As result of the Xi'an incident, the existential threat from the NRA was extinguished. The Red Army had survived its most difficult test to date and would continue its development into the professional military force that would eventually defeat the NRA and overthrow the KMT government.

Notes

1. John P. Harrison, *The Long March to Power: A History of the Chinese Communist Party, 1927-72* (New York: Praeger Publishing, 1972), 242.

2. Harrison E. Salisbury, *The Long March: The Untold Story*, (New York: Harper & Row, 1985), 52.

3. Harrison, *The Long March to Power*, 242.

4. Jun shi li shi yan jiu bu. *Zhongguo ren min jie fang jun de qi shi nian* [Seventy Years of the PLA] (Beijing: Jun shi ke xue chu ban she, 1987), 121. Hereafter cited as *Seventy years of the PLA*.

5. Harrison, *The Long March to Power*, 242.

6. Salisbury, *The Long March: The Untold Story*, 60. Garavente questioned the logic of the destination of Hunan, as it would provide little if any security, and actually increase exposure to the NRA. He argued that the most likely destination was Sichuan, with Hunan serving only as a link up point with the Second Front Red Army. See Anthony Garavente, "Commentary: Solving the Mystery of the Long March, 1934-1936" *Bulletin of Concerned Asian Scholars* 27, No. 3 (1995): 58-61.

7. *Seventy years of the PLA*, 122.

8. Garavente, "Commentary: Solving the Mystery of the Long March," 58.

9. Salisbury argued that the Long March was delayed until October because the negotiations took longer than expected. See Salisbury, *The Long March: The Untold Story*, 63.

10. Salisbury, *The Long March: The Untold Story*, 66.

11. *Seventy years of the PLA*, 122.

12. *Seventy years of the PLA*, 123.

13. Salisbury, *The Long March: The Untold Story*, 96-104.

14. Salisbury, *The Long March: The Untold Story*, 88.

15. Salisbury, *The Long March: The Untold Story*, 110.

16. *Seventy years of the PLA*, 123.

17. Yuan Wei and Zhuo Zhang, eds., *Zhongguo jun xiao fa zhan shi* [History of the Development of Military Schools in China] (Beijing: Guo fang da xue chu ban she, 2001), 361. Hereafter cited as *Chinese Military School History*.

18. Salisbury, *The Long March: The Untold Story*, 114-118.

19. There is controversy over the actual date of the conference, with previous research indicating the Zunyi Conference occurred on 6-8 January 1935. See Benjamin Yang, "The Zunyi Conference as One Step in Mao's rise to Power: A Survey of Historical Studies of the Chinese Communist Party," *The China Quarterly*, No. 106 (1986): 236-239.

20. A total of eighteen participants were at the conference, with two non-participating attendees: Wu Xiuquan, Otto Braun's interpreter, and Deng Xiaoping, a recorder for the Central Committee. See Salisbury, *The Long March:*

The Untold Story, 121; Yang, "The Zunyi Conference," 241.

21. Yang, "The Zunyi Conference," 248-249.
22. Yang, "The Zunyi Conference," 250.
23. Salisbury, *The Long March: The Untold Story*, 127.
24. Salisbury, *The Long March: The Untold Story*, 145.
25. *Seventy years of the PLA*, 125.
26. Salisbury, *The Long March: The Untold Story*, 155-162.
27. Yang, "The Zunyi Conference," 259.
28. Salisbury, *The Long March: The Untold Story*, 163-174; *Seventy years of the PLA*, 125.
29. Salisbury, *The Long March: The Untold Story*, 177-187.
30. Salisbury, *The Long March: The Untold Story*, 189.
31. At the meeting, Lin Biao criticized Mao for being reckless with the Red Army's fast pace movement. In response, Mao chastised Lin Biao, saying "You baby, what the hell do you know." The rebuke signaled the growing strength of Mao as he continued to consolidate power within the Red Army. Yang, "The Zunyi Conference," 260.
32. Salisbury, *The Long March: The Untold Story*, 198.
33. The surviving members all received a new linen tunic, a notebook, a fountain pen, an enamel bowl, an enamel pan, and a pair of chopsticks. Salisbury, *The Long March: The Untold Story*, 230.
34. Salisbury, *The Long March: The Untold Story*, 239.
35. Salisbury, *The Long March: The Untold Story*, 231-241.
36. *Seventy years of the PLA*, 126.
37. Salisbury, *The Long March: The Untold Story*, 244.
38. *Seventy years of the PLA*, 128.
39. Salisbury, *The Long March: The Untold Story*, 245-252.
40. Salisbury, *The Long March: The Untold Story*, 260.
41. Salisbury, *The Long March: The Untold Story*, 253-262.
42. Salisbury, *The Long March: The Untold Story*, 271.
43. *Seventy years of the PLA*, 129.
44. Salisbury, *The Long March: The Untold Story*, 281-282.
45. Salisbury, *The Long March: The Untold Story*, 314-317.
46. *Seventy years of the PLA*, 131.
47. *Seventy years of the PLA*, 133.
48. Harrison, *The Long March to Power*, 267.
49. *Chinese Military School History*, 283.
50. *Chinese Military School History*, 362.

51. Tetsuya Kataoka, *Resistance And Revolution in China: The Communists And the Second United Front* (Berkeley: University of California Press, 1974), 30.

52. Harrison, *The Long March to Power*, 267.

53. Harrison, *The Long March to Power*, 268.

54. Harrison, *The Long March to Power*, 268.

55. Kataoka, *Resistance And Revolution in China*, 43.

Chapter 7
Conclusion

This study examined the Chinese Red Army during the period of 1927 to 1936 to identify key adaptations and innovations that were critical in its survival. Given the historical documents and academic material available, the research attempted to present an objective analysis of the conditions and factors affecting the Red Army during this time period. The product of this work is a story of a military force growing, adapting, and improving over time while under constant threat and pressure. With concerns about China's recent military build-up on the rise, this study offers a reexamination of the origin and the early development of the Chinese People's Liberation Army within a historical context, and hopes to contribute to a more complete and deeper understanding of China and its military forces.

Evaluating the Adaptation and Development of the Chinese Red Army

Chapter 2 outlined the four categories within the study's analytical framework designed to answer the following question: How did the Chinese Red Army survive and grow from 1927 to 1936 while under constant attack from external and internal threats? Through the examination of the army's strategy, tactics, organization, and training during three discrete time periods, this study assessed change and innovation within the Chinese Red Army. It concluded that the applied analytical framework was effective in demonstrating that the Chinese Red Army was successful in adapting its organization and adopting military innovations to overcome a series of external and internal challenges to its existence. From the analysis, four broad themes emerge to describe how the Chinese Red Army was able to survive and grow during 1927 to 1936.

Pragmatic Strategy Focused on Long-term Success and Survival

When developing strategy, one key element to design is the complete and honest assessment of a unit's capabilities, limitations, and the local conditions. The success of the Chinese Red Army's adaptation was its understanding of its own capabilities and limitations, as embodied by the pragmatic strategy of "lure the enemy in deep." The army could have easily followed the Soviet military doctrinal model, especially given the experiences and education of the Whampoa graduate contingent of Red Army officers. Yet in the face of formidable criticism of "guerrillaism," "flightism," and "retreatism," the Chinese Red Army leadership, especially Mao Zedong, adopted an attrition-based strategy that shifted the focus from securing terrain to destroying the enemy.[1] The Red Army could not defeat the NRA face to face, and instead adopted a military strategy that combined guerrilla and conventional warfare. The strategy and tactics took advantage of the Red Army's strengths while at the same time exposing the weakness of the enemy. The army prepared extensively for battle by conducting detailed reconnaissance in order to understand the enemy's weakness. Armed with that knowledge, the Red Army used maneuver, terrain, and deception to isolate and gain superior firepower over the enemy, as seen in the Extermination Campaigns. The Red Army also demonstrated patience, temporarily sacrificing terrain or time now to gain the advantage later. The Red Army also continually adapted its organizational structures to its soldiers' and leaders' capabilities in order to ensure proper span of control during operations. The establishment of the 3-3-3 model and assigning key leaders to guerrilla elements were both examples of measures based on a realistic understanding of the army's military limitations and an adaptation to those conditions. Another pragmatic strategy was the establishment of alliances. The Chinese Red Army leadership constantly made deals and treaties with bandits, warlords, and minorities in order to gain security or protection. While the agreements may have gone against communist doctrine of the time, they were critical in protecting the Red Army and helped to drive a bigger wedge between those groups and the KMT.

Gaining Local Populace Support through Adaptation

Political mobilization played an instrumental role in the development of the Red Army during this time period. The Chinese Red Army leadership adapted communist policies in order to secure popular support in the rural areas with great success. Instead of targeting specific classes of people, such as landlords and rich peasants, the Chinese Red Army used selective targeting to minimize alienation while still gaining the necessary revenue and support. Certain popular landlords were not purged, though coercion was used to gain their support. Middle-class peasants were also allowed to coexist in the Soviet areas. Additionally, the Chinese Red Army instituted the three disciplines and eight points of attention out of pragmatic concerns about preventing hostilities toward Red Army operations. All these actions worked together to turn local support toward the communists. In return, the Red Army gained valuable intelligence, logistical support, protection, and revenues from the local populace. Villagers would provide information on NRA movement and assist in resupply operations during the Extermination Campaigns. These actions would become the foundation for Red Army logistical operations, and would later pay dividends in later campaigns. Yet the local populace's biggest contribution to the Red Army was volunteers to join its military force.

Strong Soldier Recruiting, Training, and Retention System

The Chinese Red Army was essentially a volunteer force and required an adjustment in policies and training procedures to properly develop and train the force. The Red Army's main force was built on the foundation of the various guerrilla units, Red Guard, and CY groups. Those volunteers who showed promise and were willing to leave the local area were moved from local security detachments of the Red Guard to the guerrilla units or the Red Army. This system pushed interested volunteers instead of uninterested citizens into the military ranks, which helped to increase the moral quality of new recruits. Once in the ranks, the Chinese Red Army focused on training soldiers. Political indoctrination helped instill loyalty within the Red Army. It also served a critical function of increasing literacy and education of the soldiers. It helped soldiers learn how to read and do basic skills needed in their jobs as well as in their regular lives. Additionally, the Red Army adjusted pedagogical methods to the soldiers, making sure esoteric lectures on military theories were limited, and more hands-on application was used to gain practical experience and keep attention spans from wavering. All these methods helped train and develop the Red Army force and increased the soldiers' morale, which was important for retention. Desertion was one of the Red Army's biggest concerns, and the army took proactive measures to improve soldiers' quality of life as part of retention. The introduction of Soldier Soviets during the Sanwan reorganization was meant to develop consensus and buy-in within the army ranks. While the Soldier Soviets went away eventually, the group discussions and debate prior to operations remained as a way for soldiers to participate in the entire planning process. Leaders also avoided beating or berating soldiers to show respect and decrease desertions. In terms of benefits, Red Army soldiers were given pocket money, their families received special benefits, and food and shelter was usually provided; all tangible benefits to the soldier. Through these initiatives, the Red Army developed a solid military force capable of conducting independent combat operations.

Comprehensive Officer Development System

With a dedicated military force and a supportive local populace, the Red Army required a competent officer corps to execute its pragmatic strategy. From its humble beginning in the Jingang Mountains, the Red Army always focused on training and developing its leaders to be successful in battle. This approach initially started with the establishment of small training units. As the Red Army became more established, it expanded the units into mobile schools, and culminated with the creation of the Red Army Academy and Red Army War College to train and develop its junior and senior officers. The Red Army also created specialty schools to develop certain skill sets needed in the military force to include artillery, engineer, communications, and medical services. The army also leveraged the political propaganda system to discuss and debate military concerns and issues as well as disseminating new tactics, which was critical for the cross-leveling of information across the army. The officers also led after-action reviews to help increase their understanding of operations and gain valuable lessons from their experience. The Red Army attempted to use every opportunity to develop and train its forces so it could overcome the numerical and material advantages of the KMT and succeed on the battlefield.

Significance of the Findings

The significance of this study is that it presents a re-examination of this neglected time period in early Republican China history. The preceding analysis demonstrated that the push for professionalization and modernization within the Chinese Red Army began earlier than many have acknowledged. Some scholars have viewed the Second Sino-Japanese War as a critical period for the development of the Red Army.[2] While the army's development and expansion during the Sino-Japanese war was critical to its later success in the Third Chinese Revolutionary War, the foundations for its growth were based on the adaptations and innovations created from 1927-1936. For Mao and other Red Army leaders, professionalization of the Red Army was always a long-term goal. In 1928, Mao outlined his view, stating, "unless we have regular armed forces of adequate strength...we certainly cannot create an independent regime, let alone an independent regime that lasts long and develops daily."[3] From its inception, the Red Army leaders adopted policies, instituted measures, and created institutions to help expand and professionalize the military force as a means of party power.

This analysis also supports the concept that a constrained Red Army should not be viewed in a negative manner. The pressures from war, lack of time, space, and resources constrained its ability to fully adapt to its challenges. With that said, these constraints also inspired innovation and forced the Chinese Red Army to create new ideas, adjust policies and measures, and experiment with new concepts for its strategy, tactics, and training methods. Red Army leaders adopted a more pragmatic attitude towards combat. The use of surprise, maneuver, deception, and night operations were developed out of necessity. Forces were used only when the long term benefit outweighed the costs. Such pragmatism only began to ebb after its success against the first three Extermination Campaigns. While it is impossible to know whether or not the Chinese Red Army would have still followed the same development track if it had had access to more resources, it is evident that the lack of resources spurred adaptation and innovation. Credit also must be given to the KMT. The Chinese Red Army's successes against the first four Extermination Campaigns moved Chiang Kai-shek and the KMT up the Clausewitzian ladder toward total war. In the Fifth Extermination Campaign, Chiang mobilized sufficient national will and resources necessary to successfully combat the Red Army. It is uncertain that any Red Army adaptation or innovation could have overcome this KMT change.

Lastly, this study provides a unique analytical framework to understand the development of an insurgent group into a professional military force. Before 1927, the Chinese Communists were a rival political party without a military force. The Nanchang and Hunan uprisings in 1927 changed the party into communist insurgent movement and began its push for a professional military force. The study outlined the Chinese Red Army's roadmap for the development of an insurgent military force operating in a specific historical context. The same analytical framework could be used on other insurgent forces to gain a better understanding of its development. This study, however, does not provide any prescriptive solutions to combat an insurgent force. Instead, broad lessons on the counterinsurgency can be gained by examining the KMT efforts, especially its use of the *baojia* system in the Fifth Extermination Campaign.[4]

Points for Consideration

These four themes should not be misconstrued as prescriptive principles for the development of any military force. Rather, these themes are simply meant to help the reader understand how internal factors contributed to the overall development of the Red Army. These factors do not highlight the other external factors that also played a role in the Red Army's success. First, the themes do not capture the large role the warlord armies and Japanese Army played in the greater Extermination Campaigns. Before the Fifth Extermination Campaign, the NRA had to contend with not only the Chinese Red Army, but also different warlord armies and an invading Japanese Army. During the Extermination campaigns, Chiang Kai-shek and the NRA forces continually battled with other warlord armies as the KMT attempted to consolidate power and control over China. Selective loyalties of warlord army leaders were a detriment to the KMT as they helped the Chinese Red Army multiple times, culminating with Feng Yuxiang's actions during the Xi'an incident. Japanese intervention was another critical factor in the success of the Red Army. The Third and Fourth Extermination Campaigns ended prematurely in part due to the KMT's response to Japanese attacks. The Japanese threat was a larger factor in pushing Chiang to accept the terms of negotiations at Xi'an.

Additionally, the limitations of the Chinese Red Army during this period cannot be understated. The strategy, tactics, and equipment of the Chinese Red Army never placed it in a superior position to gain a decisive victory over the NRA. Its success was its ability to survive the barrage of constant attacks. Additionally, its influence was limited to the rural areas. The Chinese Red Army could not extend its influence outside the Soviet areas, nor could it enter the urban areas even after several attempts. Second, the success and failure of any military force is also predicated on its political leadership. The change in the political leadership of the CCP had both positive and negative effects on the Chinese Red Army. While the professionalization and modernization efforts increased under the leadership of the Twenty-eight Bolsheviks, the Chinese Red Army also adopted a military strategy and tactics inconsistent with its capabilities and limitations. The Red Army's defeat at the Fifth Extermination Campaign demonstrates that the adoption of the four themes to develop the Red Army still did not guarantee success.

Further Research

This research on Extermination Campaigns has identified other topics concerning the Red Army's development that merit further examination. The first topic is a more comprehensive analysis of the Red Army's military culture during this early period. The examination of the Red Army's organizational structure and training programs in this study only provides a tangential explanation of the Red Army's culture. More comprehensive research on the military culture of the Red Army during this period could provide a revised understanding of the origin and evolution of the modern PLA military culture. Another area of research focuses on the operational art of the Red Army during the Extermination Campaigns. Analysis of the Red Army operations at the operational level may yield a better understanding of how its leadership and staff functioned to translate the strategy into specific engagements.

A second line of research would be the expansion of the scope of this study to include the Second Sino-Japanese War, and even the Third Chinese Revolutionary War. The survival of the Chinese Red Army after the Long March did not guarantee success for the Communists. The Red Army still faced stiff challenges from a more technologically-advanced Japanese Army. Additionally, relations with the KMT were still tenuous even at the height of the Second United Front, creating another threat to the CCP and the Red Army. Using a similar analytical framework utilized in this study, an in-depth descriptive analysis could be done on the adaptation of the Chinese Red Army through the creation of the People's Republic of China.

The last topic for further research is a reexamination of Mao's theories on guerrilla warfare, mobile warfare, and protracted war. Recent studies on counterinsurgency have led to revival in interest in Mao's military theories. Yet this interest does not include a deeper understanding of the historical context in which Mao created and developed his views. Continued research and analysis of the Extermination Campaigns and Sino-Japanese War in support of a reexamination of Mao's theories may lead to a deeper understanding of the historical context and origins of his famous writings.

Notes

1. "Flightism" is a pejorative term used by the Chinese Communists. Similar to "retreatism," flightism is used to describe what Mao called "only retreat, never advance" mentality during military operations. See Stuart Schram, ed., *Mao's Road to Power* Vol. 4 (Armonk, NY: M.E. Sharpe, 1992), 373.

2. Chalmers Johnson, *Peasant Nationalism and Communist Power* (Stanford: Stanford University Press, 1962), 49; Suzanne Pepper, *Civil War in China: The Political Struggle, 1945-1949* (Berkeley: University of California Press, 1978), 276.

3. Mao Tse-Tung, *Selected Works,* Vol. 1 (New York: International Publishers, 1954), 66-67.

4. For more information on the *baojia* system in Imperial China, see Phillip Kuhn, *Rebellion and its Enemies in Late Imperial China: Militarization and Social Structure, 1796-1864* (Cambridge: Harvard University Press, 1970). For a detailed study of the counterinsurgency techniques employed by the KMT, see William Wei, *Counterrevolution in China: the Nationalists in Jiangxi during the Soviet period* (Ann Arbor: University of Michigan Press, 1985).

Appendix A
Military Organization of Red Army

| First Extermination Campaign Red Army Table of Organization ||
| First Front Red Army ||
First Red Army Corps	Third Red Army Corps
Third Red Army	Fifth Red Army
Fourth Red Army	Eight Red Army
Twelfth Red Army	
Twentieth Red Army	
Twenty-second Red Army	

Source: Shaoqun Huang, *Zhong qu feng yun : Zhong yang Su qu di yi zhi wu ci fan "wei jiao" zhan zheng shi* [Zhong qu Feng yun: the History of the First through Fifth Extermination Campaigns in the Central Soviet] (Beijing: Zhong gong zhong yang dang xiao chu ban she, 1993), Appendix 1.

There is discrepancy on the actual size of the force numbers. Chi's source for the force numbers is from the KMT official account, *Gong fei zhan shi* (Extermination Campaign History). See Pengfeng Chi, "The Chinese Red Army and the Kiangsi Soviet," (Ph.D dissertation, George Washington University, 1977), 129. Mao stated the communists had 40,000 armed soldiers against 100,000 nationalist troops. See Mao Tse-Tung, *Selected Works*, Vol. 1 (New York: International Publishers, 1954), 227. One plausible explanation is that the NRA sent reinforcements into the area around December 1930, increasing the number to 100,000.

Second Extermination Campaign Red Army Table of Organization		
First Front Red Army		
First Red Army Corps	Third Red Army Corps	Independent Units
Third Red Army	First Red Army Division	Thirty-fifth Red Army
Fourth Red Army	Third Red Army Division	
Twelfth Red Army	Fourth Red Army Division	
	Sixth Red Army Division	

Source: Shaoqun Huang, *Zhong qu feng yun : Zhong yang Su qu di yi zhi wu ci fan "wei jiao" zhan zheng shi* [Zhong qu Feng yun: the History of the First through Fifth Extermination Campaigns in the Central Soviet] (Beijing: Zhong gong zhong yang dang xiao chu ban she, 1993), Appendix 3.

Third Extermination Campaign Red Army Table of Organization		
First Front Red Army		
First Red Army Corps	Third Red Army Corps	Independent Units
Third Red Army	First Red Army Division	Seventh Red Army
Fourth Red Army	Third Red Army Division	Thirty-fifth Red Army
Twelfth Red Army	Fourth Red Army Division	Fourth Independent Red Army Division
	Sixth Red Army Division	Fifth Independent Red Army Division

Source: Shaoqun Huang, *Zhong qu feng yun : Zhong yang Su qu di yi zhi wu ci fan "wei jiao" zhan zheng shi* [Zhong qu Feng yun: the History of the First through Fifth Extermination Campaigns in the Central Soviet] (Beijing: Zhong gong zhong yang dang xiao chu ban she, 1993), Appendix 5.

There is dispute over the number of soldiers. Snow follows Mao's estimate of 300,000. See Edgar Snow, *Red Star Over China* (New York: Grove Press, 1968), 179; *ZQFY*, 137; and Mao, *Selected Works,* Vol. 1, 230. Whereas other scholars estimated the numbers at 130,000, based on Taiwanese historical records. Chi, "The Chinese Red Army and the Kiangsi Soviet," 135.

Fourth Extermination Campaign Red Army Table of Organization			
First Front Red Army			
First Red Army Corps	Third Red Army Corps	Fifth Red Army Corps	Independent Units
Seventh Red Army Division	First Red Army Division	Thirty-eighth Red Army Division	Eleventh Red Army
Ninth Red Army Division	Third Red Army Division	Thirty-ninth Red Army Division	Twelfth Red Army
Tenth Red Army Division	Fourth Red Army Division		Twenty-first Red Army
Eleventh Red Army Division	Seventh Red Army		Twenty-second Red Army
			Jiangxi Fourth Independent Division
			Jiangxi Fifth Independent Division

Source: Shaoqun Huang, *Zhong qu feng yun : Zhong yang Su qu di yi zhi wu ci fan "wei jiao" zhan zheng shi* [Zhong qu Feng yun: the History of the First through Fifth Extermination Campaigns in the Central Soviet] (Beijing: Zhong gong zhong yang dang xiao chu ban she, 1993), Appendix 7.

Yoon noted the difficulty in fixing the correct number of soldiers n the Red Army during the Fourth Extermination Campaign, stating the number as 40,000, 65,000, or 70,000. See Chong Kun Yoon, "Mao, The Red Army, and the Chinese Soviet Republic" (Ph.D dissertation, The American University, 1968), 159-160.

Fifth Extermination Campaign Red Army Table of Organization			
First Front Red Army			
First Red Army Corps	Third Red Army Corps	Fifth Red Army Corps	Seventh Red Army Corps
First Red Army Division	Fourth Red Army Division	Thirteenth Red Army Division	Nineteenth Red Army Division
Second Red Army Division	Fifth Red Army Division	Fifteenth Red Army Division	Twentieth Red Army Division
	Sixth Red Army Division	Thirty-fourth Red Army Division	
Eighth Red Army Corps	Ninth Red Army Corps	Unassigned or Independent Subordinate Units	
Third Red Army Division	Twenty-first Red Army Division		
Fourteenth Red Army Division	Twenty-third Red Army Division		
	Twenty-second Red Army Division		
	Twenty-fourth Red Army Division		

Source: Shaoqun Huang, *Zhong qu feng yun : Zhong yang Su qu di yi zhi wu ci fan "wei jiao" zhan zheng shi* [Zhong qu Feng yun: the History of the First through Fifth Extermination Campaigns in the Central Soviet] (Beijing: Zhong gong zhong yang dang xiao chu ban she, 1993), Appendix 9.

Yoon stated the Red Army strength during this campaign to be 150,000. See Yoon, "Mao, The Red Army, and the Chinese Soviet Republic," 251. Donovan cited 80,000 as the Red Army strength during the summer of 1933. See Peter Williams Donovan, "The Chinese Red Army in the Kiangsi Soviet, 1931-1934" (Ph.D dissertation, Cornell University, 1974), 109.

Bibliography

Books

Averill, Stephen C. *Revolution in the Highlands: China's Jinggangshan Base Areas.* Lanham, MD: Rowman and Littlefield Publishers, 2006.

Benton, Gregor. *Mountain Fires: The Red Army's Three-Year War in South China, 1934-1938.* Berkeley, CA: University of California Press, 1992.

Benton, Gregor. *New Fourth Army: Communist Resistance Along the Yangtze and the Huai, 1938-1941.* Berkeley, CA: University of California Press, 1999.

Bjorge, Gary J. *Moving the Enemy: Operational Art in the Chinese PLA's Huai Hai Campaign.* Fort Leavenworth, KS: Combat Studies Institute Press, 2004.

Blasko, Dennis. *The Chinese Army Today: Tradition and Transformation for the 21st Century.* New York: Routledge, 2012.

Brady, Ann-Marie, ed. *China's Thought Management.* London: Routledge, 2011.

Bramall, Christopher. *The Industrialization of Rural China.* London: Oxford University Press, 2006.

Braun, Otto. *A Comintern Agent in China: 1932-1939.* Translated by Jeanne Moore. Stanford: Stanford University Press, 1982.

Carr, Caleb. *The Devil Soldier: the American Soldier of Fortune Who Became a God in China.* New York: Random House, 1995.

Ch'i, Hsi-sheng. *Warlord Politics in China, 1916-1928.* Stanford, CA: Stanford University Press, 1976.

Claire-Bergere, Marie. *Sun Yat-sen.* Translated by Janet Lloyd. Stanford, CA: Stanford University Press, 2000.

Clausewitz, Carl von. *On War.* Translated by Michael Howard, and Peter Paret. Princeton: Princeton University Press, 1976.

Cohen, Paul A. *A History in Three Keys: The Boxers as Event, Experience, and Myth.* New York: Columbia University Press, 1997.

Cohen, Paul A. *Discovering History in China.* New York: Columbia University Press, 1984.

Dingle, Edwin John. *China's Revolution, 1911-1912: A Historical and Political Record of the Civil War.* New York: Haskell House Publishers, 1972.

Dirlik, Arif. *The Origins of Chinese Communism.* Oxford: Oxford University Press, 1989.

Drea, Edward. *Japan's Imperial Army: Its Rise and Fall, 1853-1945.* Lawrence: University of Kansas Press, 2009.

Dreyer, Edward L. *China at War, 1901-1949.* New York: Longman Publishing, 1995.

Eastman, Lloyd. *Throne and Mandarins: China's Search for a Policy during* the *Sino-French Controversy, 1880-1885.* Cambridge, MA: Harvard University Press, 1967.

Elleman, Bruce A. *Modern Chinese Warfare, 1795-1989.* New York: Routledge, 2001.

Elleman, Bruce A. *Moscow and the Emergence of the Communist Power in China: 1925-30.* New York: Routledge, 2009.

Esherick, Joseph. *Reform and Revolution in China: The 1911 Revolution in Hunan and Hubei.* Berkeley, CA: University of California Press, 1976.

Esherick, Joseph. *The Origins of the Boxer Uprising.* Berkeley, CA: University of California Press, 1987.

Fairbank, John K., ed. *The Cambridge History of China, Vol. 12, Republican China 1912-1949, Part 1.* Cambridge: Cambridge University Press, 1983.

Fairbank, John K. *The Great Chinese Revolution, 1800-1985.* New York: Harper and Row Publishers, 1987.

Fairbank, John K. *Trade and Diplomacy on the China Coast: The Opening of the Treaty Ports, 1842-1854.* Stanford, CA: Stanford University Press, 1964.

Fairbank, John K., and Albert Feuerwerker, eds. *The Cambridge History of China, Vol. 13, Republican China 1912-1949, Part 2.* Cambridge: Cambridge University Press, 1986.

Fairbank, John K., and Kwang-Ching Liu, eds. *The Cambridge History of China, Vol. 11, Late Ch'ing, 1800-1911, Part 2.* Cambridge: Cambridge University Press, 1980.

Fairbank, John K., and Merle Goldman. *China: A New History.* Cambridge, MA: Harvard University Press, 1998.

Fay, Peter Ward. *The Opium War, 1840-1842.* Chapel Hill, NC: University of North Carolina Press, 1975.

Fisher, Richard. *China's Military Modernization: Building for Regional and Global Reach.* Stanford, CA: Stanford Security Studies, 2010.

Fung, Edmund S.K. *The Military Dimension of the Chinese Revolution: The New Army and its Role in the Revolution of 1911.* Vancouver: University of British Columbia Press, 1980.

Graff, David A., and Robin Higham, eds. *The Miltiary History of China.* Boulder, CO: Westview Press, 2002.

Harrison, John P. *The Long March to Power: A History of the Chinese Communist Party, 1927-72.* New York: Praeger Publishing, 1972.

Hsu, Immanuel C.Y. *The Ili Crisis: A Study of Sino-Russian Diplomacy 1871-1881.* Oxford: Clarendon Press, 1965.

Jacobs, Daniel N. *Borodin: Stalin's Man in China.* Cambridge, MA: Harvard University Press, 1981.

Jian, Youwen. *The Taiping Revolutionary Movement.* New Haven: Yale

University Press, 1973.

Johnson, Chalmers. *Peasant Nationalism and Communist Power.* Stanford, CA: Stanford University Press, 1962.

Jordan, Donald. *The Northern Expedition: Chinese National Revolution of 1926-1928.* Honolulu: University Press of Hawaii, 1976.

Kataoka, Tetsuya. *Resistance and Revolution in China: the Communists and the Second United Front.* Berkeley, CA: University of California Press, 1974.

Kim, Hodong. *Holy War in China: The Muslim Rebellion and State in Chinese Central Asia, 1864-1877.* Stanford, CA: Stanford University Press, 2004.

Kim, Ilpyong J. *The Politics of Chinese Communism: Kiangsi under the Soviets.* Berkeley, CA: University of California Press, 1973.

Kuhn, Philip A. *Rebellion and its Enemies in Late Imperial China: Militarization and Social Structure, 1794-1864.* Cambridge, MA: Harvard University Press, 1970.

Lary, Diana. *Warlord Soldiers: Chinese Common Soldiers, 1911-1937.* Cambridge: Cambridge University Press, 1985.

Lee, James. "Food Supply and Population Growth in Southwest China, 1250-1850." *The Journal of Asian Studies* 41, No. 7 (1982): 711-746.

Leung, Edwin Pak-Wah. "The Quasi-War in East Asia: Japan's Expedition to Taiwan and the Ryukyu Controversy." *Modern Asian Studies* 17, No. 2 (1983): 257-281.

Lew, Christopher R. *The Third Chinese Revolutionary Civil War, 1945-1949: An Analysis of Communist Strategy and Leadership.* New York: Routledge, 2009.

Li, Kwok-sing, comp. *Glossary of Political Terms of the People's Republic of China.* Translated by Mary Lok. Hong Kong: The Chinese University Press, 2005.

Li, Xiaobing. *A History of the Modern Chinese Army.* Lexington: The University Press of Kentucky, 2007.

Liddell Hart, B.H. *Strategy.* London: Faber, 1967.

Lipman, Jonathan N. *Familiar Strangers: A History of Muslims in Northwest China.* Seattle: University of Washington Press, 1998.

Liu, Frederick F. *A Military History of Modern China.* Princeton: Princeton University Press, 1956.

Lynch, Michael. *The Chinese Civil War, 1945-1949.* Oxford: Osprey Publishing, 2010.

MacKinnon, Stephen, Diana Lary, and Ezra Vogel, eds. *China at War: Regions of China, 1937-45.* Stanford, CA: Stanford University Press, 2007.

Mallory, Walter H. *China: Land of Famine.* New York: American Geographical Society, 1926.

Mao, Tse-Tung. *Selected Works,* Vol. 1. New York: International Publishers, 1954.

Marston, Daniel P. *Phoenix from the Ashes: The Indian Army in the Burma Campaign.* Westport, CT: Praeger Publishers, 2003.

Marston, Daniel P., and Carter Malkasian, eds. *Counterinsurgency in Modern Warfare.* Oxford: Osprey Publishing, 2010.

McCord, Edward. *The Power of the Gun: The Emergence of Modern Chinese Warlordism.* Berkeley, CA: University of California Press, 1993.

Nagl, John A. *Learning to Eat Soup with a Knife: Counterinsurgency Lessons from Malaya and Vietnam.* Chicago: University of Chicago Press, 2002.

North, Robert C. *Moscow and Chinese Communists.* Stanford, CA: Stanford University Press, 1963.

O'Ballance, Edgar. *The Red Army of China.* London: Farber and Farber, 1962.

Paine, S.C.M. *The Sino-Japanese War of 1894-1895: Perceptions, Power, and Primacy.* Cambridge: Cambridge University Press, 2003.

Peattie, Mark, Edward Drea, and Hans van de Ven, eds. *The Battle for China: Essays on the Military History of the Sino-Japanese War of 1937-1945.* Stanford, CA: Stanford University Press, 2010.

Peng, Dehuai. *Memoirs of a Chinese Marshal: the Autobiographical Notes of Peng Dehuai (1898-1974).* Beijing: Foreign Languages Press, 1984.

Pepper, Suzanne. *Civil War in China: The Political Struggle, 1945-1949.* Berkeley, CA: University of California Press, 1978.

Perry, Elizabeth. *Rebel and Revolutionaries in Northern China, 1845-1945.* Stanford, CA: Stanford University Press, 1980.

Polachek, James M. *The Inner Opium War.* Cambridge, MA: Harvard University Press, 1992.

Powell, Ralph L. *The Rise of Chinese Military Power: 1895-1912.* Princeton: Princeton University Press, 1955.

Price, Jane L. *Cadres, Commanders, and Commissars.* Boulder, CO: Westview Press, 1976.

Pye, Lucian W. *Warlord Politics.* New York: Praeger Press, 1971.

Reed, Bradely. *Talons and Teeth: County Clerks and Runners in the Qing Dynasty.* Stanford, CA: Stanford University Press, 2002.

Rue, John E. *Mao Tse-tung in Opposition: 1927-1935.* Stanford: Stanford University Press, 1966.

Saich, Tony. *Origin of the United Front: the Role of Sneevliet (Alias Maring).* New York: Brill, 1991.

Saich, Tony, ed. *The Rise to Power of the Chinese Communist Party.* Armonk, NY: M.E. Sharpe, 1996.

Saich, Tony, and Hans J. van de Ven, eds. *New Perspectives on the Chinese Revolution.* Armonk, NY: M.E. Sharpe, 1995.

Salisbury, Harrison E. *The Long March: the Untold Story.* New York: Harper and Row Publishers, 1985.

Schiffrin, Harold. *Sun Yat-Sen and the Origins of the Chinese Revolution.* Berkeley, CA: University of California Press, 2010.

Schram, Stuart, ed. *Mao's Road to Power.* 4 vols. Armonk, NY: M.E. Sharpe, 1992.

Schrecker, John E. *The Chinese Revolution in Historical Perspective.* Westport, CT: Praeger Press, 1991.

Schwarcz, Vera. *The Chinese Enlightenment: Intellectuals and the Legacy of the May Fourth Movement of 1919.* Berkeley, CA: University of California Press, 1990.

Shambaugh, David. *Modernizing China's Military: Progress, Problems, and Prospects.* Berkeley, CA: University of California Press, 2004.

Sheridan, James E. *China in Disintegration: The Republican Era in Chinese History, 1912-1949.* New York: Free Press, 1975.

Short, Philip. *Mao: A Life.* New York: Henry Holt and Co., 1999.

Smedley, Agnes. *The Great Road: The Life and Times of Chu Teh.* New York: Monthly Review Press, 1956.

Snow, Edgar. *Red Star Over China.* New York: Grove Press, 1968.

Snow, Helen Foster. *Inside Red China.* New York: Da Capo Press, 1979.

Spence, Jonathan D. *The Search for Modern China.* New York: W.W. Norton and Company, 1999.

Stalin, Joseph. *Marxism and the National and Colonial Question.* Honolulu: University Press of the Pacific, 2003

Suleski, Ronald, and Daniel Bays. *Early Communist China: Two Studies.* Ann Arbor: Center for Chinese Studies, Univeristy of Michigan, 1969.

Sutherland, Riley. *Army Operations in Malaya, 1947-1960.* Santa Monica: RAND, 1964.

Swarup, Shanti. *A Study of the Chinese Communist Movement.* Oxford: Clarendon Press, 1966.

Teng, Ssu-yu. *Taiping Rebellion and the Western Powers: A Comprehensive Survey.* Oxford: Oxford University Press, 1971.

Teng, Ssu-yu. *The Nien Army and their Guerrilla Warfare, 1851-1868.* Paris: Mounton Press, 1961.

Teng, Ssu-Yu, and John K. Fairbank. *China's Response to the West: A Documentary Survey, 1839-1923.* Cambridge: Harvard University Press, 1979.

Thornton, Richard C. *The Comintern and the Chinese Communists: 1928-1931.* Seattle: University of Washington Press, 1969.

Tse-tsung, Chow. *The May Fourth Movement: Intellectual Revolution in Modern China.* Stanford, CA: Stanford University Press, 1967.

van de Ven, Hans J., *From Friend to Comrade: the Founding of the Chinese Communist Party.* Berkeley, CA: University of California Press, 1991.

van de Ven, Hans J., *War and Nationalism in China.* New York: RoutledgeCruzon, 2004.

van de Ven, Hans J., ed. *Warfare in Chinese History.* Lieden: Brill, 2000.

Van Slyke, Lyman. *Enemies and Friends: the United Front in Chinese Communist History.* Stanford, CA: Stanford University Press, 1967.

Wales, Nym. *Red Dust.* Stanford, CA: Stanford University Press, 1952.

Waley, Arthur. *The Opium War through Chinese Eyes.* Stanford, CA: Stanford University Press, 1968.

Wang, Shen-tsu. *The Margary Affair and the Chefoo Agreement.* Oxford: Oxford University Press, 1940.

Wenqian, Gao. *Zhou Enlai: The Last Perfect Revolutionary.* Translated by Peter Rand and Lawerence R. Sullivan. New York: Public Affairs, 2007.

Westad, Odd Arne. *Decisive Encounters: The Chinese Civil War, 1946-1950.* Stanford, CA: Stanford University Press, 2010.

Whitson, William W. *The Chinese High Command: A History of Communist Military Politics, 1927-71.* Westport, CT: Praeger Press, 1973.

Wilson, Andrew. *The "Ever-Victorious Army": A history of the Chinese Campaign under Lt. Col. C.G. Gordon and of the Suppression of the Tai-Ping Rebellion.* Cambridge: Cambridge University Press, 2010.

Worthing, Peter. *A Military History of Modern China: from the Manchu Conquest to Tian'anmen Square.* Westport, CT: Praeger Security International, 2007.

Wright, Mary Clabaugh, ed. *China in Revolution: The First Phase 1900-1913.* New Haven: Yale University Press, 1968.

Wright, Mary Clabaugh. *The Last Stand of Chinese Conservatism: the T'ung-chih Restoration, 1862-1874.* Stanford: Stanford University Press, 1964.

Xue, Lianbi, and Zhenhua Zhang, eds. *Zhongguo jun shi jiao yu shi [History of Military Education in China].* Beijing: Guo fang da xue chu ban she, 1991.

Journals

Dirlik, Arif. "Narrativizing Revolution." Modern China 23, No. 4 (1997): 363-397.

Garavente, Anthony. "Commentary: Solving the Mystery of the Long March, 1934-1936." *Bulletin of Concerned Asian Scholars* 27, No. 3 (1995): 50-70.

Gordon, Leonard. "Japan's Abortive Colonial Venture in Taiwan, 1874." *The Journal of Modern History* 17, No. 2 (1965): 171-185.

Guillermaz, Jacques. "The Nanchang Uprising." *The China Quarterly* 11 (1964): 161-168.

Hofhejnz, Roy. "The Autumn Harvest Insurrection." *The China Quarterly* 32 (1967): 37-87.

Hsiao, Tso-Liang. "Chinese Communism and the Canton Soviet of 1927." *The China Quarterly* 30 (1967): 49-78.

Hu, Chi-Hsi. "Mao, Lin Biao, and the Fifth Encirclement Campaign." *The China Quarterly* 82 (1980): 250-280.

Ladwig III, Walter. "Supporting Allies in COIN: Britain and the Dhofar Rebellion." *Small Wars and Insurgencies* 19, No. 1 (2008): 62-88.

MacKinnon, Stephen R. "The Peiyang Army, Yüan Shih-k'ai and the Origins of Modern Chinese Warlordism." *The Journal of Asian Studies* 32, No. 3 (1973): 405-423.

Smith, Simon. "General Templer and Counter-insurgency in Malaya: Hearts and Minds, Intelligence, and Propaganda." *Intelligence and National Security* 16, No. 3 (2001): 60-78.

Suleski, Ronald. "Futian Incident Reconsidered." *The China Quarterly* 89 (1982): 97-104.

Wilbur, C. Martin. "The Ashes of Defeat." *The China Quarterly* 18 (1964): 3-54.

Wong, R. Bin. "Food Riots in the Qing Dynasty." *The Journal of Asian Studies* 41, No. 7 (1982): 767-788.

Yang, Benjamin. "The Zunyi Conference as One Step in Mao's Rise to Power: A Survey of Historical Studies of the Chinese Communist Party." *The China Quarterly* 106 (1986): 235-271.

Theses/Dissertations

Chi, Pengfeng. "The Chinese Red Army and the Kiangsi Soviet." Ph.D dissertation, George Washington University, 1977.

Chiu, Sin-Ming. "A History of the Chinese Communist Army." Ph.D dissertation, University of Southern California, Los Angeles, 1958.

Donovan, Peter Williams. "The Chinese Red Army in the Kiangsi Soviet, 1931-1934." Ph.D dissertation, Cornell University, 1974.

Jordan, James D. "Evolution of a People's Army in the People's Republic of China." Ph.D dissertation, The American University, 1975.

Yoon, Chong Kun. "Mao, The Red Army, and the Chinese Soviet Republic." Ph.D dissertation, The American University, 1968.

Chinese Language Sources

Huang, Shaoqun. *Zhong qu feng yun : Zhong yang Su qu di yi zhi wu ci fan "wei jiao" zhan zheng shi* [Zhongqu Fengyun: the History of the First through Fifth Extermination Campaigns in the Central Soviet]. Beijing: Zhong gong zhong yang dang xiao chu ban she, 1993.

Jin, Yuguo. *Zhongguo zhan shu shi* [History of Military Tactics in China]. Beijing: Jie fang jun chu ban she, 2003.

Jun shi li shi yan jiu bu. *Zhongguo ren min jie fang jun de qi shi nian* [Seventy Years of the PLA]. Beijing: Jun shi ke xue chu ban she, 1987.

Shi sou zi liao shi gong fei zi liao mu lu [Shi Sou Collection]. Stanford, CA: Hoover Institution, 1960. microfilm, 21 reels.

Yuan, Wei, and Zhuo Zhang, eds. *Zhongguo jun xiao fa zhan shi* [History of the Development of Military Schools in China]. Beijing: Guo fang da xue chu ban she, 2001.

Zhongguo gong chan dang zhong yang jun bu, ed. *Zhong yang jun shi tong xun* [Central Military Report]. Vol. 1. January 15, 1930.

Zhongguo jun dui shi zhan shi lu: Zhong ri liang jun xue zhan, guo gong liang jun xue zhan, zhong Mei liang jun xue zhan [Record of China's Military Combat: First and Second Sino-Japanese War; the Chinese Civil War; and First and Second Sino-American Wars (Korean War and Vietnam War)]. Beijing: Guo fang da xue chu ban she, 1993.

Zhongguo ren min ge ming jun shi bo wu guan. *Zhongguo zhan zheng fa zhan shi* [History of the Development of War in China]. Beijing: Ren min chu ban she, 2003.

Zhong yang jun shi tong xun, [Central Military Report], Vol. 1. Chinese Communist Party Central Military Committee, January 15, 1930.

www.ingramcontent.com/pod-product-compliance
Lightning Source LLC
Chambersburg PA
CBHW081848170426
43199CB00018B/2845